FORMING SLEEP

Cultural Inquiries in English Literature, 1400–1700

Rebecca Totaro, General Editor

ADVISORY BOARD

Joe Campana
Rice University

Vin Nardizzi
The University of British Columbia

Hillary Ecklund
Loyola University, New Orleans

Gail Kern Paster
Folger Shakespeare Library

Katherine Eggert
University of Colorado, Boulder

Garrett A. Sullivan Jr.
Penn State University

Wendy Beth Hyman
Oberlin College & Conservatory

Tiffany Werth
University of California, Davis

Julia Reinhardt Lupton
University of California, Irvine

Jessica Wolfe
University of North Carolina, Chapel Hill

Books in the Cultural Inquiries in English Literature, 1400–1700, series acknowledge the complex relationships that link disciplines in the pre-modern period and account for the lived experience represented in literary and cultural texts of the time. Scholars in this series reconnect fields often now considered distinct, including cuisine, ecology, cartography, the occult, meteorology, physiology, drama, popular print, and poetry.

OTHER BOOKS IN THE SERIES:

Emily Griffiths Jones, *Right Romance: Heroic Subjectivity and Elect Community in Seventeenth-Century England*

FORMING SLEEP

Representing Consciousness in the English Renaissance

Edited by Nancy L. Simpson-Younger
and Margaret Simon

THE PENNSYLVANIA STATE UNIVERSITY PRESS

UNIVERSITY PARK, PENNSYLVANIA

Library of Congress Cataloging-in-Publication Data

Names: Simpson-Younger, Nancy L. (Nancy Lynne), 1984– editor. Simon, Margaret,
    1975– editor.
Title: Forming sleep : representing consciousness in the English Renaissance / edited by Nancy
    L. Simpson-Younger and Margaret Simon.
Description: University Park, Pennsylvania : The Pennsylvania State University Press, [2020]
    | Series: Cultural inquiries in English literature, 1400–1700 | Includes bibliographical
    references and index.
Summary: "A collection of essays exploring how biocultural and literary dynamics acted
    together to shape conceptions of sleep states in the early modern period. Essays
    envision sleep states as a means of defining the human, both literally and metaphorically"—
    Provided by publisher.
Identifiers: LCCN 2019059745 | ISBN 9780271086118 (hardback)
Subjects: LCSH: English literature—Early modern, 1500–1700—History and criticism. |
    Consciousness in literature. | Sleep in literature.
Classification: LCC PR408.C62 2020
LC record available at https://lccn.loc.gov/2019059745

Copyright © 2020 The Pennsylvania State University
All rights reserved
Printed in the United States of America
Published by The Pennsylvania State University Press,
University Park, PA 16802–1003

The Pennsylvania State University Press is a member of the Association of University Presses.

It is the policy of The Pennsylvania State University Press to use acid-free paper. Publications
on uncoated stock satisfy the minimum requirements of American National Standard for
Information Sciences—Permanence of Paper for Printed Library Material, ANSI Z39.48–1992.

CONTENTS

Acknowledgments | vii

Introduction: Forming Sleep | 1
Margaret Simon and Nancy Simpson-Younger

PART I: SLEEP STATES AND SUBJECTIVITY
IN EARLY MODERN LYRIC

1. Thinking Sleep in the Renaissance Sonnet
   Sequence | 21
   Giulio J. Pertile

2. Rest and Rhyme in Thomas Campion's
   Poetry | 51
   Margaret Simon

3. "Still in Thought with Thee I Go":
   Epistemology and Consciousness in the
   Sidney Psalms | 69
   Nancy Simpson-Younger

PART II: SLEEP, ETHICS, AND EMBODIED
FORM IN EARLY MODERN DRAMA

4. Making the Moor: Torture, Sleep
   Deprivation, and Race in *Othello* | 89
   Timothy A. Turner

5. Sleep, Vulnerability, and Self-Knowledge in
   A Midsummer Night's Dream | 109
   Jennifer Lewin

6. "The Heaviness of Sleep": Monarchical
Exhaustion in *King Lear* | 127
Brian Chalk

PART III: SLEEP AND PERSONHOOD IN THE
EARLY MODERN VERSE EPIC AND PROSE
TREATISE

7. Life and Labor in the House of Care:
Spenserian Ethics and the Aesthetics of
Insomnia | 149
Benjamin Parris

8. "Sweet Moistning Sleepe": Perturbations of
the Mind and Rest for the Body in Robert
Burton's *Anatomy of Melancholy* | 167
Cassie M. Miura

9. The Physiology of Free Will: Faculty
Psychology and the Structure of the Miltonic
Mind | 187
N. Amos Rothschild

Afterword: Beyond the Lost World;
Early Modern Sleep Scenarios | 209
Garrett A. Sullivan Jr.

Bibliography | 217
List of Contributors | 231
Index | 233

ACKNOWLEDGMENTS

The concept for this book emerged out of conversations we had as fellows in English paleography at the Folger Shakespeare Library. While the skill of reading sixteenth- and seventeenth-century handwriting has been invaluable, so has this collaboration, and we are grateful to the Folger staff both for their research support and for bringing the two of us together so that this project could come into being. In particular, we are grateful to Heather Wolfe, Owen Williams, and all of the students and faculty participants in the seminar. We further refined the book concept through a Shakespeare Association of America seminar entitled "Sleeping Through the Renaissance." Thanks are due to all of the seminar participants, who reinforced for us that there are surprisingly many things to say about a seemingly passive state. Rebecca Totaro has been a stalwart supporter from the project's inception and has offered feedback that has strengthened the volume. We are grateful for her generosity, patience, and enthusiasm. Garrett Sullivan Jr. deserves thanks not just for contributing an afterword but also for helping to define the field of early modern sleep studies and for supporting our work and the work of our contributors. Margaret Simon is grateful to the 2015 SAA seminar participants in "Writing New Histories of Embodiment" and its facilitators, Gail Kern Paster and David Houston Wood, as well as to the Folger Faculty Seminar "The Embodied Senses" and the RSA panel "Books and Bodies," led by Jillian Linster and Harry Newman. Nancy Simpson-Younger is grateful to her colleagues at Pacific Lutheran University who provided feedback on the book proposal, as well as the Sidneians and Spenserians at Kalamazoo who heard and responded to early drafts of some of this material. All of these seminar and conference interactions helped us as editors to shape the argument and direction of the volume. Additionally, Rebecca Laroche, Jen Munroe, Amy Tigner, Elaine Leong, Hillary Nunn, and Lisa Smith, of the Early Modern Recipes Online Collective (EMROC), led us to many manuscript resources for sleep remedies and sleep states, reading that enriched the project. Additional resources and guidance were provided by Mike Witmore, Elizabeth Bearden, Ellen Samuels, Heather Dubrow, David Loewenstein, and (especially) Karen Britland, who also provided many thoughtful comments on Nancy Simpson-Younger's earlier research into sleep states. Margaret Simon's research at the British and Wellcome Libraries was supported by a faculty grant from NC State University. Most especially, we are indebted to our contributors for their hard work and patience in bringing this volume to press. Our families and children were instrumental in helping us to understand sleep, affect, and community: we'd like to thank Barbara and Nolan Simon, Marshall and Kathy Simpson, Camm and Anders Fyfe, and Lucy Younger. Finally, we would like to thank Paul Fyfe and Pippa Younger for their unwavering support in this and all our endeavors.

Introduction

Forming Sleep

MARGARET SIMON AND
NANCY L. SIMPSON-YOUNGER

MACBETH: Methought I heard a voice cry "Sleep no more!
Macbeth does murder sleep"—the innocent sleep,
Sleep that knits up the raveled sleeve of care,
The death of each day's life, sore labour's bath,
Balm of hurt minds, great nature's second course,
Chief nourisher in life's feast. (2.2.33–38)

In this familiar passage, Macbeth positions sleep as both a literal phenomenon and a literary one. Physically, Macbeth will "Sleep no more!" At the same time, he contemplates sleep's metaphorical meanings, framing the state of sleep as a daily "death" for the human body—one that is ironically positive in serving as a potent "bath," "balm," and "nourisher."[1] In these ways, Macbeth's words underscore the interplay between literary forms and forms (or states) of consciousness. *Forming Sleep* examines this interplay, considering the literary, ethical, and epistemological potentialities of representing the body at rest. In order to delve fully into these ideas, our essays employ methods and concepts from not only formalist and new formalist schools of criticism but also biopolitics, Marxist theory, trauma theory, and affect theory, among others. This multifaceted approach is particularly provocative for analyzing sleep states because it links the physical and the metaphorical, which mutually inform each other in the period.

If early modern sleep is a biocultural process, shaped by both physiological needs and social expectations (as Garrett Sullivan Jr. discusses in the afterword to this volume and as Sasha Handley has recently argued), then representations of sleep aestheticize lived experience, influencing how communities or individuals are apt to respond to a sleeping figure and how sleep itself is processed or evaluated.[2] Likewise, the historical experience of different states of consciousness, as recorded in medical and philosophical texts, offers authors ways to innovate on traditional literary forms.[3] With attention to all of these contexts and lines of influence, this volume's essays explore how literary form and the historicized body are both bioculturally inflected and mutually constituting.

This approach is particularly provocative for sleep states because, even today, so much of our physiological and perceived experience of sleep is unknown or not articulable—in part because there are so many different states of unconscious experience.[4] In this volume, we have decided to consider not just sleep itself but also moments of unconsciousness such as syncope, coma, waking sleep, and swooning, because all of these states share a vulnerability to formal manipulation—whether pathologically, religiously, humorally, or ethically. After all, an inert body is an inert body, which must become legible somehow to its onlookers (or, in some cases, to itself).[5] In other words, the unknowable mechanisms and experiences of the whole spectrum of sleep states give a particular explanatory power to forms of representation that attempt to explicate or interact with them. If Montaigne considered sleep as a practice for that ultimate unknown—death—this volume claims Montaigne's imperative in slightly different terms, suggesting that we can practice knowing multiple types of sleep by attempting to represent them.[6]

This practice can also lead to broader investigations of self. Between about 1580 and about 1670, during the period with which this volume is primarily concerned, scholars and theorists were developing questions about the capacities for self-definition (and self-formation) offered by seemingly insentient states.[7] This shift is marked in part by a philological change wherein the definition of *conscious* moves from knowing *who* one is to knowing *that* one is. In 1573 J. Foxe referred to "a pretty practise to finde out a naughty concious Byshop"; in 1592 Gabriel Harvey noted of Robert Greene that "a conscious mind, and undaunted hart, seldome dwell together."[8] In these early uses, *conscious* meant being aware of one's own predilections or failings, as an extension of the imperative to know oneself (*nosce te ipsum*). By 1725, the meaning had transitioned to its more modern psychological usage: "Conscious Beings . . . have a Power of Thought, such as the Mind of Man, God, Angels."[9] During the process of this evolution from self-knowledge to broader self-awareness, questions began to arise about the interplay of sense and sentience. If sleep was understood as a stoppage of sensory perception, it became a locus for the investigation of humanness in the era more broadly, with Descartes predicating his philosophical project on diagnosing his own consciousness and Montaigne wondering if sleeping generals were truly so virtuous as to detach themselves from worldly concerns.[10] To be conscious, in other words, meant the ability to contemplate and draw conclusions from unconsciousness.[11] At the same time, it involved forging an epistemological bridge between the two states, asking which biological, mental, and affective processes might persist in the absence of sensory awareness. Exploring what it really meant to be awake, asleep, or nonresponsive became a foundation for exploring what it really meant to be a human being. In other words, this involves a mode of self-fashioning that attends to the formation of a self through not only the conscious activities of that self but also the full spectrum of states that form bodily experience.[12]

INVESTIGATING EARLY MODERN SLEEP STATES

Because sleep can encompass a multiplicity of unconscious experiences, representations of the resting body became a major means by which early modern authors confronted these questions of consciousness and the self, as several recent studies have shown. Since sleep blurs epistemological and ontological boundaries, sliding wakefulness into unconsciousness, it provides a way for seemingly divergent concepts such as neoplatonic contemplation and bodily desire to confront each other in gray or comingled ways, as Gillian Knoll has argued about the play *Endymion*.[13] In certain cases, this divergence can render sleep an agent of paradox, allowing two potentially contradictory stances to be simultaneously true. For the kingly sleeper, as Rebecca Totaro and Benjamin Parris have shown, vigilance and somnolence are both mandatory, as the demands of self-care merge with the care of the state—even as the king's mortal body affects the level of vigilance he can generate.[14] Garrett Sullivan Jr. points out that sleep both aligns all humans with the vegetative component of the Aristotelian tripartite soul and separates the noble insomniac from the snoozing peasant.[15] While sleep can label or diagnose human statuses, though, it can also invite skepticism about ontology or even selfhood, as Jennifer Lewin has underscored.[16] Building from these ideas, a philosophical approach to sleep can dovetail with an exploration of the ethics of care in the period: the sleep of others can enable kind or unkind behavior toward those vulnerable figures, allowing critics to explore early modern constructions of practical virtue.[17] By juxtaposing conditions of being, in other words, early modern sleep performs like a rhetorical figure that merges, compares, and occasionally separates human positionalities. Whether rhetorical, philosophical, or some combination of the two, most critical approaches to early modern sleep states share the implicit conviction that the sleeping body is deeply networked within its environment, its social encounters with other living things, and what Jane Bennett has called "vibrant matter."[18] Because sleep states can serve as affective, almost gestural shorthands, representations of such states are often potent signifiers for emotive, ethical, and aesthetic concerns within these wider ecosystemic contexts.[19]

The early modern humors and passions provide a vocabulary that can help to position and interpret human consciousness within this larger ecosystem.[20] As Thomas Cogan underscores in *The Haven of Health*, sleep is one of the so-called Galenic nonnaturals in the early modern period, joining a list of six bodily states and practices that collectively constitute the health of a human being.[21] This list—"Ayre, Meat and Drinke, Sleep and Watch, Labor and Rest, Emptiness and Repletion, and affections of the mind," in Cogan's words—implies the need for a daily practice of bodily discipline in multiple areas, even as it acknowledges the cross-pollination between list elements, humoral dispositions, and environmental factors, multiple forces shaping the functional form of the body.[22] Because sleep happens when digested food is transformed into vapors, which rise up and block off sense organs such as the eyes, nose, and ears, sleep praxis and hygiene cannot be divorced from considerations of diet.[23] At the same time, they are also influenced by considerations of posture, clothing, time of day, previous exercise, current illnesses, or even susceptibility to the devil (270–77).[24] Texts such as Cogan's both describe and prescribe bodily comportment as it pertains to sleep, instituting a dynamic that plays on the distinction between *form* as a noun and *form* as a verb. Essential for human well-being, then, sleep also serves as a barometer for overall health in the early modern period, demonstrating how different medical discourses understood sleep as an agent of bodily reform.

At the same time, for Cogan, the implications of sleep are not necessarily easy to examine: "In sleepe the senses be unable to execute their office, as the eye to see, the eare to heare, the nose to smell, the mouth to tast, and all sinowy parts to feele, So that the senses for a time seem to be tyed or bound" (268). Here, Cogan equivocates subtly on the extent to which sleep binds the senses (he says they *seem* to be tied), opening the door for debates about the actual workings of the brain and body during states of unconsciousness. As he probes and expounds on these ideas, Cogan immediately turns not to bodily or empirical evidence, nor even to Aristotle, but to Seneca, Ovid, and scripture—calling sleep "the image of death," the son of justice, and the figuration of Christian resurrection hopes (269). Cogan's literary and metaphorical habit of mind in defining sleep echoes Shakespeare's *Macbeth* and speaks to sleep's status as a mediator between the physical and the metaphysical.

Perhaps because sleep states (and states of unconsciousness more generally) are so variously experienced, frequently overlap, and can be both curative and pathological, early modern philosophers and healers divided consciousness into a surprising spectrum of conditions: watch, carus, subeth, lethargie, congelation, sounding, syncope. Philip Barrough's 1583 *The Method of Phisicke* elaborates on "Lethargie," "Carus or Subeth" (a deep sleep), "Congelation or Taking" (a "sudden detention and taking of mind and body, both sense and moving being lost," whether the eyes be open or closed), and "dead sleep" (coma). Barrough works hard to distinguish these states, based on the extent to which the senses are operational. "Dead sleep," for example, can be either a "*coma somnolentum*" or a "*Vigilans spoor*," "an evill wherein the sick cannot hold open his eyes, though he be awake, but he wihnketh in hope to get sleep, and yet is altogether awake."[25] Of "Carus or Subeth" he writes, "This disease differeth from the Lethargy for that they that have the Lethargy wil answer to a question demanded, and do not lie altogether down. But they that have *Carus*, are occupied with deep sleep, and if they be stirred or pricked, although they feel, yet they will say nothing, nor once open their eies."[26] These comments can read like field notes from a long-forgotten cognitive landscape. Early moderns, no less than people today, were interested in parsing distinct cognitive states in an effort both to articulate the range of human experience and to suggest curatives when these states moved from the normal (for example, sleep) to the problematic (for example, congelation, which can include sleeping with the eyes open). Certain of these states also have provocative tie-ins with other seemingly unrelated discourses. *Sounding*, a common term for swooning in the Renaissance, was a nautical term, as today, for measuring depth. Likewise, *syncope*, a type of swoon precipitated by irregularities in the heartbeat, was a common prosodic term for the dropping or contraction of a syllable (as in syncopation). In short, such terms are rich ways of accounting for early modern cognitive experience. They tie the body, linguistically, to sound and space, their very language encapsulating the way that states like swooning and sleep negotiate body, mind, and environment.

Barrough's taxonomizing impulse imposes a legible form on states that are, as these semantic crosscurrents suggest, potentially far less distinct in experience and scope. In the face of this uncertainty, some Renaissance taxonomies of sleep states strive to offer spatial clarity, neatly organizing "sleep" and "watch" (or wakefulness) in charts and elaborating their utility in carefully labeled sections.[27] Thomas Elyot even outlines a humoral spectrum of sleep activity: "The brayne exceedyng in heat hath Slepe short and not sound" while the brain "moyst in excesse hath Slepe much and depe."[28] Texts such as Elyot's are concerned with appropriate regimens for bodily health, and these manuals provide ostensibly easy shorthand for diagnosing sleep problems within a humoral system. Taken together, Elyot's and Barrough's texts speak to the varying extents to which sixteenth-century theorists wanted to organize received knowledge of the body into accessible and useful forms, while still manifesting an interest in the margins and thresholds of observed human cognition—states that themselves resist firm categories.

By reading texts such as Elyot's and Barrough's alongside early modern lyric, epic, drama, and long-form prose, this volume continues to develop a version of new formalism that argues for form as radically embedded in a network of biocultural influences, rather than seeing it as a disconnected, purely representational literary element. This approach, of course, is rooted in the full complexity of the word *form* itself. Elizabeth Scott-Baumann and Ben Burton contend that in approaching literary texts "form is as useful as a verb as [it is as] a noun, and indeed ... many of the problems of defining form as an object come into clearer focus when we think of it as an action or series of actions."[29] The tension between form-as-action and form-as-object certainly characterizes many literary encounters with a sleeper. When early moderns look at a sleeper and diagnose their condition, as Elyot attempts to do, they may simply be describing the current "form," or visible aspect, of the figure (*OED*, noun, 1a). At the same time, they may also be labeling a "body" itself (3) or (more deeply) asking about that body's Aristotelian form or essence (4a). Their intervention could be observational, passively asking what type of consciousness is being exhibited (5b)—or, instead, active in helping to forge a new state of consciousness, literally re-forming the patient by altering their embodied circumstances ("form," verb, 1a). In light of these multifaceted perspectives on embodied form itself, the term takes on even more complex overtones as a tool of literary analysis—a use for the noun *form* that is emergent in the mid-sixteenth century (9).[30]

DIAGNOSING THE SLEEPER

While humoral guidelines provided general principles, the practical diagnosis of a sleeper depended on the sense of decorum that was cultivated within particular community settings. If a listener fell asleep during a church service, as the author of *An Alarme to Wake Church-Sleepers* (1644) peremptorily hints, the congregation ought to view this as "a breach" of the accepted code of behavior and subject that sleeper to correction.[31] In a different community context, Spenser equips his readers to judge the valences of the Redcrosse Knight's romance sleep through moralizing language: Redcrosse "slept soundly void of evill thought" before Archimago's invocation of Morpheus began to "abuse his fantasy" with "false shewes."[32] At the same time, all of these judgments could backfire, because human beings could never completely understand all of the contexts or variables in play during the sleep state, where physical, humoral, spiritual, natural, and supernatural influences coexist.

A popular pamphlet of 1646, *The True Relation of Two Wonderfull Sleepers*, implicitly highlights the danger of conflating these influences. When the virtuous Londoner Elizabeth Jefkins is discovered napping in the middle of the day, her husband (and the neighbors he eventually fetches) must make two different assessments of her condition: a spiritual diagnosis (has Jefkins

8 | FORMING SLEEP

given in to sloth?) and a medical diagnosis (is Jefkins actually ill?). Tackling both questions simultaneously, the observers experiment to see if they can wake her up. The husband drops "cold water upon her face," inserts a key into her mouth, and pulls repeatedly on her nose; later, the neighbors gawk at the sleeper, pinch her, and try verbally to shame her into waking.[33] After a number of hours, they decide that Jefkins's previous virtuous behavior, combined with her current nonresponsiveness, makes her condition a medical crisis, not a spiritual one. They spoon-feed her broth and summon a doctor—who prescribes bleeding from the nose, resulting in Jefkins's death.

Moralizing on the tale, the pamphleteer Thomas Bates called it a "wonder": Jefkins's "sanguine complexion," hardworking nature, and modest size combined to prove that "it cannot stand either in Reason or Philosophy, that such a heavines of sleep, and sloth of spirits, should proceed from any intrinsecall or inward cause."[34] In other words, human efforts have failed to judge or treat the sleeper's moral and physical conditions, because the human mind cannot understand their etiologies by deploying any epistemological tools. Only the "immediate hand of God," in Bates's phrase, could account for Jefkins's sleep—and, therefore, only God could fully understand the circumstances behind it. At the same time, there is a horrible paradox in play here. An attempt to diagnose the sleeper was necessary, because she needed help—but that attempt also meant operating without complete knowledge of the situation, in a way that led to her death.

While Bates's piece is shaped to offer a cohesive and theologically focused reading of the heretofore illegible body of Jefkins, manuscript medical case notes of the period can offer a less theologically and ethically mediated look at the epistemological crisis precipitated by the mystery of unconsciousness. Sometime in the mid-seventeenth century, Dr. John Symcotts pays a visit to Mr. Egerton, the youngest son of Lord Bridgewater. Egerton has been unconscious for many hours in an apoplexy and, by Symcotts's report, suffered "an abolition of all Animall functions." Symcotts sets about rousing Egerton, using a number of practices, poultices, and procedures. He first has "the smoke of tobacco to be blown up into his nostrills," has his head "chafed" with warm cloths, and has his neck and ears rubbed with oils of marjoram, sage, and amber, some of which is also put into his mouth and nose. This results in Egerton bleeding at the nose. Over the next few hours, Symcotts undertakes a series of increasingly invasive procedures with no evident adjustment of his uncertain diagnosis. He bathes the patient's head with sack, chafes and strikes his feet and hands, puts mustard and vinegar into his mouth, injects sneezing powder into his nose, and reapplies oils. Meeting with no success, he proceeds to hold a hot frying pan close to Egerton's head, cup his shoulders, and give the patient an enema and a suppository of allum. To his feet he applies a "black playster," and he cups and scarifies the patient's shoulders, head, and a previously bled vein in the arm. Finally, he applies leeches to the man's fundament. Sadly, it was "all in vayne for he dyed the 24th day at 12 a clock at night." Symcotts ends by noting that he avoided bleeding the vein in the man's arm or his jugular for fear it might have "bene blamed as the cause of his death."[35]

As a manuscript account of treatment, Symcotts's text stands in contrast to the published theological call to action offered by the Jefkins pamphlet. The contrasts between the texts demonstrate that different genres and even forms of textual transmission—and the extent to which these are shaped for a given audience—can provide another variation on how form might shape sleep discourses. At the same time, both of these texts take the *nosce te ipsum* imperative and apply it actively in a larger community setting: the diagnosers must know not only their own limitations but also the potentially conflated influences on the sleep state. They must also reckon with gaps in their own knowledge. In the case of *The True Relation*, this lack of knowledge is reframed as a religious teleology, meaning that those encountering the pathologized sleeper must acknowledge the superiority of the divine plan—even though this means that the sleeper can never be fully treated, or even preserved, by human mechanisms. Symcotts's account, in turn, demonstrates the limits of sleep knowledge in the medical profession, as a reminder to the practitioner and an officially documented record of practice. In both cases, interpreting sleep becomes a means by which to encounter the limits of human inquiry and agency. Yet the dynamic encounters among print, theology, and sleep (in the case of *The True Relation*) and manuscript, humoral medicine, and unconsciousness (in Symcotts's case notes) result in two very different interpretations of these limits, from religious consolation to a factual account of human powerlessness and bodily frailty. If sleepers invite observers to view, assess, and protect them within mortal boundaries, as these two cases suggest, they clearly present an epistemological puzzle, inviting speculation into the workings of not just the senses but also the soul and the conscience during states of unconsciousness.

ESSAY SUMMARIES

As literature encounters sleep, these questions of the soul, ethical judgment, taxonomy, context, and humanness are refracted through many genres and approaches. Cognizant of this fact, the essays in this collection confront questions of sleep and form from a number of perspectives, including physical form, literary form, and forms of consciousness. While many of the essays combine these perspectives in different ways, all of them use representations of sleep as a means of articulating encounters among history, embodiment, and/or genre. The through line that connects all of our approaches is attention to the implications of form for ethical definitions of the human, in multiple stages of consciousness that are bioculturally inflected.

This volume examines literary works that were created between roughly 1580 and 1667, focusing primarily on pieces written in English, with attention to Continental counterparts and classical antecedents in particular essays. Our three parts—on lyric, drama, and long-form writing (epic and prose)— focus on how genre and literary/embodied form shape and are shaped by period discourses on sleep and consciousness.

Particularly in the case of lyric poetry, the lexicons and taxonomies enabled by sleep lead to questions of literary form and signification. Three essays explore these topics in greater detail. Giulio Pertile begins the collection by engaging lyric's interest in the diction of consciousness. For Pertile, late sixteenth- and early seventeenth-century sonneteers create a rhetoric of sleep that negotiates the relationship between embodied poetics and Petrarchan conceits in the sonnet sequence. Using devices from apostrophe to oxymoron, these sonnets depict and trouble the experience of consciousness, questioning the totalizing "I" of the speaker in the process. In illustrating this, the essay reveals how soporific liminality and fluctuations of wakefulness offer a different model of lyric subjectivity that is defined by the effable and the temporary. By including Continental poets such as Della Casa and Desportes, and early women writers such as Mary Wroth, Pertile's essay introduces the collection through a multiplicity of voices, demonstrating how lyric poets from a variety of positionalities negotiate lyric subjectivity at the level of figurative language.

Margaret Simon's essay also considers how lyric strategies in representing sleep scenarios shape the subjectivities of lyric personae. Focusing on Thomas Campion's airs and epigrams, the essay traces repeated plots of half-sleep. The essay works across Campion's formal engagements, including the form of a printed song collection, songs that depict sleeping female forms, the rhyme that makes up these songs, and even the musical scores to which they were set. Rhyme and musical repetition make Campion's depictions of half-sleep open-ended and initiate a process of self-imitation. His interest in repeating scenarios of half-sleep thus becomes less about the state's dramatic possibilities than about how depicting such states might reinforce his own changing perspectives on rhyme, refrain, and poetic propagation.

To bridge between perspectives on lyric form and perspectives on embodied human forms, Nancy Simpson-Younger closes our lyric section by close-reading the Sidney Psalms. In her chapter, Simpson-Younger asks how recursive cycles of sleep and consciousness can spur reflections on human and divine knowledge. By exploring states from fetal unconsciousness to nightly slumber, and by using psalm translation as a means of repeatedly revisiting these states, she shows how Mary Sidney Herbert frames even unconscious experience as a means by which to encounter God—coming closer to an understanding of the divine, while still maintaining the Protestant conviction that the divine is never fully accessible to the human. If God's oversight and presence are palpable to human beings in utero, in slumber, in coma, and in swoon, then all human beings (not simply those who are conscious) can have access to divinely inspired learning and salvation.

Our second part, on early modern drama, begins to introduce questions of the physical human form even more deeply, since bodies are foregrounded so prominently in staged texts. Because the early modern stage is a crucible for articulating changing conceptions of personhood, the chapters in this part focus on interactions between sleeping or exhausted bodies and language, with all of the ethical ramifications that this entails.

To begin the part, Timothy Turner asks how sleep deprivation serves as a form of torture in *Othello* and *The Taming of the Shrew*. Working across dramatic genres, and using historical accounts of torture through sleep deprivation to foreground "the physiological basis upon which early modern psychology itself was founded," Turner argues that the dynamics that surround torture by sleep deprivation define it as an early modern expression of biopower. In arguing for representations of sleep deprivation as a means to explore the ontologies of other bodies and minds, Turner draws attention to the way in which sleep and its lack can form and reform the premodern person, highlighting the intersections of essentialized and socially, externally

12 | FORMING SLEEP

constructed identity. Sleep deprivation, and the language that shapes it, re-forms both Katherine and Othello, interpolating Katherine into a Foucauldian hierarchy enforced by biopower and forcing Othello to define himself through a humoral discourse of biopower that becomes racialized through Iago's manipulation.

The part continues with an essay by Jennifer Lewin. Approaching issues of hierarchical positionality from the angle of agency, Lewin argues that Puck and others use sleep as "a form of making others susceptible to magic without their understanding or consent." By analyzing the actions of Oberon and Puck vis-à-vis Titania, as well as the experience of the four young lovers in the forest, Lewin examines the perpetually shifting ways that consciousness creates and affects definitions of agency. Through a branch of philosophy known as the study of action and agency, her work seeks to understand how to account for characters whose actions and motivations are shaped by forces of which they are unaware—a frequent occurrence in *A Midsummer Night's Dream*.

Taking up these issues of constituted personhood, Brian Chalk considers the ramifications of sleep for the aging, semimonarchical figure of King Lear. While Shakespeare's earlier kings experience pressure to maintain vigilance over their bodies and realms, as Benjamin Parris and Rebecca Totaro have argued elsewhere, Shakespeare's Lear is a fascinating late exception to this rule. In his chapter, Chalk argues not only that sleep becomes necessary for Lear's ongoing personhood and relational capacities but also that sleep actively reforges the connections between Lear and his previously neglected subordinates, allowing him to understand the bonds of care and ethical obligation that subtend the early modern political hierarchy. Although Lear's understanding of these matters can be partial or temporary, given his aging condition, sleep acts as a mediating force to shore up and reconnect the former king with his relations—showing a late-career transition in Shakespeare's framing of monarchical sleep.

Our final part considers how sleep states emerge in long-form genres, such as epic and the prose treatise, that make space for sustained and sometimes recursive encounters with consciousness in both allegorical and diagnostic scenarios. These capacious genres allow authors to have ongoing engagements with philosophical conceptions of mind, at times resisting such discourses and at times nuancing them for their own purposes. Both of the epics explored in this part consider how philosophical discourses shape depictions of mind-body relations, asking how external forces are (or are not) allowed to form the inner experience of a semiconscious human being. Burton's prose treatise, meanwhile, emerges as a generic hybrid whose depiction of sleep strays from, and is skeptical of, medical and religious interpretations of sleep states.

For Benjamin Parris, the external force of labor expectations can inflect the slumber (or insomnia) of Spenserian characters such as Scudamor. In a Marxist reading of Book 4 of *The Faerie Queene*, Parris frames Scudamor's sleeplessness as a result of the demands of labor in a biopolitical context, with the figure of Care as an instantiation and exacerbation of these demands. Read in this way, the episode of the forge of Care reshapes metaphors drawn from Pythagoras to highlight the jarring sense of alienation—not harmony— in both the setting and the poetry of Scudamor's experience. In the end, Parris argues, sleep paradoxically both sustains and suspends the labor of Care, aligning Spenserian poiesis with the restless hammering of the minions.

Cassie Miura's work brings forward some of the contradictory elements of Burton's *Anatomy of Melancholy* in its encounters with sleep. Despite prominent religious discourses around sleep pathology in the period, the essay reveals Burton's view on sleep states as protosecular. Further, Burton develops a curative program that works not by balancing a patient's humors but by matching excessive sleep with curative overindulgence. At the level of genre, Burton's resistance to period orthodoxies regarding sleep transforms this aspect of his text from a medical tract to a philosophical treatise with a decidedly skeptical bent, more at home with Seneca or Montaigne than with Burton's physician peers. Tracing Burton's sustained engagement with sleep disorders, Miura's essay uses sleep as a case study to consider how Burton creates the prose treatise to forge his own identity as a philosopher-physician, indebted to—but not fully subject to and often skeptical of—the period's medical theories.

Finally, N. Amos Rothschild asks how Milton engages faculty psychology (a medieval and early modern conversation about the mind and its functional divisions) to defend the theological concept of free will in *Paradise Lost*. As the sleeping Eve is approached by Satan, many critics have wondered whether the first woman had the means to resist his incursions or whether her vulnerability actually conditioned her for an imminent fall. Rothschild's essay shows how Milton, by homing in on the human mind's balance of enclosure and exposure, not only uses contemporary scientific understandings of the faculties, but also leverages them in the service of his theodicy. He concludes that Milton highlights the interlocking but separate nature of two faculties—the Reason and the Fancy—in order to prove that Adam and Eve had the capacity not only to resist Satan's information but also to receive it without the stain of sin.

To synthesize and reflect on the implications of all of these ideas, Garrett Sullivan Jr. links back to the volume's larger focus on the biocultural contexts and inflections of the sleep state. In his afterword, he notes that sleep is "a variable somatic practice that is functionally inextricable from the social." For Sullivan, this connection offers a "horizon of expectations" that derive from the structures and parameters of sleep scenarios and also from ways of conceptualizing them.

Taken together, all of these essays demonstrate how early modern depictions of sleep shape and are shaped by the philosophical, medical, political, and, above all, formal discourses through which they are articulated. With this in mind, the question of form merges considerations of the physical and the poetic with the spiritual and the secular, highlighting the pervasiveness of sleep states as a means by which to reflect on the human condition. As this volume shows, literary forms and genres interact dynamically with embodied forms and positionalities during this process of reflection, resulting in representations of consciousness that both challenge and reify conceptions of personhood.

NOTES

1. On these topics, see Jennifer Lewin, "Murdering Sleep in *Macbeth*," *Shakespearean International Yearbook* 5 (2006): 181–88; Benjamin Parris, "'The body is with the King, but the King is not with the body': Sovereign Sleep in *Hamlet* and *Macbeth*," *Shakespeare Studies* 40 (2012): 101–42; and Sasha Handley, *Sleep in Early Modern England* (New Haven: Yale University Press, 2016).

2. Handley, *Sleep in Early Modern England*, 17.

3. As many scholars have pointed out, this often involves genres such as the dream vision or dream analysis. See, for example,

Marjorie Garber, *Dream in Shakespeare: From Metaphor to Metamorphosis* (1974; repr., New Haven: Yale University Press, 2013), and Carole Levin, *Dreaming in the English Renaissance: Politics and Desire in Court and Culture* (New York: Palgrave Macmillan, 2008).

4. Handley, *Sleep in Early Modern England*, 4.

5. See, for example, Giulio Pertile, *Feeling Faint: Affect and Consciousness in the Renaissance* (Evanston: Northwestern University Press, 2019).

6. *The Complete Essays of Montaigne*, trans. Donald M. Frame (Stanford: Stanford University Press, 1965), 268.

7. See Handley, *Sleep in Early Modern England*, 2.

8. John Foxe, *The Whole Workes of W. Tyndall, John Frith, and Doct Barnes three worthy martyrs, and principall teachers of this Churche of England collected and compiled in one tome togither, beyng before scattered, [and] now in print here exhibited to the Church. To the prayse of God, and profite of all good Christian readers* (London: John Daye, 1573), EEBO, http://gateway.proquest.com.prox.lib.ncsu.edu/openurl?ctx_ver=Z39.882003&res_id=xri:eebo&rft_id=xri:eebo:image:18327:423.330, and Gabriel Harvey, *Four letters, and certaine sonnets especially touching Robert Greene, and other parties by him abused* (London: John Wolfe, 1592), EEBO, http://gateway.proquest.com.prox.lib.ncsu.edu/openurl?ctx_ver=Z39.88-2003&res_id=xri:eebo&rft_id=xri:eebo:image:4033:4, 5. Ros King references Foxe's text and its emphasis on knowing that one has erred, noting that Shakespeare used "the much older word 'conscience' instead" that "need have no moral injunction or coloring in itself": King, "Minds at Work: Writing, Acting, Watching, Reading *Hamlet*," in *Shakespeare and Consciousness*, ed. Paul Budra and Clifford Werier (New York: Palgrave Macmillan, 2016), 140.

9. The *Oxford English Dictionary* cites this quote from Isaac Watts's *Logick* to support the definition "Having the faculty of consciousness" ("Conscious, adj. and n.," def. 8).

10. Philip van der Eijk, *Medicine and Philosophy in Classical Antiquity* (Cambridge: Cambridge University Press, 2005), 169–71; Sir Thomas Elyot, *The Castell of Health corrected, and in some places augmented by the first author thereof, Sir Thomas Elyot Knight* (London: Widdow Orwin, 1595), 3v; Michel de Montaigne, *Essays*, trans. John Florio (London: Valentine Sims for Edward Blount, 1603), 146–47; René Descartes, *Meditations on First Philosophy*, trans. and ed. John Cottingham (Cambridge: Cambridge University Press, 2017), 16.

11. Over the past decade, literary scholars have become increasingly interested in how the language of and discoveries in the cognitive sciences can help us better to understand how early moderns theorized and represented the mind within a network of subjectivities. See, for example, John A. Teske, "From Embodied to Extended Cognition," *Zygon* 48, no. 3 (2013): 759–87; John Henry Adams, "Agentive Objects and Protestant Idolatry in *Arden of Faversham*," *Studies in English Literature 1500–1900*, 57, no. 2 (2017): 231–51; Drew Daniel, *The Melancholy Assemblage: Affect and Epistemology in the English Renaissance* (New York: Fordham University Press, 2013); Christopher Tilmouth, "Passions and Intersubjectivity in Early Modern Literature," in *Passions and Subjectivity in Early Modern Culture*, ed. Brian Cummings and Freya Sierhuis (Farnham: Ashgate, 2013), 13–32; Bruce R. Smith, *Phenomenal Shakespeare* (Chichester, U.K.: Wiley-Blackwell, 2010), e.g., 180. Scholars have in some cases claimed this modern language as a way to speak more precisely about what we commonly think of (perhaps too strictly) as the pre-Cartesian integration of body and mind.

12. On self-fashioning, see Stephen Greenblatt, *Renaissance Self-Fashioning: From More to Shakespeare* (Chicago: University of Chicago Press, 1980).

13. Gillian Knoll, "How to Make Love to the Moon: Intimacy and Erotic Distance in John Lyly's *Endymion*," *Shakespeare Quarterly* 65, no. 2 (2014): 164–79. Similarly interested in the intersectionality offered by embodied states, Giulio Pertile finds threshold states of consciousness as points of connection between the literal and allegorical in Spenser's *Faerie Queene* as he argues that moments of astonishment ("stounds") "mark the places where the allegorical and literal levels of the poem, by means of the 'spirits,' interpenetrate most fully": Giulio Pertile, "'And All His Senses Stound': The Physiology of Stupefaction in Spenser's *Faerie Queene*," *English Literary Renaissance* 44, no. 3 (2014), 451.

14. Parris, "The body is with the King," 101–42; Rebecca Totaro, "Securing Sleep in

Hamlet," *Studies in English Literature, 1500–1900* 50, no. 2 (2010): 407–26.

15. Garrett Sullivan Jr., *Sleep, Romance, and Human Embodiment: Vitality from Spenser to Milton* (Cambridge: Cambridge University Press, 2012), e.g., 95.

16. Jennifer Lewin, "'Your Actions Are My Dreams': Sleepy Minds in Shakespeare's Last Plays," *Shakespeare Studies* 31 (2003): 184–204.

17. Megan Leitch, "'Grete luste to slepe': Somatic Ethics and the Sleep of Romance from *Sir Gawain and the Green Knight* to Shakespeare," *Parergon* 32, no. 1 (2015): 103–28; Nancy Simpson-Younger, "'The Garments of Posthumus': Identifying the Non-responsive Body in *Cymbeline,*" in *Staging the Blazon in Early Modern Theater,* ed. Sara Morrison and Deborah Uman (Farnham, U.K.: Ashgate, 2013), 177–88; Simpson-Younger, "'I become a vision': Seeing and the Reader in Sidney's *Old Arcadia,*" *Sidney Journal* 30, no. 2 (2012): 57–85; Simpson-Younger, "Watching the Sleeper in *Macbeth,*" *Shakespeare* 12, no. 3 (2016): 260–73.

18. Jane Bennett, *Vibrant Matter: An Ecology of Things* (Durham: Duke University Press, 2010). See in particular the chapter "The Force of Things," which traces the extent to which the inanimate world has been theorized as having agency over human experience, beginning with Foucault and working back to Spinoza.

19. For a reading of this process in medieval texts, see Barry Windeatt, "The Art of Swooning in Middle English," in *Medieval Latin and Middle English Literature,* ed. Christopher Canon and Maura Nolan (Cambridge, U.K.: Brewer, 2011), 211–30.

20. Gail Kern Paster, *Humoring the Body: Emotions and the Shakespearean Stage* (Chicago: University of Chicago Press, 2004), e.g., 4–5.

21. L. J. Rather points out that the term *nonnatural* was never used by Galen and elaborates on the complexity of this term; see Rather, "The 'Six Things Non-Natural': A Note on the Origins and Fate of a Doctrine and a Phrase," *Clio Medica* 3 (1968): 337–47.

22. Thomas Cogan, *The Haven of Health [. . .] Hereunto Is added a preservation from the pestilence, with a short censure of the late sicknes at Oxford* (London: Anne Griffin for Roger Ball, 1636), Internet Archive, 20, https://archive.org/details/havenofhealth chioocoga/page/20. Subsequent references to Cogan in this introduction are from the 1636 edition and will be made parenthetically.

23. The humoral coldness of the brain encountering these vapors triggers the sensory blockage for Cogan (ibid., 269). See also John Lydgate, following Aristotle, in his *Governall of Helthe*: "He that slepeth so moche th[at] he have no hevynes in his wombe of the meate that he toke before need not drede of ony great syckenes nor of the goute" ([London: Wynkyn de Worde, 1506], 2v). The digestive activities of the body in sleep could be preservative to health, at least in the vernacular understanding of Aristotelian physiology.

24. On the final point, see Thomas Nashe, *The Terrors of the Night* (London: John Danter for William Jones, 1594), B2v–B3r.

25. Philip Barrough, *The Methode of Phisicke, Conteyning the Causes, Signes, and Cures of Inward Diseases in Mans Body* (London: Thomas Vautroullier, 1583), 30–31.

26. Barrough, *The Methode of Phisicke,* 29.

27. See Elyot, *Castell of Health* (1595), 1–23. This taxonomy is commonplace in the sixteenth and early seventeenth centuries. Thomas Cogan, in his *Haven of Health* (1636), quotes Elyot on the subject (4r).

28. Elyot, *Castell of Health.* 5–6.

29. Elizabeth Scott-Bauman and Ben Burton, eds., *The Work of Form: Poetics and Materiality in Early Modern Culture* (Oxford: Oxford University Press, 2014), 5.

30. As Burton and Scott-Bauman demonstrate, George Puttenham's *The Arte of English Poesie* (1589) was written just after "a time when 'form' becomes associated with literary composition (*OED* 9)" (*Work of Form,* 8).

31. *An Alarme to Wake Church-Sleepers* (London: Matthew Symmons, 1644), 39.

32. Edmund Spenser, *The Faerie Queene,* ed. Thomas P. Roche (New York: Penguin,

1987), 52, 1.1.446.3–4. For more on Spenser's Redcrosse Knight, see Benjamin Parris, "'Watching to banish Care': Sleep and Insomnia in Book 1 of *The Faerie Queene*," *Modern Philology* 113, no. 2 (2015): 151–77.

33. Thomas Bates, *The True Relation of Two Wonderfull Sleepers*, reprinted in *Reprints of English Books, 1475–1700*, ed. Joseph Arnold Foster, no. 42 (East Lansing, Mich., 1945), 4–5. [Source text: British Museum, E.349.]

34. Bates, *The True Relation of Two Wonderfull Sleepers*, 10.

35. W. Welles, John Symcotts, and C. Haslam, Wellcome MS 798, 1635–59, Wellcome Library, London, 21v. Symcotts is probably best known for being doctor to Oliver Cromwell. See F. N. L. Poynter, *A Seventeenth Century Doctor and His Patients* (Bedfordshire, U.K.: The Society, 1951), vii.

Part I

SLEEP STATES AND SUBJECTIVITY IN EARLY MODERN LYRIC

CHAPTER 1

Thinking Sleep in the Renaissance Sonnet Sequence

GIULIO J. PERTILE

Sonnet sequences have long been a central testing ground for claims about subjectivity in the Renaissance. Perhaps most famously, in *Shakespeare's Perjured Eye*, Joel Fineman argued that "in his sonnets Shakespeare invents a genuinely new poetic subjectivity," one he characterizes in terms of a "broken identity that carves out in the poet's self a syncopated hollowness that accounts for the deep personal interiority of the sonnets' poetic persona."[1] More recent work on sonnets has emphasized the political and social entanglements of these seemingly most personal utterances, drawing on Arthur Marotti's influential claim that in Renaissance sonnet sequences "love is not love" but rather an expression of social ambition.[2] Christopher Warley, for example, argues that Sir Philip Sidney's *Astrophil and Stella* "differs from other Petrarchan work . . . in the degree to which it stages the failure of Astrophil's autoreflexivity and the degree to which it views such autoreflexivity as itself conditioned by a broader social field"; "the desire for autoreflexivity itself," he continues, "is a socially distinct position."[3]

Despite their differences, Fineman and Warley both define subjectivity in the same way: as the speaker's tendency to reflect and report on his or her own experience—in other words, as what Warley here calls "autoreflexivity."

We might well ask whether this autoreflexivity, and the "deep personal interiority" that it opens up, exhausts the possible forms of subjectivity in the sonnet sequence. Scholarship on the body, for example, has shown the degree to which Renaissance subjectivity is tied to somatic experience, in particular as it is shaped by the four humors. In *Bodies and Selves in Early Modern England*, Michael Schoenfeldt demonstrates "the profound medical and physiological underpinnings of Shakespeare's acute vocabulary of psychological inwardness" in the *Sonnets*.[4] This humoral conception of the subject grounds autoreflexivity—whether socially embedded or autonomous—in the working of impersonal substances. Yet while accounts such as Schoenfeldt's insist that mental and emotional states in the Renaissance were experienced through and as the operations of bodily substances, they do not always fully capture what *happens* to subjective experience when we understand it as embodied. They tend either (as in the quotation above) to preserve the language of "inwardness" or to replace it with a humoral body that may well seem to lack self-consciousness altogether. Philosophers and scientists working on consciousness today agree that it is embodied but, for them (as, perhaps, for most of us today), consciousness is primarily defined not as interior reflection but rather as, in John Searle's words, "those states of sentience or awareness that typically begin when we wake up in the morning from a dreamless sleep and continue throughout the day until we fall asleep again." When subjectivity is understood in these terms, the autoreflexivity of an incorporeal subject is replaced by the sentient states of an embodied one; on this account, subjective experience is less a matter of a stable self reflecting in inward space on a range of thoughts and experiences than of the phenomenological texture of sentient experience as such. In this sense, Searle suggests, consciousness can be found not only in human beings but in "higher animals" as well.[5] Can we find Renaissance poems in which awareness is a felt rather than an abstract phenomenon, affective and sensory in nature rather than discursive and self-reflective—in which, in other words, consciousness extends beyond the rationality and reflectiveness that are the traditional prerogatives of "the human"?

In the following pages I make what may at first seem to be a counterintuitive argument: in sonnets about and addressed to sleep, the felt experience of consciousness (which necessarily underlies all more elaborate conceptions of the subject) most fully comes to the fore. In the sonnet *ad somnum*, which emerges as a distinctive subgenre of post-Petrarchan lyric in

Italy, France, and England, sleep is in fact both proximate and tantalizingly remote.[6] Thus the experience of insomnia such sonnets frequently describe involves not persistent wakefulness but rather a borderland between sleep and waking. And at that border, consciousness is transformed into a state of sheer, unwilled feeling—one that we might well still characterize in terms of "awareness," and yet, necessarily, of an awareness that is not directed to *objects*, whether inner or outer. Instead, for poets including Giovanni Della Casa, Philippe Desportes, Mary Wroth, and others, the inability to sleep gives rise to a unique phenomenological state: the frustratingly ongoing fact of feeling and sensing that is, to his or her vexation, the one thing of which the insomniac remains helplessly aware. In such states, that is, awareness is directed to nothing more than awareness itself. Paradoxically, the vanishing of sensory objects and the receding of agency undergone near sleep, in experiences of what Emmanuel Levinas describes as a "wakefulness without intentionality," bring sentience as such into view.[7] When they are no longer directed to outward things, the senses sense nothing but their own continuing activity, nothing but feeling as such.

In dream poetry, the dream is usually recounted *as if* it were happening to waking consciousness. Falling asleep, then, is merely a transitional state between two different forms of consciousness, both conceived as forms of vision. But as we move beyond Petrarch and into sixteenth-century lyric, sleep itself becomes the main focus while dreams recede in importance. Thus rather than replacing one form of consciousness with another, poems about sleep explore a liminal condition in which waking consciousness has been diminished by night and exhaustion even as some form of awareness, unwanted and undirected, continues to be present. And as we will see, when thought is unwilled it is present as such, rather than as an instrument or medium for the transmission of something outside it. The poems depict consciousness as a felt experience of sensing per se rather than as a form of reflection or vision. Where consciousness persists in the absence of both exterior and interior objects, the affective life underlying all conscious experience is laid bare, and vision is replaced by a feeling that cannot be clearly transmuted into an object of any kind, whether material or intangible. In writing from the borderland between wakefulness and sleep, therefore, Renaissance poets move beyond the standard Aristotelian account of sleep that remained dominant in the Renaissance, in which sleep and waking are two mutually exclusive states that do not permit any middle ground:

"No animal which has sense-perception can be neither asleep nor awake."[8] Instead, they open up that phenomenological and philosophical terrain most fully described by the twentieth-century philosopher Emmanuel Levinas, in which subjectivity, trapped at the periphery between sleep and waking, becomes exclusively "constituted by the consciousness that it will never finish."[9]

Aristotle's account of sleep—and his concern to distinguish it clearly from waking—stems from his influential distinction between what he saw as three interrelated but clearly separate forms of life: human, animal, and vegetable. As Garrett Sullivan Jr. has shown, in the late Renaissance that distinction was beginning to weaken. Sullivan's *Sleep, Romance, and Human Embodiment: Vitality from Spenser to Milton* shows in persuasive detail how within the genre of epic the "romance episode" works to blur the line between forms of life. In lyric poetry of the same period, we can see poets from Della Casa to Wroth exploiting and extending the traditional contours of the sonnet form to a similar end. By creating analogies between states of consciousness and the internal formal articulations of the sonnet, these poets—and in particular Wroth—can then use the sonnet to show how consciousness may transgress its own boundaries and elude the distinctions between reason, sensation, and affect on which traditional definitions of the human being depend.

It might be objected that the states of consciousness explored in the sonnet *ad somnum* are marginal and transient and thus cannot constitute an alternative to the self-consciousness and sense of identity that comprise what we might think of as "mainstream" accounts of the human subject. In Sidney's *Astrophil and Stella*, however, sleep and near-sleep states provide the impetus for the most extensive subsequence of poems, the so-called Morpheus sonnets; the nocturnal motif also recurs near the end of the sequence. And Mary Wroth's *Pamphilia to Amphilanthus*, one of the last seventeenth-century English sonnet sequences, and the only secular sequence written by a woman, is composed under the sign of night and sleep from the beginning. Indeed, Wroth's sequence will allow us to see, in the final pages of this essay, that when the gendered gaze so central to much of the Petrarchan tradition fades out—when, in other words, vision weakens in proximity to sleep—we are left not merely with the desensitized privation of Aristotelian sleep but rather with a liminal condition in which the senses sense nothing but themselves.[10] Such a state, I suggest in conclusion, forms the basis for much of Wroth's sequence and offers a form of poetic subjectivity that is not merely gendered "female" but rather eludes, at least tentatively, the gender distinctions built into a poetics premised on the centrality of vision and the gaze. While it perhaps falls short of a fully fledged alternate model of the self, the kind of subjectivity unveiled in proximity to sleep nevertheless offers an important and powerful glimpse of how human experience—and the human itself—might be conceived beyond dichotomies such as reason and passion, activity and passivity, and the gender divisions onto which, in the early modern period, they were inevitably mapped.

WAKING, THINKING, BURNING, CRYING: CONTINENTAL MODELS

In much love poetry, sleep is perhaps most conspicuous when it is absent, in the motif of the lover's insomnia. The motif goes back at least to Dido in Book 4 of Virgil's *Aeneid* and to Ovid's *Amores* 1.2, and it recurs throughout Petrarch's *Rerum Vulgarium Fragmenta* (*RVF*; see, for instance, 23, 50, 83, 164, 216, 223, 226, 234, 237, 255, 332, 360). It is perhaps most vividly expressed by 164:

> Or che 'l ciel et la terra e 'l vento tace
> et le fere e gli augelli il sonno affrena,
> Notte il carro stellato in giro mena
> et nel suo letto il mar senz'onda giace,
>
> vegghio, penso, ardo, piango; et chi mi sface
> sempre m'è inanzi per mia dolce pena:
> guerra è 'l mio stato, d'ira et di duol piena,
> et sol di lei pensando ò qualche pace.
>
> Così sol d'una chiara fonte viva
> move 'l dolce et l'amaro ond'io mi pasco;
> una man sola mi risana et punge;
>
> e perché 'l mio martir non giunga a riva,
> mille volte il dí moro et mille nasco,
> tanto da la salute mia son lunge.[11]

> Now that the heavens and the earth and the wind are silent, and
> sleep reins in the beasts and the birds, Night drives her starry car
> about, and in its bed the sea lies without a wave,
>
> I am awake, I think, I burn, I weep; and she who destroys me is
> always before me, to my sweet pain: war is my state, full of sorrow
> and suffering, and only thinking of her do I have any peace.
>
> Thus from one clear living fountain alone spring the sweet and the
> bitter on which I feed; one hand alone heals me and pierces me.
>
> And that my suffering may not reach an end, a thousand times a
> day I die and a thousand am born, so distant am I from health.

The second quatrain opens by providing, in the rapid succession of an asyndeton, the main verbs of the first sentence. They express, in a sharp contrast to the peaceful state of the world around him, the lover's tormented and unwilled wakefulness: "vegghio, penso, ardo, piango." The asyndeton turns each verb into a synonym for a single underlying state in which waking, thinking, burning, and crying, usually separate activities, are all identified—a state in which, in short, consciousness persists as the self-expression of sheer affect. The implicit contrast with the sea lying peacefully on its "bed" leads us to imagine the speaker's thoughts and tears as relentless waves; he is tossing and turning both physically and in his restless thought.

The Earl of Surrey's translation omits not only the asyndeton but also the sharp transition from the first to the second stanza by which it is emphasized in Petrarch:

> Alas, so all thinges nowe doe holde their peace,
> Heaven and earth disturbed in nothing;
> The beasts, the ayer, the birdes their song doe cease;
> The nightes chare the starres aboute dothe bring.
> Calme is the sea, the waves worke lesse and lesse;
> So am not I, whom love alas doth wring,
> Bringing before my face the great encrease
> Of my desires, whereat I wepe and syng
> In joye and wo as in a doubtfull ease.
> For my swete thoughtes sometyme doe pleasure bring,

But by and by the cause of my disease
Geves me a pang that inwardly dothe sting,
When that I thinke what griefe it is again
To live and lacke the thing should ridde my paine.[12]

The final lines of Petrarch's 164 suggest, in a subtle *volta*, that Petrarch himself wants his torment to continue and hence does not want to sleep. Surrey's translation of the ending does away with this nuance. Indeed, although he does not invoke sleep explicitly, the two exclamations of "alas" suggest that, in contrast to Petrarch, Surrey does desire rest and release. Thus, despite his more outspoken longing for sleep and rest, Surrey actually lessens the insomniac fervor of Petrarch's poem, replacing it with a more languid and lethargic state. We rarely encounter Petrarch himself longing for sleep—unless that sleep, like Endymion's, is tinged by a dream of his beloved, as in *RVF* 237 ("Non à tanti animali il mar fra l'onde"): "Deh or foss'io col vago de la luna / adormentato in qua' che verdi boschi" ["Ah, would that with the lover of the moon / I had fallen asleep in some green wood"]. Even at a point of explicitly low ebb, in *RVF* 83, Petrarch tells us that "può turbarmi il sonno, / ma romper no, l'imagine aspra et cruda" ["the harsh cruel image can disturb my sleep, but not break it"]; a merely "disturbed" sleep, it would seem, is the lowest degree of intensity Petrarch can imagine his amorous passion having.

Yet despite these differences, both Petrarch's and Surrey's sonnets show us how proximity to sleep actually brings into focus what it feels like *not* to sleep—what it feels like, in other words, to be aware when one does not wish to be and when awareness lacks any particular object beyond its own state. Though both refer to an image of the beloved present "before" the speaker in some way, that image is not described in visual detail. Rather, Petrarch and Surrey describe a state of Levinasian "wakefulness without intentionality" in which the objects of the senses and of thinking have been replaced by sheer feeling. Both poets long for this wakefulness to dissolve into a state of insentient oblivion associated with animals and nonhuman nature. In this regard, *RVF* 164 and its translation differ in important ways from sonnets about dreams, in which the sleeper has some sort of visual encounter with the beloved in sleep, a quasi-erotic experience that he longs to recapture. Petrarch himself wrote several sonnets, mostly concentrated in the *in morte* section of the *RVF*, in which the spirit of Laura appears to him in a vision;

in many of his sixteenth-century imitators, if not in Petrarch himself, that vision becomes erotic in nature. Jacopo Sannazaro's *Sonetti e canzoni* 62, for example, is explicitly addressed to sleep, but its focus, like that of the cluster of poems surrounding it (60–68), is ultimately on the dream to which sleep leads:

> O sonno, o requie e triegua degli affanni,
> che acqueti e plachi i miseri mortali,
> da qual parte del ciel movendo l'ali
> venisti a consolare i nostri danni?
> Io per te lodo e benedico gli anni
> che ardendo ho spesi in seguitar miei mali;
> e s'e' piacer non sono al pianto eguali,
> ringrazio pur tuo' dolci e cari inganni.
> Sì bella e sì pietosa in vista umile
> madonna apparve al cor doglioso e stanco,
> che agguagliar non la pòte ingegno o stile;
> tal che, pensando e desïando, io manco,
> qual vidi e strinsi quella man gentile,
> e qual vendetta fei del velo bianco.[13]

O sleep, O respite and truce of troubles, you who assuage and pacify miserable mortals, from what part of the sky, moving your wings, did you come to console our wrongs?

For your sake I praise and bless the years that I have spent following my ills; and if my pleasures have not equaled my complaints, I still thank your sweet dear delusions.

So beautiful and full of pity, with her humble looks, does my lady appear to the doleful and tired heart that wit and style cannot match her—

so much so that I faint, thinking and desiring that hand that I saw and held, and the revenge that I had on her white veil.

While the poem opens with a classical invocation of sleep as peace and rest, it quickly becomes apparent that the "consolation" sleep provides is not merely rest but rather the presence of the beloved in "dolci e cari inganni" that are quasi-erotic in nature. Sleeping is a gateway to dreaming, and dreaming in turn is construed as a form of sight fixed on an object, fully parallel to waking consciousness. Indeed, Sanazaro's *Sonetti e canzoni* 61 is actually structured as a blazon, in which he describes each part of his beloved only to have them all vanish with the appearance of the sun. In English verse, a similar idea is picked up in Sir Thomas Wyatt's "Unstable dream," first printed in Tottel's *Miscellany* (1557):

Unstable dream, according to the place,
Be steadfast once, or else at least be true.
By tasted sweetness make me not to rue
The sudden loss of thy false feignèd grace.
By good respect in such a dangerous case
Thou broughtest not her into this tossing mew
But madest my sprite live, my care to renew,
My body in tempest her succour to embrace.
The body dead, the sprite had his desire,
Painless was th'one, th'other in delight.
Why then, alas, did it not keep it right,
Returning, to leap into the fire?
And where it was at wish, it could not remain,
Such mocks of dreams they turn to deadly pain.[14]

It is hard to imagine Petrarch, with his deep-seated conflicts about the nature of his love and his consistent anxiety about "error," longing for "dolci e cari inganni" or "false feignèd grace" in such an explicit and unambiguous way. At least when it comes to nocturnal sonnets, the objectifying gaze is more central in Petrarchan poetry than it is in Petrarch himself.

While most Italian sonneteers of the sixteenth century invoke sleep primarily for the sake of the visual dreams to which it leads, Giovanni Della Casa's *Rime* (1558) 54 returns to the precedent set by Petrarch in its focus on sleep in disjunction from dreaming. In Della Casa, however, sleep and insomnia are no longer treated only as symptoms of lovesickness.[15] Love, if present at all, is only obliquely alluded to in the poem. Sleep has now become the central motif. Unlike the classical poets to whom he alludes

(Virgil, Ovid, and Tibullus), moreover, Della Casa describes sleep and sleep-lessness in terms of first-person experience:

> O sonno, o della queta, umida, ombrosa
> notte placido figlio; o de' mortali
> egri conforto, oblio dolce de' mali
> sì gravi, ond'è la vita aspra e noiosa;
> soccorri al cor omai, che langu' e posa
> non have, e queste membra stanch' e frali
> solleva: a me ten vola, o sonno, e l'ali
> tue brune sovra me distendi e posa.
> Ov'è 'l silentio che'l dì fugge e'l lume?
> E i lievi sogni, che con non secure
> vestigia di seguirti han per costume?
> Lasso, ch'invan te chiamo, e queste oscure
> e gelide ombre invan lusingo. O piume
> d'asprezza colme! O notti acerb' e dure![16]

O sleep, O peaceful son of humid, quiet, shady night, comfort of sickly mortals and sweet oblivion of those heavy cares that make life sour and tedious,

succor my heart at last, which languishes and yet cannot find rest, and relieve these frail and tired limbs: fly to me, o sleep, and extend and rest over me your tawny wings.

Where is the silence that flees the day and light? And the light dreams, which are wont to follow you with uncertain steps?

Alas, in vain I call you, and in vain I flatter these obscure and frigid shades. O feathers full of harshness! O hard and bitter nights!

The poem tracks an evolving series of relationships to sleep moment by moment, almost in the manner of a dramatic monologue. After the allusive and mythological address to sleep of the first quatrain, the four imperatives in the second quatrain summon sleep with gentle insistence; Della Casa's characteristic enjambments and inversions space them out so as to avoid any hint, as yet, of anxiety or insomnia. In tandem with its many elisions, these features serve to slow down the pace of the poem, so that his language seems almost to take on the peaceful quality of the repose he is invoking—as if he could lull himself into the state he desires by approximating its qualities in his verse. With its long syllables and elision, the concluding "distendi e posa" aurally enacts the actions not only of sleep, imagined as a bird that spreads its peaceful wings over the speaker, but also of his own tired limbs distending and sinking quietly and conclusively into rest.

The eighth line of the sonnet thus brings to a head the desire for sleep that guides the whole octave; for the duration of the *volta*, that desire seems to have been fulfilled. But the illusion of softness and tranquility created by the gradual ritardando of the first two quatrains is shattered with the first line of the sestet, in which the speaker, in a newly pained tone of voice, asks after the silence that this very question disrupts. In contrast to the "lievi sogni" he desired, what the speaker finds instead is the continued and unpleasant insistence of his own inner voice. Since that voice is itself what breaks the silence for which it longs, it speaks of nothing but the fact that it continues. To put it differently, consciousness is perceiving nothing but itself, and that self-perception is experienced as a form of pain and vexation. The form of the sonnet, and specifically the use of the *volta*, is crucial in conveying the reflexive affectivity that consciousness takes on in such a moment. It is as if the speaker momentarily succeeds in experiencing a willed "posa" at the end of the second stanza, only to find consciousness, against his will, quickly and vexingly returning—thus bearing out formally Levinas's description of insomnia as "constituted by the consciousness that it will never finish— that is, that there is no longer any way of withdrawing from the vigilance to which one is held."[17] The transition to the sestet thus captures this experience in which consciousness becomes its own object. Consciousness does not see or grasp itself. It simply feels itself, neither inwardly nor outwardly, in and as an experience of unwilled, persistent affect.

Thus, it is on the basis of the experience recorded by and through the progress of the sonnet itself that, in the final tercet, Della Casa rewrites the encomiastic apostrophe with which the poem began. What he had falsely and even magniloquently invoked as "della queta, umida, ombrosa / notte placido figlio" is now reconceived in the more realistic guise of "oscure / e gelide ombre." Likewise, the merely "aspra e noiosa" life he complains of in the first stanza has now become much more acute, much harder to bear after this interval of near-peace: "O notti acerb' e dure!" And perhaps

32 | SLEEP STATES AND SUBJECTIVITY

most pointedly, the soft and gentle "wings" of sleep have instead become the irritating feathers of the pillow—less an object of consciousness than a metonymy for the painful feeling of consciousness's involuntary persistence. For as the sleeper struggles to feel nothing and fails, even something that should be pleasant becomes an irritant simply insofar as it reminds him that feeling continues. The sonnet has evolved from fantasy to reality in the "real time" of consciousness thinking and feeling out loud as it seeks, counter-productively and with increasing desperation, to switch itself off. Petrarch's sonnets, although they are of course full of intense emotion, tend neverthe-less to describe that emotion in terms of semipermanent conditions rather than of particular and more transient phenomenological states. In contrast, Della Casa's sonnet tracks the changes of an inner state as it evolves in the lived present, and he makes the form of the sonnet crucial to this depiction. The unwilled consciousness characteristic of insomnia is itself captured by the sonnet's relentless unfolding of its form. Ironically enough, therefore, a poem addressed to sleep finishes not merely by describing insomnia but also, through that description, by isolating what we might understand as a state of pure consciousness. In contrast to the visual experience charac-teristic of dream sonnets, Della Casa inaugurates a tradition in which the sleep sonnet instead tracks the twists and turns of the speaker's own felt consciousness—in which consciousness is experienced as felt affect, rather than the eidetic vision of an intangible object.

Philippe Desportes's sonnet to sleep, in his *Les Amours d'Hippolyte* (1573), is a fairly close translation of Della Casa's. In Desportes, however, the outburst of frustration is moved into the second quatrain, so that some of the artfulness with which Della Casa tracks the evolving consciousness of the insomniac is lost:

> Sommeil, paisible fils de la Nuict solitaire,
> Père alme nourricier de tous les animaux,
> Enchanteur gracieux, doux oubli de nos maux,
> Et des esprits blessez l'appareil salutaire:
> Dieu favorable à tous, pourquoy m'es-tu contraire?
> Pourquoi suis-je tout seul rechargé de travaux,
> Or' que l'humide nuict guide ses noirs chevaux,
> Et que chacun jouit de ta grace ordinaire?
> Ton silence où est-il? ton repos et ta paix,

Et ces songes vollans comme un nuage espais,
Qui des ondes d'Oubli vont lavant nos pensées?
O frere de la Mort, que tu m'es ennemi!
Je t'invoque au secours: mais tu es endormi,
Et j'ards, toujours veillant, en tes horreurs glacées.[18]

Sleep, peaceful son of solitary night, mild father, nourisher of all animals, gracious enchanter, sweet oblivion of our ills, and healing help to our wounded souls:

God favorable to all, why are you contrary to me? Why am I alone burdened by cares, now that humid night guides its black horses and every being rejoices in your ordinary grace?

Where is your silence? Where are your repose and peace, and the dreams that fly like a thick cloud, which wash our thoughts in waves of forgetfulness?

O brother of Death, how much of an enemy you are to me! I invoke your aid: but you are asleep, and I continue to burn, waking, amid your frigid horrors.

Desportes's description of dreams in the first tercet differs significantly from that which we find in other sonnets: "Et ces songes vollans comme un nuage espais, / Qui des ondes d'Oubli vont lavant nos pensées." For Desportes, dreams are a means of forgetfulness, cloud-like not because they shift shapes according to the whims of imagination but rather because they wash away our thoughts and leave the mind empty of any content whatsoever. The dissipation of consciousness implied by this image of clouds suggests that the rest of the poem is about its opposite: consciousness's persistence. As with Della Casa, the poem addressed to sleep ends up ironically isolating what is present when sleep is absent—namely, consciousness: "j'ards, toujours veillant, en tes horreurs glacées." Thus, like Della Casa, Desportes also concludes by revising his original flattery of sleep. But the possessive pronoun "tes" introduces a wrinkle into the description of this wakeful state. Though "toujours veillant," he still finds himself, somehow, confined or entrapped by sleep. For while he is clearly not enjoying the happy animal oblivion of sleep, he also lacks the self-possession of full wakefulness. Awake yet unable

34 | SLEEP STATES AND SUBJECTIVITY

to think about anything except being awake itself, he inhabits a hazy borderland, inside sleep's kingdom without actually being asleep. Paradoxically entranced by his own wakefulness, Desportes experiences the mere fact of continued consciousness itself as a kind of nightmare.

"SIGHT'S DECAY": DANIEL AND SIDNEY

As we have seen, Della Casa and Desportes make use of the sonnet form to track the conscious experience of an insomniac speaker as he tries to fall asleep. In the sleep sonnet, the *volta*, or "turn," built in to the sonnet structure becomes an image of the speaker's mental tossing and turning as he seeks a respite from his own frustratingly persistent consciousness. Paradoxically and painfully, in the surrounding darkness and in their proximity to unconsciousness—in "queste umide ombre" or the "horreurs glacées" of sleep itself—the speakers discover that the felt experience of consciousness, in the absence of external stimuli, is actually heightened. For these two poets—in contrast to many of their contemporaries—sleep leads not to dreams but to an anguished exploration of what Emmanuel Levinas describes as the "il y a," the "there is": "One watches on when there is nothing to watch and despite the absence of any reason for remaining watchful. The bare fact of presence is oppressive; one is held by being, held to be. One is detached from any object, any content, yet there is presence. The presence that arises behind nothingness is neither *a being*, nor consciousness functioning in a void, but the universal fact of the *there is*, which encompasses things and consciousness."[19] As we will now see, English sonneteers including Samuel Daniel, Philip Sidney, and Mary Wroth also use the sonnet form to explore the "bare fact of presence" exposed by insomnia. And while all English poets writing about sleep do return to the motif of dreaming, in their poems dreaming comes to represent not an escape from nocturnal consciousness but rather an intensification of its particular form of phenomenological torment.

Samuel Daniel included one sonnet to sleep, probably inspired by Desportes's sonnet on the subject, in his sequence *Delia* (1592):

> Care-charmer sleep, son of the sable night,
> Brother to death, in silent darkness born:
> Relieve my languish, and restore the light,
> With dark forgetting of my cares, return;

And let the day be time enough to mourn
The shipwreck of my ill-adventured youth:
Let waking eyes suffice to wail their scorn
Without the torment of the night's untruth.
Cease dreams, th' imagery of our day-desires,
To model forth the passions of the morrow;
Never let rising sun approve you liars,
To add more grief to aggravate my sorrow.
Still let me sleep, embracing clouds in vain;
And never wake to feel the day's disdain.[20]

Like the sonnets by Della Casa and Desportes, Daniel's sonnet to sleep is in fact a sonnet about insomnia. But it describes, even more precisely, insomnia's hybrid phenomenology: it is a state of consciousness with neither the full clarity of waking nor the peaceful release of real sleep. Daniel asks sleep both to "restore the light" and "with dark forgetting of my cares, return." Insofar as he is still awake, he wishes for darkness, but insofar as he is tormented by obscure, indistinct thoughts, he wishes for light. In their seeming contradiction, these descriptions evoke powerfully the nature of that unwilled, painful consciousness described by Della Casa as well. It is a form of thinking that, lacking any clear object on which to focus, is like a light that shows nothing—a light, then, that is really a kind of darkness. Indeed, the imperative that opens the second quatrain suggests that his present state is an almost unnatural continuation of the day ("let the day be time enough") into night: a brooding chiaroscuro in which the line between daytime thinking and the oblivion of sleep is blurred. Persisting into night, consciousness is left with nothing to be conscious of except the "languish" and the "care" with which it has become identical.

But, for Daniel, nocturnal consciousness does not merely prolong the torments of the day; it also involves its own distinctive form of pain, what he calls the "night's untruth." This is a reference, as the third quatrain clarifies, to dreams: "Cease dreams, th' imagery of our day-desires / To model forth the passions of the morrow." The poem here becomes rather tricky. Lines 7–8 appear to be uttered in parallel to lines 5–6, and yet where 5–6, developing the first stanza, suggest a state of insomniac wakefulness, lines 7–8 would seem to refer to dreams—a feature of sleeping rather than "waking eyes." Similarly, the imperative that opens the third quatrain seems to be in parallel to the summons to sleep, yet it implies that the speaker is now dreaming. Perhaps one should understand Daniel as addressing dreams in general, rather than as speaking to specific dreams tormenting him in the fictional present of the poem's utterance. But it is also possible to imagine the speaker as somehow tormented by dreams even though he is still awake—a reading that aligns with the mingling of dark and light described in the first quatrain. In his short treatise *On Dreams*, Aristotle draws a distinction between the dreams of which we are aware and those of which we are not; some such distinction can perhaps help us to understand the liminal state in which Daniel finds himself here: "Just in the same way in sleep, if a man is conscious that he is asleep, i.e., of the sleeping state in which the perception occurs, the appearance is there, but something within him tells him that although it appears to be Coriscus, it is not really Coriscus (for often when a man is asleep something tells him that what appears to him is a dream); but if he is unaware that he is asleep there is nothing to contradict the imagination."[21] It is the former kind of dream, in which "something within" the dreamer acknowledges the dream's unreality, that Daniel appears to describe in his sonnet. The speaker's dreams are contaminated by a continued awareness that they are nothing but dreams. Thus, Daniel commands them not to cease altogether but rather to cease "to model forth passions" that, even though he is in or near sleep, he knows will be proven false. But where Aristotle, despite the distinction he draws here, does not allow for states between sleep and waking, Daniel's poem can be taken as describing a liminal state in which he is neither fully awake nor asleep. It dedicates six lines to one side of that state (insomnia) and six lines to the other (a shallow sleep in which dreams can still be known as false), slipping between the two inconspicuously to show that for the speaker, in the fictional lived present of the poem's utterance, they cannot be distinguished.

For Daniel, then, these dreams are not significant on account of their visual content, since he knows that content to be false. What his poem dwells on is this state in which dreams continue to happen despite that knowledge. The poem thus bears witness to the torment of a conscious state that escapes the speaker's control and yet leaves him with just enough awareness to recognize that fact. Like Della Casa and Desportes, Daniel testifies not only to the persistence of unwanted consciousness in close proximity to sleep but also to a mental state that is aware, above all, of itself. And, for Daniel, as for his precursors, that self-awareness is a form not of mastery but of its opposite—of passivity and frustration. In the final lines of this quatrain and the concluding couplet, Daniel appears to lower his defenses, and to desire, more conventionally, that he might simply continue dreaming without the epistemological pain of waking up (as in Wyatt's "Unstable dream"). But if my reading of the first twelve lines is correct, what Daniel more specifically desires are dreams unmitigated by the awareness that they are dreams—the second kind of dreaming described by Aristotle. He longs for a resolution to the in-between state described by the rest of the poem and hinging on the transition from line 6 to 7, in which the persistence of daytime consciousness into night is indistinguishable from a superficial kind of dream that is still subject to residual awareness from the day.

In the cluster of sonnets he dedicates to sleep, Sir Philip Sidney, too, is tormented by indistinct images of his beloved. Again, those images tell us more about the lover's own phenomenological condition than about the beloved herself.[22] Sidney describes the conditions under which such images appear in *Astrophil and Stella* (1591) 39, one of the last of his Morpheus sonnets, and the one that is most closely modeled on Continental precursors:

> Come sleep, oh sleep, the certain knot of peace,
> The baiting place of wit, the balm of woe,
> The poor man's wealth, the prisoner's release,
> Th'indifferent judge between the high and low;
> With shield of proof shield me from out the prease
> Of those fierce darts, Despair at me doth throw:
> Oh make in me those civil wars to cease;
> I will good tribute pay if thou do so:
> Take thou of me smooth pillows, sweetest bed,
> A chamber deaf to noise and blind to light;
> A rosy garland, and a weary head;
> And if these things, as being thine by right,
> Move not thy heavy Grace, thou shalt in me
> Livelier than elsewhere Stella's image see.[23]

Like Della Casa's, Desportes's, and Daniel's sonnets to sleep, *AS* 39 begins with a series of apostrophes designed to seduce sleep, and indeed the sonnet sustains the imperatives of Della Casa's octave into its third quatrain. Unlike Della Casa's sonnet, however, the poem does not evolve in

38 | SLEEP STATES AND SUBJECTIVITY

"real time." Instead, it is structured as a sort of prayer to sleep delivered at a single moment. Its *volta* leads not to vituperation of a god he has failed to summon but rather to a conditional promise—one that suggests he has often stayed awake thinking of Stella in the past but leaves open the possibility he might fall asleep in the present. And yet the *volta* still works in parallel to Della Casa's, aligning Astrophil's insomniac visions of Stella with Della Casa's tormented wakefulness. Inasmuch as, at the end of the sonnet, it is not Astrophil himself but rather Sleep who will see Stella's image implanted in his wakeful mind, Astrophil suggests that his sense-experience will become something involuntary and impersonal. Though still awake, consciousness will experience its own persistence as something alien and forced on it from without—and, indeed, actually experienced from without, rather than from within. Admittedly, subjectivity here remains structured as a gaze, but unlike the waking gaze of the blazon, the gaze of the insomniac lover is involuntary and incapable of looking carefully or of controlling its direction. In the neighborhood of sleep, vision is no longer, in Gary Waller's words, "a substitute for . . . actual physical control."[24] Stella's image is not described in any detail, and its significance now lies in the fact that he is experiencing it at all, rather than in its visual details. Again, therefore, in the sleep sonnet the focal point of consciousness is turned away from the beloved and recursively trained back on consciousness itself. In the process, the sense of a "male-viewer/female-object exchange" that defines the Petrarchan gaze is greatly weakened.[25]

A similar experience is recounted in *AS* 38. Here, however, "Stella's image" appears not to insomniac consciousness but rather in a hypnopompic condition that befalls Astrophil just as he begins to fall asleep:

> This night, while sleep begins with heavy wings
> To hatch mine eyes, and that unbitted thought
> Doth fall to stray, and my chief powers are brought
> To leave the scepter of all subject things,
> The first that straight my fancy's error brings
> Unto my mind, is Stella's image, wrought
> By love's own self; but with so curious draught
> That she, methinks, not only shines, but sings.
> I start, look, heark; but what in closed-up sense
> Was held, in opened sense it flies away,

Leaving me nought but wailing eloquence.
I, seeing better sights in sight's decay,
Called it anew, and wooed sleep again:
But him, her host, that unkind guest had slain.

As in the other nocturnal sonnets we have been examining, proximity to sleep, in the first quatrain of the sonnet, does not simply mean the eclipse of consciousness. For Sidney, as for Della Casa before him, it instead seems to trigger an "unbitted" or unwilled mode of thought. Thought, he writes, "doth fall to stray," which may well suggest that it becomes undisciplined and unreliable. Indeed, he describes the image of Stella that emerges as brought to him by "fancy's error." Yet Sidney here does not seem troubled, as Daniel is, by the question of whether or not the image is true. Instead, the sonnet focuses on the fleeting nature of the mental state in which he is privy to it: "I start, look, hark; but what in closed-up sense / Was held," he tells us, "in opened sense it flies away." *Start, look, hark*: all of these verbs suggest an effort to make his hypnopompic experience the *object* of a conscious thought, to look at what he is already seeing and to hark at what he is already hearing. But these efforts all fail, for there are "better sights in sight's decay." We have here explicitly the paradox of an "image" that is only accessed by means of "sight's decay." It is not simply, as in more conventional dream poems, that one form of gaze has been replaced by another; again, "Stella's image" is not described in much detail at all. Astrophil accesses that image not in deep sleep but rather in a threshold state between consciousness and its absence—a state in which sensory experience persists but is uncoupled from the first-person consciousness that could make it the object of focused attention and description.[26] In his sestet, Sidney describes the return to that insomniac state described by Della Casa, in which the senses are left with nothing but their own helpless persistence, captured in the empty "wailing eloquence" of the sonnet itself. In contrast to Della Casa, then, Sidney's poem appears to articulate two distinct states—one of light sleep and one of insomnia. The first is tenuous and fleeting, while the second is vexingly tenacious. In the first, we have an object without consciousness, and in the second, consciousness without an object. Yet, as in Daniel, they are woven together in the state of hypnopompic transition ("while sleep begins") in which the poem opens, and what they share is "sight's decay": a sense that consciousness has become unmoored and uncontrolled, subject to its own motions rather than to first-person control, and thus intractable to intentional awareness.

It is when consciousness is "unbitted" in this way that the sonnet form can really track thought's twists and turns, as opposed to merely providing a vehicle for it to reflect on itself. The opening of *AS* 40 captures consciousness's unwilled persistence with the dramatic immediacy of a monologue unfolding in the real time:[27]

> As good to write, as for to lie and groan.
> O Stella dear, how much thy power hath wrought,
> That hath my mind, none of the basest, brought,
> My still kept course, while others sleep, to moan.

The first line reads as the spontaneous declaration of a speaker who has been trying to sleep and failing, and decides at this moment to bring his helpless awareness into focus on Stella. Like Della Casa's *volta*, the movement from the first line here into the rest of the poem suggests the movement of a consciousness that cannot willfully turn itself off. The subsequent thirteen lines, like Della Casa's sestet, are written under the sign of the unwilled consciousness of an insomniac. The sonnet's structuring fiction is thus that its own composition is coterminous with a state in which, sleep being denied, the speaker persists in a state of involuntary, discomfiting awareness. In this poem, the formal unfolding of the sonnet itself testifies to a state of awareness identified fully with pain rather than with vision or reflection: "to lie and groan."

Whether they are describing a vision that just eludes the grasp of awareness or a waking awareness that itself has become entirely involuntary in nature, Sidney's Morpheus sonnets testify to a form of interiority that is sentient rather than intelligible—that consists fundamentally of felt experiences rather than of detached self-reflection. The content of such thinking is less significant than the mere fact of its happening—than expressing what it feels like to be aware in the first place. When Sidney returns to the nocturnal motif in a series of sonnets near the end of *Astrophil and Stella*, dreams and images are pointedly absent, fully replaced by a nonvisual, shapeless affect only dimly available to Astrophil himself:

> Grief, find the words; for thou hast made my brain
> So dark with misty vapours, which arise

From out thy heavy mould, that inbent eyes
Can scarce discern the shape of mine own pain. (94)

When far spent night persuades each mortal eye,
To whom nor art nor nature granteth light,
To lay his then mark-wanting shafts of sight,
Closed with their quivers, in sleep's armoury;
With windows open then most my mind doth lie,
Viewing the shape of darkness and delight,
Takes in that sad hue, which with the inward night
Of his mazed powers keeps perfect harmony. (99)

In the first of these poems, both outer and inner ("inbent") vision have been replaced with "misty vapours" that, darkening the brain, are palpable rather than visible. The same idea structures sonnet 99. Despite the mind's "windows open," sight has lain down its metaphorical arrows for want of "marks"—in other words, objects on which it could focus. Faced, as in the Morpheus sonnets, with "sight's decay," the mind instead "view[s] the shape of darkness and delight." Darkness, of course, has no shape; the "viewing" involved here cannot be conventional vision. Again, we are speaking of an entirely nonvisual, affective experience, one that blurs the line between inner and outer and in which the senses take in, above all, their own state.

AS 96 ("Thought with good cause thou likest so well the night") draws an extensive series of parallels between night and thought only to point out, at the end, that where night "at length yet doth invite some rest, / Thou though still tired, yet still doost it detest." Insofar as Astrophil addresses his own thought here, the sonnet might well be taken as representing a pinnacle of Renaissance "autoreflexivity." Yet what Astrophil experiences is not the transparency of the first person thinking to itself but rather an involuntary, unsettling presence he characterizes as almost demonic in quality: "In night, of sprites the ghastly powers stir, / In thee, or sprites, or sprited ghastliness." Like Della Casa's anguished question in the first tercet of his *Rime* 54, *AS* 96 enacts in its self-address the unfolding of a "thought" that has no content other than itself and its own depersonalizing persistence. In the isolation of insomnia, consciousness has become pure sentience, severed from self and identity and devoid of any object other than the feeling of its own continued existence. This point, at which Sidney is almost ready

42 | SLEEP STATES AND SUBJECTIVITY

to leave off, is where, in *Pamphilia to Amphilanthus*, his niece Mary Wroth will pick up.

THINKING SLEEP IN MARY WROTH'S *PAMPHILIA TO AMPHILANTHUS*

Sidney expanded the motif of sleep, which was the subject of only one sonnet in Della Casa and Daniel, to a small cluster of poems. Mary Wroth, who was the daughter of his brother Robert, expanded the motif still further. As its opening sonnet suggests, her sequence *Pamphilia to Amphilanthus* (1621) is entirely written under sleep's auspices:

> When nights black mantle could most darknes prove,
> And sleepe deaths Image did my senceses hiere
> From knowledge of my self, then thoughts did move
> Swifter then those most swiftnes need require:
>
> In sleepe, a Chariot drawne by wing'd desire
> I sawe: wher sate bright Venus Queene of love,
> And att her feete her sonne, still adding fire
> To burning hearts which she did hold above,
>
> Butt one hart flaming more then all the rest
> The goddess held, and putt it to my brest,
> Deare sonne, now shutt sayd she: thus must wee winn;
>
> Hee her obay'd, and martir'd my poore hart,
> I, waking hop'd as dreames it would depart
> Yett since: O mee: a lover I have binn. (P1)[28]

As in the other poems we have been considering, Wroth's opening quatrain implies clearly that sleep does not merely cause consciousness to fade. Rather, it severs the senses and thought from self-knowledge, suggesting that sentient life persists even in the absence of a self who is fully aware of it. And on the other hand, as Wroth's concluding couplet implies, such consciousness is not equivalent to dreams. Throughout the sequence, the phrase "my thoughts" frequently recurs, situated (as this opening sonnet suggests) somewhere between full self-knowledge and the oblivion of dreams. The content of these thoughts is often left unspecified, for as we will see it is the mere fact of their existence and happening that Wroth most values. In this final section, then, I consider Wroth's sleep sonnets in the context of those by her predecessors to reveal how Wroth expands to its fullest extent a possibility only glimpsed by those earlier figures. Her nocturnal "thoughts" are not merely an interiority cultivated in parallel or reaction to male subjectivity but rather a form of sentient awareness—as we have already begun to see—fundamentally distinct from the autonomous "reflexivity" usually associated with a prototypically male subject as well as with the "rational" soul traditionally taken to separate the human from other forms of life.

Pamphilia to Amphilanthus has, in fact, been a crucial point of reference in discussions surrounding early modern subjectivity. Does it represent the participation of women in a form of subjectivity heretofore confined to men—a bid, in other words, for "the possibility of emulating or stealing for themselves the autonomy apparently enjoyed by men"?[29] Or is it one of several literary "vehicles for exploring women's rather than men's consciousness and fantasies," thus seeking not participation but distinction?[30] Or, as Jeffrey Masten has argued, is Wroth's subjectivity necessarily not only "private but [also] privative," figured only "in terms of emptiness, lack, loss, and absence" by means of which "*Pamphilia to Apmhilanthus* clears a space for a nascent subject without articulating what it is that fills that emergent private space"?[31] A poetics centered on the descriptive blazon and the gaze that gives rise to it is necessarily a gendered poetics. While Aemilia Lanyer does describe Christ with a blazon in *Salve Deus Rex Judaeorum*, the erotic visuality of the typical blazon would not have been available as such to a female poet such as Wroth.[32] Yet in the forms of subjectivity experienced in proximity to sleep—in what Sidney calls "sight's decay"—that gaze is disabled. (As we have seen, in this regard sleep poems are distinct from dream poems such as those by Sannazaro, in which the blazon is still active.) Similarly, inasmuch as thinking in proximity to sleep is, as Sidney puts it, "unbitted," the kind of subjectivity to which that thinking gives rise is not necessarily linked to agency or its absence. It is perhaps not surprising, then, that Wroth should find, in moments of "sight's decay," a source of inspiration for her own forms of lyric subjectivity—a subjectivity that goes beyond what Naomi Miller describes as "mirror-image gender differentiation, where female constancy is opposed to male inconstancy, feminine victimization to masculine agency."[33] Masten argues that in *Pamphilia to Amphilanthus* Wroth "deploys images of night, blackness, darkness, and

44 | SLEEP STATES AND SUBJECTIVITY

sleep to register privacy and privation."[34] Yet sleep, I would argue, is much more than a negative state characteristic of a subjectivity premised on lack. For Wroth, sleep discloses a phenomenologically rich experience in which "thoughts," though unable to know themselves, feel themselves instead.

Although the opening poem suggests that all of the poems in *Pamphilia to Amphilanthus* are, in a sense, sleep poems, like *Astrophil and Stella* Wroth's sequence—in its final, published version—does cluster closely together a sequence of sonnets (P17–P24) specifically focused on sleep.[35] P18 echoes Daniel and Sidney in its opening apostrophe to sleep:

> Sleepe fy possess mee nott, nor doe nott fright
> Mee with thy heavy, and thy deathlike might
> For counterfetting's vilder then deaths sight,
> And such deluding more my thoughts doe spite.
> Thou suff'rest faulsest shapes my soule t'affright
> Some times in liknes of a hopefull spright,
> And oft times like my love as in dispite
> Joying thou canst with mallice kill delight,
> When I (a poore foole made by thee) think joy
> Doth flow, when thy fond shadows doe destroy
> My that while senceles self, left free to thee,
> Butt now doe well, lett mee for ever sleepe,
> And soe for ever that deare Image keepe,
> Or still wake, that my sences may be free. (P18)

Despite the initial echo, however, Wroth's command in the first line represents a startling revision of Sidney's and Daniel's poems, as well as of their Continental and English precursors. Della Casa, Desportes, Sidney, and Daniel all start out by invoking or summoning sleep. (Though Petrarch does not, he clearly suffers from its absence.) Wroth, on the contrary, is attempting to hold it off. Like earlier nocturnal sonnets, then, this poem is written from a state that is *near* sleep—yet whereas other writers hope to pass from such a state to complete sleep, Wroth struggles in the other direction, actively resisting sleep's onset, for she fears its "counterfetting." This sonnet thus confirms the impression created by the first poem in *Pamphilia to Amphilanthus*—namely, that Wroth's nocturnal *thoughts*, though proximal to sleep, are to be clearly distinguished from dreams. "And such deluding more my thoughts do spite": whether we read "my thoughts" or "deluding" as the subject here, it is clear that her nocturnal thoughts are more truthful than dreams. It is almost as if Wroth relishes the insomniac state so unpleasant to many of her male forerunners. If darkness and solitude allow her the experience and expression of a form of subjectivity ("my thoughts") that she is otherwise denied, then we can perhaps see why she resists sleep and the total eclipse of consciousness it brings, where male poets tend to welcome it. Indeed, in P26 ("When every one to pleasing pastime hies"), she favorably contrasts the pleasure of her inner life—of its mere existence rather than of any particular content it may have—to the vacuous pastimes of those around her: "Yet I my thoughts doe farr above thes prise."

In the second quatrain and first tercet, Wroth's language becomes extremely convoluted, capturing the torment of inexpressible desire for a sexual encounter that she seems almost, in sleep, to experience ("When I . . . think joy / Doth flow"); a state in which, as she puts it in P24, "some pleasure shadowe-like is wrought." But whereas in that poem the dream is imagined simply as a form of fulfillment, here its untruth is presented as a form of torment—images of fulfillment are offset by images of frustration, presented to her by sleep "as in dispite," and whenever she "thinks joy / Doth flow," sleep's "fond shadows" destroy that "sencelesse selfe." Here, paradoxically, it is *sleep*'s shadows that destroy the formerly "sencelesse selfe" who thinks that joy doth flow, pointing to a distinction between sleep that is senseless and sleep that is not. Like Daniel, perhaps, Wroth is lamenting the torments of a specific form of sleep, one that does not allow her to enjoy her dreams with unqualified abandon. She, too, may be drawing the Aristotelian distinction between sleep that lacks self-knowledge ("senseless," then, also in the sense of mad) and sleep tormented by an awareness of its falsehood. Indeed, the two alternatives proposed by the last three lines situate the speaker between deep sleep and full waking, between senses that are fettered and senses that are "free." Thus, Wroth ultimately identifies the quality of her predicament more precisely than Daniel. Where he simply longs to sleep at the end of his sonnet, she wishes to resolve the state into one or the other of its constituent elements.

The writing of this sonnet is itself a form of subjectivity, but not as an "act of self-assertion" or of a more masculine agency that critics often seek to attribute to women's writing in this era. Rather, subjectivity emerges as the ineluctable experience of a felt consciousness that cannot easily be categorized as active or passive.[36] It is never clear, moreover, what she sees in sleep or what she wants to see in the poem. Indeed, the obscurities of her language suggest a visual object whose presence, like that of "Stella's image" in *AS* 38, is palpable but whose outlines rarely come into focus (see P98 for an exception). The poem replaces the subjectivity of vision with the dramatic immediacy of consciousness unfolding in "real time." Its conceit is that the speaker is wrangling with insomnia and with sleep in the present moment, captured in and as the sonnet's formal unfolding (in particular in the *volta* to the second tercet). Its consciousness is not trained on an object, whether visual or otherwise, but rather on its own persistent presence in the face of "sight's decay"—as the pure feeling of being aware without a clear object to be aware *of*. And, at least initially, she does not want that feeling to cease. For Wroth takes pleasure not in the surrogate satisfaction and proxy form of possession offered by representation but rather in the activity of a feeling that operates without objects altogether: in the obscure yet intense self-apprehension of what she calls "my thoughts."

It may seem naive to suggest that such apprehension could in any way transcend the formidable gender dichotomies of Jacobean England, let alone distinctions between the human and its others inherited from the classical world. For a male poet writing at this time, privacy would have been a choice; for Wroth, it was enforced. Thus, inasmuch as her "thoughts"—the fruit of a mental experience that Wroth is forced to keep private—dominate her sequence, they do unquestionably represent a gendered form of subjectivity. But the terms of this account can also be reversed, so that Wroth's gender can actually be seen as enabling a philosophical perspective absent in her male peers. For whereas Wroth's male precursors long for sleep and cannot tolerate the painful isolation of a thought that refuses to subside into "animal" oblivion, at least at times she proves able to relish this liminal condition:

> Then kinde thought my phant'sie guide
> Lett mee never haples slide;
> Still maintaine thy force in mee,
> Let mee thinking still be free:
> Nor leave thy might untill my death
> But let mee thinking yeeld up breath. (P21)

Wroth's arresting vision of continuing to think in and through her final breath resonates with the way in which, as we have seen, her "thoughts" straddle the boundary between sleeping and waking, between consciousness and its absence. Her desire to persist in this state also contrasts, in philosophically significant ways, with the longing for thoughtless sleep characteristic of sonnets written by male poets on the subject. For in the very intensity of their longing for an "animal" oblivion untroubled by thinking, sonneteers from Petrarch to Sidney ultimately adhere to the clear-cut Aristotelian distinction between a purportedly human form of consciousness and its absence in sleep (analogous to the distinction between reason and passion, which is important for several of these poets as well), even as they testify to a condition that poses serious problems for that distinction. For Wroth, in contrast, proximity to insentience activates a greater attunement to a sensible flux of "thoughts" that do not fit neatly into categorical distinctions between thought and its less-than-human others, a troubling of philosophical and ideological boundaries she is considerably more willing to countenance, and that she uses the formal resources of the sonnet tradition to reimagine and revalue. Indeed, in her poetry, the felt experience of thinking becomes a distinctive form of subjectivity unto itself, in which awareness, in the absence of self-knowledge, is given unique access to itself. Far from seeing such subjectivity as a pallid or incomplete version of full and "masculine" self-consciousness, one might instead start to see it for the startling new discovery that it was.

NOTES

1. Joel Fineman, *Shakespeare's Perjured Eye* (Berkeley: University of California Press, 1986), 1, 25. For the idea of a "new conception of inward experience" in Sidney's and Shakespeare's sonnets, see also Anne Ferry, *The "Inward" Language: Sonnets of Wyatt, Sidney, Shakespeare, Donne* (Chicago: University of Chicago Press, 1983).

2. See Arthur Marotti, "'Love is not Love': Elizabethan Sonnet Sequences and the Social Order," *English Literary History* 49, no. 2 (1982). For a recent study that takes Marotti's claim as its starting point, see Melissa Sanchez, *Erotic Subjects:*

The Sexuality of Politics in Early Modern English Literature (Oxford: Oxford University Press, 2011). For a powerful critique of Marotti's position, see Emily Vasiliauskas, "The Outmodedness of Shakespeare's Sonnets," *English Literary History* 82, no. 3 (2015): 759–87.

3. Christopher Warley, *Sonnet Sequences and Social Distinction in Renaissance England* (Cambridge: Cambridge University Press, 2005), 78, 79.

4. Michael Schoenfeldt, *Bodies and Selves in Early Modern England: Physiology and Inwardness in Spenser, Shakespeare,*

Herbert, and Milton (Cambridge: Cambridge University Press, 1999), 75.

5. See John Searle, "The Mystery of Consciousness," *New York Review of Books*, November 2, 1995.

6. For the only comprehensive study of sonnets addressed to sleep, see Stefano Carrai, *Ad somnum: L'invocazione al sonno nella lirica italiana* (Padua, Italy: Antenore, 1990). Carrai's valuable study focuses on sleep's function as a poetic topos rather than on its phenomenological articulations.

7. Emmanuel Levinas, *Of God Who Comes to Mind*, trans. Bettina Bergo (Stanford: Stanford University Press, 1998), 59.

8. Aristotle, *On the Soul; Parva naturalia; On Breath*, trans. W. S. Hett (Cambridge, Mass.: Harvard University Press, 1936), 323. Aristotle argues that sleep and waking are contraries and that "of two contraries one must be present and the other not." For an important account of sleep in the Renaissance in an Aristotelian context, see Garrett Sullivan Jr., *Sleep, Romance, and Human Embodiment: Vitality from Spenser to Milton* (Cambridge: Cambridge University Press, 2012).

9. Emmanuel Levinas, *Time and the Other*, trans. Richard Cohen (Pittsburgh: Duquesne University Press, 1985), 48.

10. For an account of "the power [Petrarchism] affords to sight, specifically the voyeuristic gaze," see Gary Waller, *The Sidney Family Romance: Mary Wroth, William Herbert, and the Early Modern Construction of Gender* (Detroit: Wayne State University Press, 1993), 149: "The male gaze is predominantly directed, most obviously in the blazon, at a woman as the sum of separable parts" (150). Waller draws on Nancy J. Vickers's influential article "Diana Described: Scattered Woman and Scattered Rhyme," in *Critical Inquiry* 8, no. 2 (Winter 1981): 265–89. For a recent critical take on Vickers's account, see Sara Morrison and Deborah Uman, eds., *Staging the Blazon in Early Modern English Theater* (London: Routledge, 2016).

11. Francesco Petrarca, *Canzoniere*, ed. Marco Santagata (Milan: Mondadori, 2004). English translations are from *Petrarch's Lyric Poems: The "Rime sparse"*

and Other Lyrics, trans. and ed. Robert M. Durling (Cambridge, Mass.: Harvard University Press, 1976).

12. Henry Howard, Earl of Surrey, *Poems*, ed. Emrys Jones (Oxford: Clarendon, 1964).

13. I follow Jacopo Sannazaro, *Opere volgari*, ed. Alfredo Mauro (Bari, Italy: Laterza, 1961). Translations are my own. Pietro Bembo's *Rime* 89–90 also describe a quasi-erotic dream of the beloved that disappears on waking. See Pietro Bembo, *Prose e rime*, ed. Carlo Dionisotti (Turin, Italy: Unione Tipografico-Editrice Torinese, 1960). For a comprehensive anthology of Italian sonnets to sleep, see Stefano Carrai, *Ad Somnum*, 142–221.

14. Sir Thomas Wyatt, *The Complete Poems*, ed. R. A. Rebholz (New York: Penguin, 1985), 85.

15. As Carrai notes. See *Ad somnum*, 63–64.

16. I follow Giovanni Della Casa, *Rime*, ed. Stefano Carrai (Milan: Mimesis, 2014). Translations are my own.

17. Levinas, *Time and the Other*, 48.

18. I follow Philippe Desportes, *Les Amours d'Hippolyte*, ed. Victor E. Graham (Geneva: Droz, 1960). Translation is my own.

19. Emmanuel Levinas, *Existence and Existents*, trans. Alphonso Lingis (Dordrecht, Netherlands: Kluwer, 1988), 65.

20. Samuel Daniel, *Selected Poetry and "A Defense of Rhyme,"* ed. Geoffrey G. Hiller and Peter L. Groves (Asheville, N.C.: Pegasus Press, 1998). Although it was probably written after Sidney's Morpheus sonnets, I discuss this poem first because it seems to me that the Continental influence on it is greater. For Daniel and Desportes, see Joan Rees, *Samuel Daniel: A Critical and Biographical Study* (Liverpool: Liverpool University Press, 1964), 22–26, and Anne Lake Prescott, *French Poets and the English Renaissance: Studies in Fame and Transformation* (New Haven: Yale University Press, 1978), 146–48.

21. Aristotle, *On Dreams*, 367.

22. For a different perspective on the beloved in Sidney's sequence, see Margaret Simon's essay in this volume.

23. Sir Philip Sidney, *The Major Works*, ed. Katherine Duncan-Jones (Oxford: Oxford University Press, 2008).

24. Waller, *Sidney Family Romance*, 149.

25. Vickers, "Diana Described," 277.

26. That the traditional notion of interiority is unable to account fully for such a state is, I think, demonstrated by the contradiction in Anne Ferry's account of this sonnet. On the one hand, she argues that "the dream is at the same distance from inward experience, has the same capacity to alter it, as poetry" (*"Inward" Language*, 151–52). On the other hand, she suggests that Astrophil's vision is elusive not because it is superficial or unreliable but because it is, somehow, *too* inward to be fully grasped: "His moment of vision escapes, leaving him only with 'wailing eloquence,' which is the husk of poetry. It is uttered, it is skillful, but it cannot hold inward experience. . . . This dream the poet experiences inwardly, but cannot capture in his verse" (154). Understanding this sonnet requires us to think of inner experience not as the transparency of thought to itself but as a form of felt experience only partly palpable to the subject undergoing it.

27. Anne Ferry writes, "In sonnet 40 the first line is understood as spoken by Astrophil to himself when no one can hear him. It is therefore like an aside, giving a momentary glimpse of what is in his heart, or a piece of soliloquy, in that it illustrates the way he talks aloud to himself" (*"Inward" Language*, 150).

28. *The Poems of Lady Mary Wroth*, ed. Josephine A. Roberts (Baton Rouge: Louisiana State University Press, 1983). Roberts's edition follows the text of the Folger manuscript (V.a. 104) of *Pamphilia to Amphilanthus* but orders the poems as they appeared in print at the end of *The Countesse of Montgomeries Urania* (1621), numbering them as P1, P2, etc.

29. Waller, *Sidney Family Romance*, 205.

30. Barbara Kiefer Lewalski, *Writing Women in Jacobean England* (Cambridge, Mass.: Harvard University Press, 1993), 244. See also Naomi J. Miller, *Changing the Subject: Mary Wroth and Figurations of Gender in Early Modern England* (Lexington: University Press of Kentucky, 1996).

31. Jeffrey Masten, "'Shall I turne blabb?': Circulation, Gender, and Subjectivity in Mary Wroth's Sonnets," in *Reading Mary Wroth: Representing Alternatives in Early Modern England*, ed. Naomi J. Miller and Gary Waller (Knoxville: University of Tennessee Press, 1991), 81.

32. Waller himself notes the degree to which subjectivity in Petrarch sonnets "assumes a 'universal' gaze that in fact is that of the dominant male"—based, therefore, on "gender-specific stereotypes." As he writes, "Women display for men; men display for themselves, and then are authorized to display, in writing, their accounts of the experience." See Waller, *Sidney Family Romance*, 214. For Lanyer's blazon of Christ, see *The Poems of Aemilia Lanyer: Salve Deus Rex Judaeorum*, ed. Susanne Woods (Oxford: Oxford University Press, 1993), 107.

33. Miller, *Changing the Subject*, 5.

34. Masten, "'Shall I turne blabb?,'" 70.

35. In the earlier version of *Pamphilia* represented by the Folger manuscript, P17, P18, and P19 appear later in the sequence and separately from one another (Roberts, introduction to *The Poems of Lady Mary Wroth*, 64). It would appear, then, that in preparing the sequence for print, Wroth clustered all eight poems together.

36. Waller, *Sidney Family Romance*, 204.

CHAPTER 2

Rest and Rhyme in
Thomas Campion's Poetry

MARGARET SIMON

Thomas Campion's poetry has long been noted for its innovative use of the dramatic monologue, particularly for female speakers. Several articles take up Campion's relatively frequent use of female persona poems and his progressive representation of female characters in general. Catherine Ing writes that his English personae "have their individuality and it arises partly from the fact that Campion draws attention to qualities in them hardly noticed by other poets. They may have golden wires for hair and pearls for teeth, but he is not particularly interested if they have. Yet if they move or speak or sing his awareness quickens at once."[1] Campion, while working from classical and ballad precedents, innovates on the typical poems that address such women, giving them often complex voices and forms of agency. And this, Ing suggests, emerges at the level of poetic strategy. Rather than engaging in the tradition of the objectifying blazon, which requires a relatively static and generally voiceless figure, Campion often creates dramatic monologues. Gail Reitenbach, crediting Ing's view, focuses her work on these monologues spoken by women, bringing attention to "their strongly delineated speakers, implied auditors, and social . . . contexts."[2] This emphasis on how Campion's female personae resist blazon through their more active role as speakers, while valid, suppresses some of the nuance in Campion's portrayal of female agency and embodiment.

While Campion certainly riffs on the period's practice of having male poets write in a female voice to develop *ethopoeia*,[3] creating diverse and surprising female speakers, he is also provocatively fixated on the inactive or liminal female body. In particular, across his airs and his epigrams Campion replays the scenario of female erotic experience in half-sleep or sleep-waking. As a writer so interested in how the mode of music interacts with the language of poetry, Campion, perhaps unsurprisingly, is likewise invested in connecting bodily experience to different generic modes and formal strategies. This essay considers the poetic possibilities Campion discovers in representing liminal states of consciousness. Positioning female sleep states as generally associated with poetic strategies of blazon or narratives of transgression, I consider how Campion uses nuanced engagements with threshold states of consciousness to retool the traditional formal strategies that shape the female body in verse.

Beyond his collaborations with musician Philip Rosseter[4] and his mastery of both music and prosody, a rarity in writers of early modern lyric, Campion is perhaps best known for his polemical view of rhyme. Rhyme takes poetry away from its classical quantitative roots, often causing a "confused inequalitie of sillables" relative to the meter.[5] Further, rhyme causes a writer "oftentimes to abjure his matter and extend a short conceit beyond all bounds of art" (295). As evidence of the formal connection between poetry and music, Campion's view on rests in certain types of music accords with his view on rhyme as he notes that "in Ayres I find no use they have, unlesse it be to make a vulgar and triviall modulation seem to the ignorant strange, and to the judicial tedious."[6] Ironically, the very indeterminacy and lengthening that rests in music and rhyming in verse create are thematic elements that sometimes preoccupy the narratives of Campion's verse across a number of lyric subgenres. Specifically, this essay looks to four poems, the eighth air in *A Booke of Ayres* (1601) and three subsequent epigrams, two in Latin and one in English, that take up the same narrative situation, wherein a woman, depicted in half-sleep, has an erotic encounter with a wakeful suitor. Placing these poems in the context of the period's theorizing of half-sleep and the poems' formal concerns, this essay demonstrates how Campion connects the thematic representation of half-sleep to his vexed use of formal elements including, most prominently, rhyme. In so doing, Campion makes the repetition of his poems across genres surprisingly dependent on their shared plots, thus connecting representations of the body to certain poetic forms and forms of poetic production.

1

Campion's lyric description of sleep-waking in the eighth song uses formal strategies that make space for an extended, reciprocal erotic encounter:

> It fell on a sommers day,
> While sweete Bessie sleeping laie
> In her bowre, on her bed,
> Light with curtaines shadowed;
> Jamy came, shee him spies,
> Opning halfe her heavie eies.
>
> Jamy stole in through the dore,
> She lay slumbring as before;
> Softly to her he drew neere,
> She heard him, yet would not heare;
> Bessie vow'd not to speake,
> He resolved that dumpe to breake.
>
> First a soft kiss he doth take,
> She lay still, and would not wake;
> Then his hands learn'd to woo,
> She dreamp't not what he would doo,
> But still slept, while he smild
> To see love by sleepe beguild.
>
> Jamy then began to play,
> Bessie as one buried lay,
> Gladly still through this sleight
> Deceiv'd in her owne deceit;
> And, since this traunce begoon,
> She sleepes ev're afternoone. (31)

Bessie's experience is described as a complicated intertwining of somatic lassitude and volition, an interstitial state reinforced by the seemingly accidental nature of the dramatic situation, which "fell on a sommers day." The poem's interest in the vagaries of erotic opportunity and agency continue as the poem begins from a perspective more aligned with Jamy—Bessie, with eyes closed, would not be aware of the room's lighting. And Jamy interprets her state as sleep. By the second stanza, however, we see that Bessie's state is a bit more complex. She sees him, initially, but with heavy eyes, suggesting that elements of the sleep state are still affecting her. By the second stanza both Jamy and Bessie begin to question her state, as she finds herself able to hear and he "resolve[s]" her "dumpe to breake." She wishes to preserve the half-sleep that would allow her erotic license. By the third stanza she exercises agency over sleep, imposing it (or at least its appearance) on herself. The line "She dreamp't not what he would doo" emphasizes this enabling double unconsciousness, as it could be meant metaphorically, conveying that she never expected his advances. Or it may be, more obliquely, that she is not dreaming but rather experiencing his undreamed-of ministrations in real time. The joke finally seems to be on Jamy, who believes he is having a transgressive one-sided encounter, seeing "love by sleepe beguild" while in fact he is beguiled by her seeming sleep. Though, because he has just resolved to wake her from her "dumpe"—to break her out of her melancholy state, rather than her sleep—it may be that Jamy knows that she is somewhat awake but continues the ruse. Finally, Bessie finds herself "as one buried," perhaps experiencing the "little death" as she feigns death. And this finitude ironically initiates a cognitive refrain, as she plans now to sleep every afternoon. It is never clear, through the duration of the poem, if Bessie experiences some sort of half-sleep or if she is merely feigning. But this undecidability becomes useful in considering the narrative's form and reforming, as it moves from the rhyming song to the unrhymed epigram.

Recognizing the credibility of Campion's depiction of half-sleep is important to parsing how embodied and literary form interact across Campion's use and reuse of this narrative scenario. In 1603, just two years after Campion publishes his *Booke of Ayres*, Richard Haydocke, a noted preacher, is called to account by King James. James had heard of Haydocke's rising popularity due to the fact that "two or three times a week he was preaching in his sleep."[7] As punishment for what James condemned as falsity, Haydocke is tasked with writing a learned disquisition on why such activity is impossible, a task he completes in a visually lovely manuscript addressed to the king. He offers a genealogy of theories on sleep-waking:

Vives seemeth to putt a midde disposition beetweene wake=inge and sleepeinge, which hee calleth Dormitatio or Slumbringe, wherein Fernelius [marginal annotation: De funct: nat:] agreeth, both of them groundeinge uppon Aristo: sayeinge thus [marginal annotation: De Insomn:]. If one sleepe but perfunctorily and sleightly, soe that abundance of vapours oppresse not the imaginative power, then though many visions thwart his conceit, yet may those bee noe more called dreames, then that disposition which insensibly or very litle differeth from wakeinge may bee accounted Sleepe: soe that here is rather a quiet stillnes, and vacuitie of outward objects, then a binde=inge of the Senses, which is true sleepe: but in this case they saye men heare the croweinge of Cockes, and barkeinge of dogges, which must needs argue sense. Againe his words are, quiete com=positi, not somno ligati: in the still and silent repose of the night, when the braine is kindely heated, and the grosse vapours consumed.[8]

Due to the influence of Galen, much theorizing around sleep has to do with the extent to which it binds or disables the sensing body.[9] This "perfunctory" sleep is marked by a loosening of this binding, wherein the sleeper can hear and, by implication, use other senses. Haydocke makes it clear that, grounding in Aristotle and moving up through Vives, there is a recognition of this state between sleep and waking, a state defined by a more sensible body. Haydocke's brief overview of this state as it was understood from classical to early modern theorists usefully identifies reactivation of sense perception as a key feature of the state.[10] Campion engages with this state across lyric subgenres, not so much attempting a direct correlation between poetic representation and the period's cognitive theories but rather exploiting it for his lyric persona and, as I will discuss, his formal agenda. The sensing but passive body, suspended between the diurnal rhythms that constitute cycles of sleep and waking, is able to have an unbounded, and ultimately proleptic, erotic experience. Fully awake, Bessie would have to deny her own desires. In half-sleep she can both explore and deny them.

If from one perspective this is an apt use of the subtleties of sleep states to create provocative lyric narratives, it is also a surprising intervention in normative lyric depictions of female sleep prominent in the period. The scenario has roots going at least back to Ovid, with his story of Priapus and

56 | SLEEP STATES AND SUBJECTIVITY

Lotis in the *Fasti*.[11] In this scene, Priapus is interrupted in his lechery against the sleeping nymph and ends up an object of derision.[12] In Campion's day, Philip Sidney's second song in *Astrophil and Stella* creates a version of this scenario less punitive for the male agent. Sidney's speaker, Astrophil, finds his beloved, Stella, asleep. This sends him into a moral quandary, in which he resolves to "invade the fort," taking by force what the waking Stella would deny him.[13] Though he uses the future refrain of "Now will I" seven times as he plans each new transgression, he ultimately settles for a stolen kiss, refraining in refrain (2.3, 7, 11, 15, 19, 23, 27). Even the stolen kiss raises Stella's ire, as her wakeful and "lowring beauty" chastens Astrophil (26). It also provides him the chance for a puckish rejoinder, as he counts himself a "fool for no more taking" (28). While this poem famously complicates Astrophil's extensive lyric tousle with his own fleshly desires, the moral situation is clear: Astrophil transgresses; the chaste and honorable Stella resists and punishes. Again, we might look to Sidney, whose unrevised prose romance the *Arcadia* includes another famous passage of sleep-watching (also indebted, I have argued, to Ovid's rendering of the Priapus and Lotis story),[14] wherein the otherwise honorable prince Musidorus almost rapes his beloved princess Pamela after being inflamed by her unguarded beauty while she sleeps. Musidorus is interrupted by a band of "clownish villains" who prevent his transgression and obliquely allude to his own moral failing.[15] As David Lindley notes of another of Campion's verses, "Sleep, angry beauty," in the case of Campion's eighth air, convention is similarly subverted: "Though underpinned by convention . . . [the poem] manipulates the reader's pre-set knowledge of its literary stereotype in subtle, dislocatory fashion."[16] While the lady's sleep state may be subtly undecidable, this poem, as compared to "Sleep, angry beauty," is less subtle in its sexual result, though certainly not as decisively predatory as its Ovidian and Sidneian precursors.

2

Specific formal warrants underlie and shape Campion's and Sidney's depictions. Linear, narrative prose, as Sidney practices in the *Arcadia*, requires that Pamela cede narrative control until she wakes, thus ending the interstitial lyric blazon with which Musidorus arouses himself while he watches her sleep and effectively allowing the prose narrative to scold Musidorus's lyric digression. The dynamics of refrain in Sidney's second song hold the speaker in a state of lyric contemplation that, in an ironic bit of wordplay, forces the speaker to at once refrain from violating Stella while allowing him to express frustration at this self-imposed constraint.[17] Like Sidney's second song, Campion's eighth is one of the more narrative in its volume. Unlike Sidney's, however, it does not make use of repetition and refrain as formal elements, even as its narrative predicts the repetition of its erotic situation. The refrain in Sidney's song signals the narrative's transgression and its one-off nature—Astrophil will not find Stella so compromised by sleep again. Campion's own third air, in the same volume as "It fell on a sommers day," also uses refrain to contemplate repeated desire. In this poem, the speaker seeks a simple country girl, not "these ladies / That must be woode and praide." Instead, he prefers "kind Amarillis / The wanton countrey maide." He likes the (supposed) game of consent they play: "Her when we court and kiss, / She cries forsooth, let go: / But when we come where comfort is, / She never will say no" (5.1–4, 5–8). This refrain, repeated three times, signals repeated desire. But this desire, according to the conditional ("when") and future ("will"), is never fulfilled within the poem. He, like Sidney's speaker, ultimately refrains in refrain. Jamy, on the other hand, will find Bessie available each afternoon, with no grammatical ambiguity. Campion's poem thus links the song form's capacity to convey a narrative without refrain with a more capacious depiction of embodied fulfillment. Bessie's own liminal state helps to authorize this formal choice.

Rather than refrain or repetition, the primary formal driver of Campion's song is a fairly simple pattern of end-rhymed couplets, which may seem surprising given Campion's oft-noted criticism of rhymed verse briefly mentioned above. In his address "To the Reader" in *Two Bookes of Ayres*, Campion aims to couple "his Words and Notes lovingly together" (55). Campion plans to harmonize the measure of his music with the meter of his verse, where possible. The emotive description ("lovingly") of this process demonstrates a formal interest in intertwining his poetry with adjacent creative forms. This formal hybridity, described in affective terms, informs depictions of the resting body. In *Two Bookes of Ayres*, part of this loving coupling involves the use of rhyme. Campion's relationship to rhyme in English poetry is complex. He associates his use throughout this collection of "ear-pleasing rimes without Arte" with their subject—"for the most part amorous"—finding rhyme useful for creating a new range of poems in English. As he puts it, "Why not amorous songs, as well as amorous attires?

Or why not new Ayres, as well as new fascions?" The subject and the rhyme dress up the "Note and Tableture" that "if they satisfie the most, we have our desire" (15). Rhyme, it seems, is useful as an accessory, and emotive, amplifier to certain musical and poetic experiments.

Rhyme is also surprisingly useful in reinforcing the themes of embodiment and the temporal disposition of the eighth air. While Campion happily associates rhyme with amorous themes in his "To the Reader," about a decade earlier Campion's *Observations on the Art of English Poesie* impugned rhyme for just this association. In this treatise, Campion calls for an English version of quantitative verse, crediting classical Greek and Roman poets who abandoned "the childish titillation of riming" (295). The titillation, by implication, comes from the satisfaction in maintaining the rhyme, an almost formal consummation, or a punning coupling. Through reference to Procrustes, Campion suggests that rhyme causes writers to make lines artificially long or short to accomplish the form. Most often, we remember, rhyme causes the poet "to abjure his matter and extend a short conceit beyond all bounds of art." The "bed" in the eighth air is far from Procrustean, as the desire it houses extends; the poem's lack of refrain and its proleptic, renewing pattern of desire are reinforced by its unbounded view of desire, coded in the endless movement of repeated end rhyme.

At the same time, rhyme is a type of "continual repetition" and can result in "tedious affectation." Poets might "rime a man to death" (293). This combination of arousal and tedium reinforces Bessie's intransigence as she continues in her feigned (or real) half-sleep despite Jamy's presence (like the indefatigable rhyme, she won't change). It also speaks to the satisfying arousal both Jamy and Bessie achieve—Bessie and, we assume, Jamy are rhymed not "to death" but to a "little death." Rhyming couplets are particularly given to the "continual repetition," and amorous resurrection, that Bessie hopes for. On the one hand, the lighthearted, titillating rhyme gives voice to Bessie's unvoiced enjoyment. At the same time, its repetition can make this liveliness predictable, instead bringing a focus to the poem's temporal horizon—Bessie hopes that she can linger in half-sleep each afternoon. It is almost proverbial that rhyme is a poetic techinique that aids memory. Amanda Watson, in putting forth a new early modern model of forgetting, one "based on the proliferation of impressions rather than their burial or disappearance," looks unexpectedly to the relationship Campion draws between rhyme and forgetting. She traces this to George

Gascoigne, who fears that the pursuit of rhyme will derail poets from their subject.[18] For Bessie, the rhyme shapes her experience in a way that can be replicated, thus, in a fashion, remembered. But while this very repetition, with its potential for unbounded proliferation, means Bessie may, perhaps, also forget herself as she gives over to the rhythms both of the poem and of her desires. The rhyme itself performs a sort of willful negligence reflective of Bessie's actual or performed half-sleep.

The rhymed couplet is lively in the moment: the first stanza of the eighth air bounces from "day" to "laie." But Campion alters it at certain points to draw attention to key shifts in the poem. The next couplet moves from "bed," slowing to "shadowed." The poem asks us to pause over the liminal lighting, a feature that might prevent both Jamy and Bessie from fully interpreting the other's state and intentions. Then the poem picks up with a declarative line emphasized with a caesura: "Jamy came, shee him spies." The stanza ends with another quick rhyme with "eies." In the second stanza, Campion uses the rhyme to accentuate Jamy's and Bessie's efforts to control her (performed) cognitive state: "Bessie vow'd not to speake, / He resolved that dumpe to breake." Campion's off rhyme of "speake" and "breake" marks a turn in the poem, as Jamy solicits her wakeful participation by physical means. The stanza that follows, and the first couplet of the final stanza, progress through simple end rhymes as he kisses and touches Bessie. The rhyme alters as her state is described again: "Gladly still through this sleight / Deceiv'd in her own deceit." If the juxtaposition of "speake" and "breake" in the previous stanza spoke to Jamy's change in strategy, the move from "sleight" to "deceit" speaks to Bessie's. Deferred agency and self-doubling are common lyric strategies, from Queen Elizabeth's speaker's claim that "from myself another self I turned" to Sidney's Astrophil's claim that "I am not I, pity the tale of me" or, after stealing a kiss from Stella, "It was saucy Love, not humble I."[19] Campion's poem introduces half-sleep, described in off rhyme, as a way to further blur his character's agency. Jamy's play operates through clear erotic action, Bessie's through undecidable cognitive performance, both reinforced by Campion's intermittent use of end and off rhyme.

3

As Kristen Gibson has noted, songs in print "become mutually informing of each other as they are gathered together to form a discrete collection."[20]

60 | SLEEP STATES AND SUBJECTIVITY

The narrative openness of Bessie's experience, its both forward-looking and cyclical narrative, interact provocatively with Campion's song collection, aspects of which call into question Bessie's idealized fulfillment through sleep-waking. While one interaction is the shift from refrain to rhyme in similar seduction poems discussed above, another occurs at the level of narrative. In the eighth song, the final lines convey Bessie's participation in a repeated sexual encounter, a plot reinforced by the continuous rhymed couplets. The fifth air, however, is a narrative about a woman whose chastity is taken, we assume only once, by a man who breaks his promise to her. In this case, the man is a "dissembling wretch." After getting his desire, he acts to her as "a stranger," "the vile guise of men / When a woman is in danger." She regrets having trusted "a fained toong" (5.15, 19–21). Jamy and Bessie form a closed erotic system as their beguiling, sleighting, and deceiving serve their mutual satisfaction. Yet the certainty of Bessie's untroubled, daily half-naps is called into question preemptively by the fifth air, its language of dissembling and male trickery suggesting the consequences Bessie might endure beyond "her bowre" as she allows her chastity to be compromised.

Despite being categorized as an air, and the designation on the title page that the airs are "set foorth to be song to the Lute, Orpherian, and Base Violl by Philip Rosseter, Lutenist," the eighth air does not draw attention to itself as a type of song. Sarah Iovan, in her work on Sir Thomas Wyatt's lute poems, considers the sometimes tense relationship Wyatt develops "between the poetic voice of the speaker and the musical voice of lute" as a way to reconsider "the problems presented by the early modern understanding of song as a mode of discourse between two related, but ultimately irreconcilable, types of voices."[21] If Wyatt struggles with his sluggish lute, challenging his poetic voice to wake up the instrument, Campion uses musical liveliness to counterintuitively propel Bessie's feigned rest. This musical feigning reinforces the poem's complex portrayal of agency and consciousness. Returning to Campion's view of rests mentioned above, he asserts that "in Ayres . . . no use they have, unlesse it be to make a vulgar and triviall modulation seem to the ignorant strange, and to the judicial tedious" (15). Campion, in a version of the period's penchant for performed modesty, depicts these poems as light, even unimportant, and accepts that the sometimes ponderous absence introduced by a rest is false to the spirit of the verse. And the volume manifests this theory. The musical scores that accompany each air use rests sometimes to emphasize a turn in the lyric's plot but otherwise avoid what seems, as he implies, an artificial lengthening and complicating of the form. The pacing Campion accomplishes through rhyme, slowing down occasionally but generally keeping with quick-paced couplets, is supported by the music, letting the poem's formal elements foreground Bessie's and Jamy's quickened desire, and further suggesting Bessie's state of physical stillness and amorous excitement.

The musical score also interacts provocatively with the temporal claims of the rhyme. While Campion's poem, in this case, might not include refrain, the music for the air is repeated for each stanza, again reinforcing the sense that what Bessie and Jamy experience can be repeated in an unchanging way. Robert Toft underscores how in the early modern period music and poetry are often interdependent and rely on a shared affect.[22] Of course, in practice the embodied experience of creating instrumental music, like singing or reciting a song, like sleeping, waking, and loving, is not fully documented by score or script. So again, the printed elements, in this case the score, at once reinforce the feasibility of the lovers' plans while also reminding us that what they experience "ev'rie afternoone" is subject to the vagaries of the body and performance.

The idea of a song in general also offers a greater sense of both physical immediacy (someone sings) and ephemerality (the voice dissipates) than a printed poem. This is what has led scholars to suggest that "the title 'Song' is used as cover for many lyrics with bawdy inclinations in this period because it carries some license: what is sung is less 'meant' than what is said."[23] And the printed verse collection might gain license for its bawdy contents by categorizing its poems as songs. Nonetheless, in print the song or air's supposed ephemerality becomes a metaphor. In actuality, readers would likely encounter the fifth air fixed in print on the page and prior to reading the eighth air. The narrative of the fifth air, sharing language with that of the eighth, calls into question the feasibility of Bessie's experience. This is reinforced by the first-person perspective of the fifth air, wherein the lady laments her fallen state, versus the third-person perspective of air eight. Air eight comes to seem more of a titillating story, while the fifth is more like a dispatch from lived experience. The eighth air's very position within Campion's collection reinforces Bessie's uncertain cognitive state and the uncertainty of the lovers' experience. In short, Campion brings together rhyme, music, print, and sleep states to present a poem about bodily experience, explicating this experience through the intersection of poetics (the pattern of end-rhymed

62 | SLEEP STATES AND SUBJECTIVITY

couplets) and textual materiality (the paradoxical ephemeral permanency of the printed song). While Bessie's state may be legible through early modern theorizing on sleep states, its explanatory force comes through the material and poetic mechanisms that represent it.

4

Campion's lively, earthy song, with its everyday English personae, is part of a group of poems with a similar narrative: an epigram from 1595, one from 1619, and another shorter poem from the same collection.[24]

> 1595 in *Poemata*: "De Thermanio et Glaia" "Thermius, a boy, saw Glaia, a girl, stretched out in sleep. With stealthy hand he drew apart her loosened garments, took her leg, and kissed her smooth lips. She kept silent, as if in the tomb. The boy smiled and attempted the ultimate joy; she still did not stir but gladly submitted to all his tricks—the sly girl. What novel slumber is this, Glaia, defeating the gentle goose and the wakeful Sibyl? As if overcome by a great lethargy you sleep away your nights and days.[25]

> 1619: II. 60. The boy Lycius, seeing the girl Clytha reclined in sleep, furtively approached her and, taking her by the cheeks, he planted a kiss on her lips. Seeing she remained motionless, he gave her more kisses, and soon they became stronger. She remained as still as if she were in her tomb. The boy smiled, and attempted to gain the ultimate consolation. She still remains unmoving, but deceitfully endures all his deceits. What kind of slumber is this? Neither that goose nor the Sibyl were as wakeful as she. Now, seized by the same weariness, she daily returns to the same slumber.

> II.61. ON THE SAME
> Lycius constantly smiles when his Clytha is asleep. In her sleep Clytha smiles even more.[26]

Epigrams have long been noted as some of the most mobile forms of writing in the early modern period. Since they are short, prime for collecting, and often tantalizingly topical or titillating, it comes as no surprise that epigrams circulated widely in manuscript (both in miscellanies and in gift manuscripts) and in print. Campion writes in the mode of Martial and sets out his philosophy in an epigram on the poet:

> Cantabat Veneres meras Catullus;
> Quasvis sed quasi silva Martialis
> Miscet materias suis libellis,
> Ludes, stigmata, gratulationes,
> contemptus, ioca, seria, ima, summa;
> multis magnus hic est, bene ille cultis.

> Catullus used to sing mere love songs. But, like a forest, in his slim volumes Martial commingled all sorts of material: praises and reproaches, congratulations and diatribes, witticism and serious stuff, the highest and the lowest. So the former is great in the eyes of the multitudes, while the latter is well liked by those of cultivated taste.[27]

In the case of air eight and its epigrammatic compeers, Campion seems to have pursued formal variety while replaying the same plot. In his poem on Lycius and Clytha, the lady's sleep state, in which she "deceitfully endures all his deceits" causes the poet to ask, "What kind of slumber is this?" The kind, it seems, that she can conjure "daily." In the next poem, he writes, "Lycius constantly smiles when his Clytha is asleep. In her sleep Clytha smiles even more." The lady's plan for daily sleep is tied to the repeated scenario of the epigrams, as her pleasure in half-sleep allows him to write another poem. While Campion does have other linked epigrams, noted by the title "To the Same" or "On the Same," none extend the poem's temporal claims or are linked in a plotted way, as these two are.

By exploiting his characters' ambiguous sleep states, both in the song and in the epigrams, Campion can extend the erotic encounter, conceptually lengthening the normally brief confines of the air and the epigram and again raising questions about how represented embodiment, plot, and formal strategies interact across his oeuvre. George Puttenham famously considered epigrams to be poems that exist on a specific surface and that, like the instruments that inscribe them, are pointed.[28] Perhaps with an eye to their frequently more bawdy content, Campion sees epigrams as similar to airs: "What epigrams are in Poetrie, the same are Ayres in musicke, then

64 | SLEEP STATES AND SUBJECTIVITY

in their chiefe perfection when they are short and well seasoned" (15). For Campion, epigrams are not pointed but piquant. The physical metaphor implies more pleasure than pain. It also suggests a greater ephemerality, as the pleasure of taste is fleeting while the pain of a barb might linger.

In the three epigrams that presage and replay the dramatic scenario of the eighth air, Campion engages in a form of poetic remembering that accords with this reworked plot. In the eighth air he uses rhyme as a way to both "forget the classical tradition"[29] formally, while remembering a classical scenario in terms of content (the Ovidian referent already discussed, and his own Latin epigram). In bringing this scenario into the Latin epigram form three times, he relies on a scenario of feigned consciousness to reinforce his own feigned formal forgetfulness. If rhyme, as he sees it, "enforceth man" to act against his will, then the complex and troubling play of consent and resistance in these poems codes his own seduction by rhyme. The prolepsis and repetition of these three poems' amorous scenario reinforces their formal strategies as deeply memorial, embodied, and erotic. The interplay these poems create between classical form and contemporary rhyme, linked by the seduction plot, is further evidence for what David Lindley identified as Campion's "double direction." Lindley argues that his "poetry seems to be poised between the old and the new."[30] Lindley goes on to specify how certain of his musical experiments (monody, for example) are forward looking while his use of quantitative verse is decidedly backward looking. This methodological double direction is supported in the lyric plot with which he shows such fascination, the desire to look back and repeat what has gone before, but that also moves forward in the process of repetition. Including this plot in both the rhymed English song and the Latin epigrams is a version of this double direction at the level of dramatic action, and based within the somatic experiences he imagines for his characters.

Epigrams were routinely adapted and changed by copyists.[31] Campion, however, as the poem above suggests, allied himself with Martial as a poet who advocated the exclusivity of his epigrams and therefore tightly controlled their circulation.[32] Campion in one sense serves as his own copyist, using the epigram and its provocative subject as a means to expand his poetic collection. If the epigram is known to be a "self-conscious form in imitation of the classics,"[33] Campion takes this self-consciousness rather more literally. He undertakes self-imitation authorized by the formal choices that define the air and its epigrammatic cousins, and by the liminal consciousness of his characters, whose proliferating encounters call for further poems. In copying and adapting his own work, Campion creates a system as dichotomously closed yet open-ended as that between the lovers he imagines. He can allow his verse to propagate and participate in a performance of what Arthur Marotti calls "social textuality" without risking the extra-authorial changes or corruptions such circulation would require.[34] Further, though rhyme is exchanged for quantitative verse, the repetition associated with rhyme is reformed into a dramatic refrain, the repeated plot of the epigrams. He thus brings the poetic present into contact with the poetic past in part through the mechanism of a dramatic situation that relies on the possibilities of half-sleep. In one sense, then, the license sleep gives to the lovers in these poems is re-created as a form of poetic license. Campion uses this sleep scenario to initiate a type of procedural mimesis for the repetition and transmission of his verse. The editor of the scholarly online edition of Campion's Latin verse notes of his poems on half-sleep, quite rightly, that Campion must have "liked this erotic situation."[35] His investment in this plot may ultimately be less about its erotic possibilities than about the way liminal cognitive experiences were useful topics for his experiments in different forms of prosody, flexible and indeterminate plots that might accord with his own shifting ideas about rhyme, refrain, and poetic propagation.

NOTES

1. Catharine Ing, *Elizabethan Lyrics: A Study of the Development of English Metres and Their Relation to Poetic Effect* (London: Chatto and Windus, 1951), 173.

2. Gail Reitenbach, "'Maydes Are Simple, Some Men Say': Thomas Campion's Female Persona Poems," in *The Renaissance Englishwoman in Print: Counterbalancing the Canon*, ed. Anne M. Haselkorn and Betty Travitsky (Amherst: University of Massachusetts Press, 1990), 80–96.

3. Richard Rainholde offers a succinct period definition: "Ethopoeia is a certaine Oracion made by voice, and lamentable imitacion, upon the state of any one." He goes on to suggest the mode's frequent use of a female speaker by offering as an example "what patheticall and dolefull oracion, Hecuba the quene made, the citee of Troie destroied, her housbande, her children

slaine." See *A Booke Called the Foundacion of Rhetorike: because all other partes of rhetorike are grounded thereupon, every parte sette forthe in an oracion upon questions, verie profitable to bee knowen and redde* (London: John Kingston, 1563), fol. xlix.

4. David Lindley describes Campion as "an amateur musician whose compositions were born in private circumstances" and elaborates on Campion's collaboration with court lutenist Philip Rosseter, coproducer of *A Booke of Ayres*. See Lindley, *Thomas Campion* (Leiden, Netherlands: E. J. Brill, 1986), 66–68.

5. Thomas Campion, "Observations in the Art of English Poesie," in *The Works of Thomas Campion*, ed. Walter R. Davis (London: Doubleday, 1969), 294. Unless otherwise noted, all references to Campion's

poetry in this chapter come from this edition and will be made parenthetically in the text.

6. *A Booke of Ayres, Set foorth to be song to the Lute, Orpherian, and Base Violl, by Philip Rosseter, Lutenist*, in Davis, *Works of Thomas Campion*, 15.

7. Carole Levin, *Dreaming the English Renaissance: Politics and Desire in Court Culture* (New York: Palgrave Macmillan, 2008), 16.

8. Aristotle talks about the moments when we fall asleep and when we wake up as being particular moments of awareness where we can recognize dreams as dreams. He writes, "For in the case of waking and sleeping, when one of these states is present in the ordinary way, it is possible for the other to be present in a certain manner": *Aristotle on Sleep and Dreams*, trans. David Gallop (Warminster, U.K.: Aris & Phillips 1996), 103. Juan Luis Vives discusses "Phantasma. Cicero calls him Visus, or Vision, in Latin, because he represents himself to our senses when we are half-asleep, neither fully awake nor with our bodies yet completely surrendered in submission to Sleep, and so find ourselves in the two powerful kingdoms of Slumber and Wakefulness": *Somnium et vigilia in "Somnium Scipionis" (Commentary on "The Dream of Scipio")*, trans. Edward V. George (Greenwood, S.C.: Attic Press, 1989), 21. I would like to thank Nancy Simpson-Younger for this transcription of Folger MS J.a.1 (5), *Oneirologia, or, A Brief Discourse of the Nature of Dreames* (1605), 59v.

9. See, for example, Thomas Cogan, who gives a confident appraisal of what attaining the sleep state involves, based on Aristotle: "Because in sleepe the senses be unable to execute their office, as the eye to see, the eare to heare, the nose to smell, the mouth to tast, and all sinowy parts to feele, So that the sense for a time seem to be tyed or bound." See *The Haven of Health, Chiefly gathered for the comfort of students, and consequently of all those that have a care of their health, amplified upon five words of Hippocrates, written Epid. 6. Labour, cibus, potio, somnus, Venus. Hereunto is added a preservation from the pestilence, with a*

short censure of the late sicknes at Oxford (London: Anne Griffin for Roger Ball, 1636), EEBO. See also Garrett Sullivan Jr., *Sleep, Romance, and Human Embodiment: Vitality from Spenser to Milton* (Cambridge: Cambridge University Press, 2012), 17–18.

10. Michel de Montaigne agrees in his essay "Of Practice," noting, "So it happens to us in the early stages of sleep, before it has seized us completely, to sense as in a dream what is happening around us, and to follow voices with a blurred and uncertain hearing which seems to touch only the edges of the soul." See *The Complete Essays of Montaigne*, trans. Donald M. Frame (Palo Alto: Stanford University Press, 1998), 271. For more on Montaigne and sleep, see pages 178–79 of Cassie Miura's essay in this volume.

11. Mary Chan, "The Strife of Love in a Dream and Sidney's Second Song in *Astrophil and Stella*," *Sidney Newsletter* 3, no. 1 (1982): 3–9.

12. Ovid, *Times and Reasons: A New Translation of Fasti*, trans. Anne Wiseman and Peter Wiseman (Oxford: Oxford University Press, 2011), 1.432.

13. Sir Philip Sidney, *Astrophil and Stella*, in *English Sixteenth-Century Verse: An Anthology*, ed. Richard S. Sylvester (New York: W. W. Norton, 1984), 2.15.

14. Margaret Simon, "Collaborative Writing and Lyric Interchange in Philip Sidney's *Old Arcadia*," *Early Modern Literary Studies* 19, no. 2 (2017): 14.

15. Sir Philip Sidney, *The Countess of Pembroke's Arcadia (The Old Arcadia)*, ed. Jean Robertson (Oxford: Clarendon Press, 1973), 201–2.

16. See Lindley's discussion of "Sleep Angry Beauty" in *Thomas Campion*, 43.

17. Margaret Simon, "Refraining Songs: The Dynamics of Form in Philip Sidney's *Astrophil and Stella*," *Studies in Philology* 109, no. 1 (Winter 2012): 92.

18. Amanda Watson, "Off the Subject: Early Modern Poets on Rhyme, Distraction, and Forgetfulness," in *Forgetting in Early Modern English Literature and Culture: Lethe's Legacies*, ed. Christopher Ivic and Grant Williams (London: Routledge, 2004), 84–85.

19. Sidney, *Astrophil and Stella*, 73.8, 45.14.

20. Kristen Gibson, "The Order of the Book: Materiality, Narrative and Authorial Voice in John Dowland's *First Booke of Songs or Ayres*," *Renaissance Studies* 26, no. 1 (2012): 24.

21. Sarah Iovan, "Singers and Lutes, Lutes and Singers: Musical Performance and Poetic Discourse in Early Modern Songs," *Sixteenth Century Journal* 47, no. 3 (2016): 555.

22. Robert Toft, "Musicke a Sister to Poetrie: Rhetorical Artifice in the Passionate Airs of John Dowland," *Early Music* 12, no. 2 (May 1984): 191.

23. Pamela Coren, "In the Person of Womankind: Female Persona Poems by Campion, Donne, Jonson," *Studies in Philology* 98, no. 2 (Spring 2001): 227.

24. David Lindley writes briefly of this relationship, focusing on the shift in narrative pace and closure from the eighth air to the epigram versions (*Thomas Campion*, 55).

25. *Thomae Campiani poemata* (London: Richard Field, 1595), Doc. Image 37. The translation is from Dana F. Sutton in the note to epigram 60 in her edition of "The Second Book of Thomas Campion's Epigrams," in *The Latin Poetry of Thomas Campion* (Birmingham, U.K.: Philological Museum, 2016), http://www.philological .bham.ac.uk/campion/notes.html#II.60.

26. Sutton, "Second Book," 60, 61, http:// www.philological.bham.ac.uk/campion/epigrams_2_trans.html.

27. Ibid., 27.

28. George Puttenham, *The Art of English Poesy*, ed. Frank Whigham and Wayne A. Rebhorn (Ithaca: Cornell University Press, 2007), 27. As Joel Swann puts it, "The epigram could lend itself to different practices of transcription, since it was often the 'point' or 'sharpness' of an epigram that early modern commentators regarded as important." See Swann, "Copying Epigrams in Manuscript Miscellanies," in *Manuscript Miscellanies in Early Modern England*, ed. Joshua Eckhardt and Daniel Starza Smith (London: Ashgate, 2016), 151.

29. Watson, "Off the Subject," 86.

30. Lindley, *Thomas Campion*, 136.

31. Swann, "Copying Epigrams," 153.

32. James Doelman, "Circulation of the Late Elizabethan and Early Stuart Epigram," *Renaissance and Reformation* 29, no. 1 (Winter 2005): 67.

33. Ibid., 60.

34. Arthur Marotti, *Manuscript, Print, and the Renaissance Lyric* (Ithaca: Cornell University Press 1995), 135.

35. Sutton, "Second Book," note to epigram 60, http://www.philological.bham .ac.uk/campion/notes.html#II.60.

CHAPTER 3

"Still in Thought with Thee I Go"

Epistemology and Consciousness in the Sidney Psalms

NANCY L. SIMPSON-YOUNGER

Does a person have to be conscious in order to think about God or to learn from his instruction? This question has important theological implications for early modern Christians, who might experience the stillbirths of children or outbreaks of deadly illnesses such as sleeping sickness—with the threat of nocturnal visitations from the devil during periods of ill health, as well.[1] If God could not only be present during states of human unconsciousness but also actively assist or even teach the sleeping, the comatose, and the unborn, then religious hopes of salvation could be extended to all human beings, whether they ever (re)attain consciousness or not. At the same time, if God is actively protecting and instructing those who cannot access the faculty of reason, questions might arise about free will and about the relationship between human bodies and minds. For Mary Sidney Herbert, a sixteenth-century translator of religious texts, the Psalms became a vehicle by which to explore these ideas and their implications. By rooting her project in the idea that God is present (and active) during every state of human consciousness, Sidney Herbert frames a range of embodied sleep states as an educational means through which to access knowledge about the divine.

70 | SLEEP STATES AND SUBJECTIVITY

In the early modern period, the use of the human body as a conduit to divine encounters could be a controversial subject. In the aftermath of the Protestant Reformation, for example, theologian John Calvin framed the physical as a sign of the spiritual, in a way that prioritized the latter. For example, Calvin believed that communicants could know God by eating bread that symbolized the "spiritual presence" of the divine, which was true but not "local": the bread itself was not Christ's body, but only a sacramental "sign."[2] Similarly, Reformed sinners could express contrition before God when they offered a spiritual "sacrifice of praise," instead of performing physical rites of penance.[3] As Calvin developed his ideas, the book of Psalms served as a key intertext, providing him with body-based metaphors to interpret in spiritual ways. Reading Psalm 139, for example, Calvin notes that the "worde [*face*] is putte for knowledge or syghte" and "the word [*hand*] is here put for power."[4] In Calvin's Psalm exegesis, which builds on Augustine's, the body becomes an allegorical means to an end: its physical substance becomes a sort of shorthand for the metaphysical ideas that lead to spiritual edification. At the same time, while this discourse of the metaphorical body was gaining traction, the psalm translator Mary Sidney Herbert—who used Calvin as one of her sources—was implicitly asking if the physical human body could also be used as a pathway toward the knowledge of God. Without emphasizing the material over the spiritual, or investing too much in the transient flesh, could a Protestant working with Calvin's ideas still use concrete human embodiment to come to a better understanding of the divine? For Sidney Herbert, I argue, the answer is yes. In her psalms, especially Psalm 139, repeated experiences of physical consciousness and unconsciousness become the precondition for (limited) knowledge about God to be recursively and thoroughly learned. This idea is both encouraged and mediated by the recursive experience of psalm interaction itself.

To investigate consciousness, metaphors, and embodied religious knowledge, we need to investigate sleep. In the period, sleep was often used as a religious metaphor for a distracted or an unattentive state, using the body as an instrumental means to convey a spiritual concept. This is the case even though the scriptures themselves can use sleep to highlight the concrete consequences of human embodiment, as when Jesus admonishes his sleepy disciples to "watch [or stay awake] and pray, that ye enter not into temptation: the spirit indeed is willing, but the flesh is weak" (Matthew 26:41). Still, while acknowledging the physical fact of flesh that needs sleep, early modern commentators tended to emphasize sleep as a launchpad for alle-gory. Leonard Wright's 1589 *A summons for sleepers* uses Romans 13:11–12 to describe the sleep of "ignorance, darkness, and sin." Wright's goal in writ-ing is "to wake up this kinde of sleepers, and to rebuke the world."[5] In 1638 *The Drowsie Disease* acknowledged both the positive and negative meta-phorical valences of sleep—godly rest and sinful sloth—using the latter to discourage napping during worship.[6] Here, an embodied form of sleep is condemned because of its metaphorical antecedents, to which it is onto-logically subordinate. Knowledge of embodied sleep, in other words, was primarily valuable as a subsidiary stepping stone to the metaphysical knowl-edge of good and evil, righteousness and sin.

This metaphorical reading of sleep dovetails nicely with the Protes-tant emphasis on typological or figural strategies for reading scripture. As Rivkah Zim and Hannibal Hamlin point out, the Psalms were particularly privileged as texts that not only encapsulated knowledge about God but also dispensed that knowledge to individuals by "wrapp[ing] up things in types & figures" or "describing them under borowed personages," as Arthur Golding put it in 1571.[7] The epistemological consequences of this perspective come through when Richard Hooker asks, "What is there necessary for man to know which the Psalmes are not able to teach?"[8] If the speaker of a given psalm is simultaneously (or alternately) David, Christ, a translator, a con-gregation, and every Christian, then the Psalms are not only a *nosce te ipsum* workbook for individuals but also a theologically complex set of allusions that can generate knowledge by asking a reader to unpack a series of nom-inally embodied metaphors in a typological framework.[9] Here, an example might be helpful. If a soul "pants" for God like a deer pants for water in Psalm 42:1, that image of a thirsty animal body can unlock self-reflexive insight for individual readers, while simultaneously teaching them about David's his-torical suffering and broader human affective experience on earth.[10] When the Psalms teach readers to know themselves, they also attend diligently to the religious contexts of those selves, conveying knowledge about God, fellow believers, and historical figures through multilayered metaphors.

As one might expect, though, the role of the physical body in these ped-agogical metaphors was highly debated. In 1528 the *Opusculum in Psalmos* recommended psalm study for all those who "desire to know the savior in the body (*in corpore*)"—an ambiguous phrase that signaled both knowledge of the Savior himself, in the flesh, and knowledge of Christ that is, in itself,

72 | SLEEP STATES AND SUBJECTIVITY

somehow physical knowledge.[11] This idea builds on the Augustinian model of reading the Psalms typologically as lyrics that simultaneously prefigure and remember the human experiences of Christ—the figure who merges divine and mortal attributes through incarnation in a single body, paving the way both for salvation and for (partial) human learning about God.[12] So far, this tradition frames the Psalms as a teaching tool that can leverage the human body in pursuit of epistemological and theological inquiry. At the same time, though, knowing Christ *in corpore* leans toward a Catholic model of the Eucharist, which is decidedly unmetaphorical. For Catholics, transubstantiation turns a piece of bread into the actual body of Christ and a drink of wine into the actual blood of Christ, allowing both to be swallowed and incorporated into a practitioner's own body.[13] (Luther modified this slightly with the concept of consubstantiation, in which God imbues and contextualizes the bread through his "real presence," which coexists with the substance of the bread. Calvin rejected this model in favor of "spiritual presence.")[14] The relative alignment of the Psalms with the rhetoric of embodied, flesh-based learning thereby becomes a doctrinal issue for the Sidneys to confront. As Margaret Hannay points out, Mary Sidney Herbert in particular rooted her psalm translations in sources like the Geneva Bible and Calvin's commentaries, putting the lyrics in a left-leaning Protestant context that tended to prioritize the spiritual above the bodily.[15] If the Psalms are meant to teach, but teaching about the embodied physical knowledge of Christ can be linked to Catholic or Lutheran Eucharistic practice, then psalm translators such as the Sidneys, building on Genevan source texts, must find a way to negotiate these tensions.

One solution is to portray an embodied but metaphorically distanced God. Philip Sidney does this when describing the poetry of the Psalms in the *Defense*: "For what else [are David's] . . . notable prosopopoeias, when he makes you, as it were, see God coming in His majesty . . . but a heavenly poesy, wherein almost he shows himself a passionate lover of that unspeakable and everlasting beauty to be seen by the eyes of the mind?"[16] Here, to use Anne Lake Prescott's phrase, Sidney sees the original psalmist as a feigner of "allegories and metaphors," using figurative language to personify the unspeakable divine.[17] Qualified by "as it were" and "almost," Sidney's description insists on the metaphorically distanced nature of David's poetic project, enabling later readers to approach the words typologically, pedagogically, and with the humble knowledge of incomplete perception. At the same time, with the phrasing "makes you, as it were, see God," Sidney prioritizes the metaphysical sight of the mind in a way that relies on (first) the physical incarnation of God and (second) the usefulness of the human senses in learning, partially, about that God. While David's psalms operate inherently by metaphor, for Sidney, they are also at their core poetic instruments that can make the invisible God somehow visible, despite the distancing that figurative language can create. The beauty of this God is discussable only in the terms of metaphorical embodiment: God takes on a physical presence, and his essence is partially available to his people by means of their (figuratively) embodied perceptions.

This stance leads Sidney to invest his own psalm translations with a surprising number of bodily references, because they provide the fresh, striking imagery that can enable metaphysical (but physically informed) "seeing." Before his death, Sidney translated Psalms 1–43. His speaker describes both God and himself as embodied beings. God's "brest" is the "neast" that enables the speaker's safe "rest" in the final stanza of Psalm 4, for example. In Psalm 30, "Well may the Evening cloathe the eyes / In clouds of teares," even though none of Sidney's sources mention tears.[18] Tracking Sidney's choices as a translator and consultor of psalm commentaries, Zim argues that his goal was to create "palpable effects" on readers.[19] Because his readers are human beings, stuck within the "clayey lodgings" or "fleshly darkness" of the body, these palpable effects have to resonate with the fallen but unavoidable context of embodied being—reflecting a sensorial, affective, pain-conscious engagement with the created environment, in order to capture and teach an audience.[20] In this, Sidney adapts a Calvinist idea. Just as physical symbols represent spiritual truths during the sacraments, constituting the "visible signs" that "our infirmity requires," concrete bodily imagery embedded within poetry can point toward transcendent spiritual ideas.[21] For Sidney, this makes the human body both corrupt and essential: it is the raw material that enables poetic expression, links us to the incarnate Christ, and thereby allows for (limited) theological didacticism.

Here, we reach an important crux. While all of these ideas are true, they also depend on human consciousness. After all, only a body that is wakeful and aware can process or analyze a metaphor, and metaphor itself most often draws on conscious, wakeful human experience. This raises a troubling question. Can God still reach, and even educate, a body that does not harbor conscious thought of its own? (In other words, can God teach

74 | SLEEP STATES AND SUBJECTIVITY

those who cannot hear or process metaphorically rooted language?) Sidney begins to approach this question in his psalms, outlining the problem without quite tackling it. In 3:5 (lines 15–17) the speaker reports, "I layd me down and slept / For he me safely kept / And safe again He rear'd mee."[22] In 16:7 (lines 19–24), he goes a bit further:

> Ever, lord, I will blesse Thee,
> Who dost ever counsell mee,
> Ev'n when night with his black wing
> Sleepy darkness doth o're cast,
> In my inward reynes I taste
> Of my faults and chastening. (*Poems*, 288)

Taken together, these passages from Sidney's initial psalms create a picture of a God who actively supervises the speaker at all times of the day and night. This supervision not only guarantees the sleeper's safety but also enables divine "counsel," or pedagogy. Under the cover of night, the speaker—perhaps awake, perhaps asleep—experiences an internal and bodily process of "chastening" that involves both his sense of taste and the idea of renal ("reins"-based) filtration.[23] The combination is uniquely Sidneian. Gilby's translation of Théodore de Bèze says simply, "Thou doest teach mee inwardly everie night," and the Geneva Bible of 1560 says, "My reines also teach me in the nights," with a gloss that moves immediately to the metaphorical: "God teacheth me continually by secret inspiration."[24] For Sidney, who adds the idea of "taste," God provides instruction by allowing the nocturnal speaker to perceive sinful faults in an embodied way, shunted through the kidneys with a "taste" that gives sensory, conscious notice to an unconscious process.

If this is a simple metaphor, then Sidney just demands attention to the daily inward processing of sin. If this is both a metaphor and a concrete assertion of divine intervention in the human body, then something more is at stake. The nocturnal "safety" that God provides must be aligned—or even synonymous—with the fact of his physical, sensorily palpable intervention during a time of rest, if not necessarily slumber. Under faculty psychology, if this divine intervention is concretely tasteable, then the brain is either conscious (because sleep obstructs sensory perception) or asleep and experiencing a divine rerouting of normal procedure, by which the senses can be associated with unconscious processes for educational purposes.[25] Sidney leaves this ambivalent—he does not establish firmly that the speaker is sleeping, although the night is "sleepy"—but he leaves the door open for the second possibility. Sidney's speaker, in other words, raises the notion that God might purge, teach, and even protect through unconscious but sensorily embodied experience.

While Sidney stops short of fully exploring this idea, making his speaker ambiguously conscious, his sister Mary Sidney Herbert develops it to a much greater degree. As Gary Waller points out, after Sidney's death, Sidney Herbert used her brother's psalm translations as a poetic training ground, making judicious tweaks to his wording. One of Sidney Herbert's tweaks was to lines 13–14 of Sidney's third psalm. Instead of "I layed mee downe and slept / For hee mee safely kept," Sidney Herbert writes, "I layed mee downe and slept / *While* hee mee safely kept" (my emphasis)—emphasizing the duration of God's watchfulness instead of the speaker's causal logic in choosing to sleep.[26] (In doing so, she also departs from Gilby's paraphrase of Bèze's reading, which uses "for" as well.)[27] This is the first step in moving toward a portrayal of the God-human relationship that downplays the speaker's conscious decision-making agency. It also begins to develop implicit epistemological claims. While Sidney's speaker knows that God is keeping him safe before he chooses to sleep, using that knowledge to justify his slumber, Sidney Herbert's speaker may not have this knowledge in advance. Only in retrospect, reporting in the past tense, can the poet realize the duration of God's watch time, this temporal "while"—meaning that God's knowledge is shown to be both vaster and more dominant than the speaker's in the new revision. Though it's a small step, Sidney Herbert here alters the text to suggest that the speaker's preemptive, conscious agency is not always tied to divine oversight—and that God guards even those who do not consciously decide to sleep under his aegis.

Theologically, this brings up the sticky question of free will. If God can safeguard or even teach a body that is not conscious, that might seem to indicate that humans have very little agency in soliciting or accepting divine instruction. While this might seem threatening on the surface, conjuring up images of a God who interposes himself upon the unwilling sleeper, two considerations mitigate this threat: (1) the sleeper's ability to reject or embrace the teaching upon waking, and (2) the substantive hope that this teaching offers in a Christian context for those who are stillborn, comatose, drugged, or experiencing other alternative states of consciousness.

76 | SLEEP STATES AND SUBJECTIVITY

As Margaret Hannay has argued, Sidney Herbert repeatedly deepens and expands psalm imagery of the unborn or embryonic body, adding details that signal God's presence with and instruction of that individual life.[28] Psalm 51 features an unborn child who has learned "inward truth" in the "hid school" (probably the womb) because of God's actions (lines 20–21); Psalm 71 reports that "with my childish understanding / Nay, with life my hopes began"—emphasizing that God's provision of "hope" predates the speaker's memories of rational cognition (lines 17–18). When the psalmist describes her enemies' condemnation in a famous passage, she compares them to a stillborn child deprived of God's presence. Sidney Herbert's early drafts of 58:8 describe "the Embrio, whose vitall band / Breakes er[e] it hold, and formlesse eyes do faile / to see the sunn, though brought to lightfull land" (Penshurst ms, 22–24).[29] Metaphorically, going back to the language in Philip Sidney's *Defence*, these enemies have no capacity to "see" (or learn from) God's created world. Concretely, the most chilling measure of doom that the psalmist can articulate is the lack of divine instruction for a vulnerable, unconscious, unborn soul—hinting that this instruction would otherwise be present and available. In this light, acknowledging God's teaching of the unconscious means acknowledging God's ability to provide care to those who can exercise neither agency nor free will—those who are subsumed in a prolonged, sleeplike state.

Mary Sidney Herbert's Psalm 139 takes these ideas a step further, exploring both conscious and unconscious interactions with God from an epistemological, physical standpoint. Ever since the work of editor J. C. A. Rathmell, this psalm has been central to the analysis of Sidney Herbert's poetic project, particularly from the angle of gender critique. Margaret Hannay reads it as a defense of the speaker's voice, which argues that all those with knowledge—even women—must praise God publicly. Hannay, Zim, and Michele Osherow also use 139 to track Sidney Herbert's deep, often gendered engagements with the Calvin commentary and the Marot-Bèze translation of the Psalms into French, from which the composer drew metaphors of embroidery and building construction to describe God's creation of a fetus.[30] At the same time, less attention has been paid to the poem's views of epistemology and human embodiment from the perspective of consciousness. Still, the entire poem is about knowledge, which comes in two subvarieties: God's omniscient knowledge of human beings, and human beings' limited knowledge of God. If one of the ancient and early modern goals of the Psalms was to "set forth and celebrate all the considerations and operations that belong to God," in Richard Hooker's words, preparing humans to be receptive to these teachings, it makes sense to ask how Sidney Herbert is using Psalm 139 to participate in this tradition, while keeping questions of consciousness in mind.[31]

In Sidney Herbert's text (and most other versions of the psalm), the speaker begins by asking if he can ever escape from God's oversight—for example, by flying into space or hiding in hell. This very embodied way to frame an epistemological problem allows Sidney Herbert to build on her brother's ideas about poetic metaphor in the Psalms. Clearly, the speaker is not proposing an actual, physical trip to hell, but grounding a thought experiment about divine and human perception in physical terms. At the same time, though, under the umbrella of that metaphorical thought experiment, the psalm begins to ask how the concrete human body can shape levels of knowledge about God. Here are verses 3 through 7, in Sidney Herbert's translation:

> When I sit
> Thou markest it;
> No less thou notest when I rise:
> Yea, closest closet of my thought
> Hath open windows to thine eyes.[32]

Here, the concrete human body is actively shaping the speaker's knowledge of God—who is, in turn, figured as the omnipresent perceiver of human physicality. The speaker sits, and God sees; the speaker rises, and God sees that; the speaker thinks, and God sees this, as well. For the commentator Augustine, reflecting on these verses, all of this is instantly and almost completely metaphorical: it reflects the death and resurrection of Christ (in sitting and rising) and also the repentence and forgiveness of the sinner. (In fact, for Augustine, a "body"-focused reading of the passage simply applies its allegory to the "body" of the Church, the congregation, instead of its "head," which is Christ.)[33] In Sidney Herbert's hands, though, *copia* extends the passage to foreground and centralize physical details of personal embodiment. Even thought now happens in a spatial, physicalized way: it is both enclosed in the body (a closet) and viewable by God, in a way that cannot be understood, let alone troped, without the material body. While Augustine sees the

78 | SLEEP STATES AND SUBJECTIVITY

body simply as a point of departure for the principal metaphors in the passage, Sidney Herbert roots even the abstract notion of thinking firmly in a physicalized reality, refusing to make the body simply a launching pad for a spiritual exercise. In doing so, she shares common ground with the Geneva Bible and the Sternhold and Hopkins Psalter, which emphasize the physical in lines such as "Thou holdest me strait behind and before, and layest thine hand upon me" (Psalm 139:4). Nonmetaphorical readings of these lines uphold the dignity of human embodiment, framing incarnation itself as a dignified mechanism for human instruction.[34]

One payoff of this emphasis on the physical, for Mary Sidney Herbert, is increased self-knowledge for the speaker, based on God's omniscient perceptions of her own physical movements. If God can see and know the speaker's instantiated thoughts, for example, but the speaker can't equally see and know God, this allows the speaker to confess her physical and metaphysical subordination in a healthy way. (The idea resonates intertextually with Psalm 8:3–4, which famously studies divine creation and then wonders, "What is man . . . that thou art mindful of him?" In case anyone misses the point, the Geneva gloss helpfully answers the question: "Man . . . is but dust.")[35] As Katherine Eisaman Maus argues, this set of contemplations also establishes the speakers like this one as a human being with inwardness, who must understand both their own interior being and God's surveillance of that being as preconditions for early modern personhood.[36] Even while this learning reinforces the speaker's identity and hierarchical positioning, though, it also creates further learning opportunities. As Katherine Larson points out, the speaker's exploration of knowledge becomes the catalyst for a conversational relationship between God and the human that nests the two of them together, creating a productive intimacy that enables the human first to learn and then to speak publicly about her learning.[37] In other words, the speaker's understanding of God's constant oversight is both galvanized and informed by thinking about physical positions, and this understanding crystallizes both the speaker's self-knowledge and her productive intimacy with God.

At the same time, in order to understand God's omnipresent surveillance fully, a human needs to move further. It's one thing to know that God sees human bodies and minds all the time; it's quite another thing for the *human* to know that all the time, internalizing the knowledge of God's presence in every possible situation. This idea builds from Calvin's notion of the "overcarelessness of the flesh," discussed in his commentary on this psalm. For Calvin, the corruptness of embodiment means that humans usually fail to internalize the true omnipresence, power, and mastery of the divine, even though they know the concepts in general.[38] For Mary Sidney Herbert, though, even if the flesh is corrupt, it can still be used in itself to counteract overcarelessness: it can act as a reminder of God's presence during every increment of existence, enabling stronger (though still inevitably limited) knowledge of the divine. If God knows humans across temporal and spatial boundaries, after all, humans cannot hope to understand this without at least trying to know God in a similar way—around the clock, sleeping and waking, even before and after death.

This is where Sidney Herbert's translation of Psalm 139 becomes particularly compelling at an epistemological level. Picturing her own being as it is crafted in the womb, the speaker writes:

> Thou, how my back was beam-wise laid,
> and raftering of my ribs dost know;
> knowest every point
> of bone and joint
> how to the whole these parts did grow;
> in brave embroidery fair arrayed
> though wrought in shop both dark and low. (50–56)

In his commentary on this psalm, Calvin (following Augustine) jumps immediately to metaphor here, saying, "Whether [the psalmist] meane our bones, or whether he meane oure strengthe: it skilles little to the effect of the matter: howbeit I had lever understand it of the bones."[39] By contrast, Sidney Herbert expands this verse to dwell on the intimate, domestic details of physical construction. Splicing lines 2 and 3 together with the back-to-back repetition of "know" (a verb that differs from the Geneva translation, which reads, "My bones are not hid from thee"),[40] Sidney Herbert frames the body as a poem-house with components that are literally held together by means of divine understanding. Moreover, God's technical ability coincides here with his theoretical and transhistorical knowing, in a way that bridges past and present tense: God acted previously, and knows now. To try to understand this, the speaker needs to try to view herself before she was a self. In the process, she feebly tries to emulate divine transtemporality, in a limited and human way, through rhyme: *know/know* becomes recursive, and gives rise to its echoes in "grow" and "low," as the living human speaker turns back the clock to gaze on her own creation. This attempt to limn the transtemporal divine taps into the goal that Arthur Golding articulates for the Psalms in general. "Speaking of things too come as if they were past or present, and of things past as if they were in doing," these texts aim to make each reader "a bewrayer of his own heart"—or, in this case, an observer of it.[41] For Sidney Herbert's speaker, this observation function provides more than an allegory of sin, framing the fetus/believer within a womb that "symbolizes the [immoral] standards of the city to which I then belonged . . . Babylon."[42] Instead, the verse becomes a moment when the conscious psalmist can reflect deliberately on the details of her unconscious body's concrete construction—never quite reaching the knowledge of God but making a move toward a recursive, transtemporal, transconscious understanding of God's active presence.

This transconscious understanding of God operates on a number of levels. First, it allows the conscious speaker to create a narrative in which God has supervised her physical life, even when she could not perceive that supervision. The ability to fill in these gaps, once again, creates a picture of a caretaker God that looks after not only the conscious or the intellectually active. Second, by reflecting on this narrative, the speaker is able to understand how her state of unconsciousness has actually helped to lay the emotional and intellectual groundwork for her own knowledge of this caretaker God:

> All that me clad
> From thee I had.
> Thou in my frame hast strangely dealt:
> Needs in my praise thy works must shine
> So inly them my thoughts have felt. (45–49)

Here, Sidney Herbert puts pressure on the idea of the speaker's "thoughts" in a new way, by rooting them in reflections on an experience that, by default, could not have involved conscious thinking. Residually, in fact, the thoughts show their origins in unconscious fetal life: they literally "feel" the "works" of God, and these feelings are based on inward bodily experience. While the culminating ideas of praise and thinking are necessarily abstract, then, they are also the literal effects of embodied feeling, triggered initially by God's physical intervention during a state of unconsciousness in the womb.

Although the speaker is a fetus only once, she can use daily moments of unconsciousness to remember God's style of physical, caring intervention in a didactic way. Sidney Herbert writes, "I lie to sleep, from sleep I rise, / Yet still in thought with thee I go" (69–70). Like the passage on fetal experience, this passage on sleep posits a set of speakerly "thoughts" that actively connect the vulnerable, unconscious body with the divine mind, against all human logic. In other words, the speaker is thinking along with God before, during, and after sleep. The surprisingness of this idea is signaled by the "yet" at the start of the line. It does not make sense that human thoughts happen during sleep, but still, they do, and they have a connective force: "with thee I go." This doesn't happen in other translations. Sternhold and Hopkins follow the Geneva translation closely in saying, "Whensoever I awake / I present am with thee," for example (stanza 16; Geneva 265r). Gilby's translation of Bèze sees sleep as a sort of necessary but irritating pause, when rest can rejuvenate the body to enable more conscious thought later on: "Though sleepe come uppon me thinking uppon these thinges, I never awake againe, but a newe matter and cause of praysing thee doth offer it selfe."[43] By departing from these examples, Sidney Herbert posits clearly that the cycles and rhythms of human consciousness do not obstruct access to God but instead allow a particular type of contemplative merger with the divine. God is in sleep, as well as wakefulness. While this merger does not indicate equality or complete knowledge of God in any way, it does offer the worshipper an intellectual encounter with God that is verified and enabled by means of the body's concrete processes.

With this idea comes the element of recursivity that helps the speaker catch just a glimpse of divine existence. If God is transtemporally omniscient, knowing all things at all times, then the speaker (who must necessarily be born, sleep, and die) can only fuzzily comprehend this omniscience by thinking embodied thoughts of God and by asking how those thoughts might be somehow continuous—or, at least, recurring—across different states of consciousness. As these thoughts recur through the speaker's memory, sleep, and moments of wakeful praise, they function as a thread that unifies all of the stages of embodied Christian life, focusing each stage on the contemplation of God. From human fetal sleep (Psalm 51) to daily sleep (139) and the sleep of death (76, 90)—and even under God's omnipresent surveillance (3,

4) or the surface appearance of divine slumber (44, 78, and 121)—thoughts and images of God are enabled by the body itself, both as the foundation for metaphor and as the material means of encountering the divine. As sleep recurs throughout the Psalms, it invites human beings to contemplate God's omnipresence as extensively as they can, by linking the knowledge of omnipresence with cycles of consciousness.

Ultimately, portrayals of sleep in the Psalms are one recursive element in a larger recursive structure, since the Psalms are described by early modern commentators as repeatable reminders of ideas about God. Richard Hooker points out that the Psalms educate all levels of learner equally well, with the beginner finding "an easie and familiar introduction" and more advanced students finding "a mightie augmentation of all vertue and knowledge."[44] Since the Psalms were impossible to outgrow, releasing more insight with each subsequent revisitation, they were repeated as part of the school curriculum and in private household devotions—forming, as Margaret Hannay points out, an integral part of daily worship services at Ludlow during Sidney Herbert's childhood.[45] While worshippers sang many of the Psalms in daily or weekly settings, Beth Quitslund notes that it would be "difficult if not impossible" to sing the Sidney Psalms, with their enjambment and metrical variation, even though there was at least one manuscript of a scored Sidney psalm lyric.[46] Whether or not these particular psalms were intended to be sung, though, the texts themselves were repeatedly revisited. Gary Waller describes Sidney Herbert's intensive process of psalm revision, involving one manuscript at Wilton and one in London; more succinctly, William Ringler calls the countess an "inveterate tinkerer," perpetually tweaking the phrasing or imagery in her work.[47] As part of her devotional process, as well as her editorial one, Sidney Herbert visited and revisited each text, rooting her poetic voice in extended meditation and frequent check-ins with each segment.

Conscious of the recursive cultural uses of the Psalms themselves, Sidney Herbert calls for repeated, recursive attention to the role that the body plays in spiritual epistemology. Her work means that bodies could serve purposes beyond the metaphorical in Protestant interpretations of scripture, and it also implies that bodily consciousness is not a prerequisite for didactic interactions with the divine. While states like sleep and fetal life seem on the surface to block human rationality, Sidney Herbert frames them as opportunities for the embodied speaker to access both the divine presence and a form of knowledge about that presence, in recursive ways. Though aspects of this process can have metaphorical valences, Sidney Herbert repeatedly and emphatically roots the whole project in the concrete human body and its states of consciousness, emphasizing God's omniscient oversight and also the flexible range of embodied human thought. In doing so, Sidney Herbert posits that the cycles and rhythms of human consciousness do not obstruct access to God but instead allow a particular type of contemplative merger with the divine.

NOTES

1. On sleeping sickness, see the account of Elizabeth Jefkins in Thomas Bates, *The True Relation of Two Wonderfull Sleepers* (1646), reprinted in *Reprints of English Books, 1475–1700*, ed. Joseph Arnold Foster (East Lansing, Mich., 1945). On demonic visitation, see, for example, Thomas Nashe, *The Terrors of the Night* (London: John Danter for William Jones, 1594), Biiir.

2. For Calvin's stance, see Christopher Elwood, *The Body Broken: The Calvinist Doctrine of the Eucharist and the Symbolization of Power in Sixteenth-Century France* (Oxford: Oxford University Press, 1999), 62–65. Calvin's Reformed view splits from Luther's stance on "consubstantiation," in which Christ is in, near, and around the Eucharist, but the bread does not actually become Christ. On the broader question of the metaphoricity of the Eucharist during this period, see Antony Dawson and Paul Yachnin, *The Culture of Playgoing in Shakespeare's England: A Collaborative Debate* (Cambridge: Cambridge University Press, 2001), 23–26.

3. On the "sacrifice of praise," and Mary Sidney Herbert's more "concrete" recharacterization of this Protestant metaphor, see Mary Trull, "'Theise Dearest Offrings of my Heart': The Sacrifice of Praise in Mary Sidney Herbert, Countess of Pembroke's Psalms," in *English Women, Religion, and Textual Production, 1500–1625*, ed. Micheline White (New York: Routledge, 2011), 37, 39, 47–48.

4. *The Psalmes of David and Others: With M. John Calvins Commentaries*, trans. Arthur Golding (London: [Thomas East and Henry Middleton for Lucas Harison and George Byshop], 1571), 230v.

5. Leonard Wright, *A Summons for Sleepers, Wherein most Grievous and Notorious Offenders Are Cited to Bring Forth True Frutes of Repentance, Before the Day of the Lord Now at Hand. Hereunto Is Annexed a Pattern for Pastors, Deciphering Briefly the Dueties Pertaining to that Function* (London: J. Wolfe, 1589), A1r.

6. *The drowsie disease, or, an alarum to wake church sleepers* (London: J. D., 1638), 8–11, 32–33.

7. Golding, "Epistle dedicatorie," in *Psalmes of David and Others*, *iiiiv. Rivkah Zim quotes and analyzes Golding's phrase in *English Metrical Psalms: Poetry as Praise and Prayer, 1535–1601* (Cambridge: Cambridge University Press, 1987), 32. See also Hannibal Hamlin, *Psalm Culture and Early Modern English Literature* (Cambridge: Cambridge University Press, 2004), 2.

8. Richard Hooker, *Of the Laws of Ecclesiastical Polity: A Critical Edition*, ed. Arthur Stephen McGrade (Oxford: Oxford University Press, 2013), 100.

9. On the multiple speakers and voices of the Psalms, see Danielle Clarke, "Mary Sidney Herbert and Women's Religious Verse," in *Early Modern English Poetry: A Critical Companion*, ed. Patrick Cheney, Andrew Hadfield, and Garrett A. Sullivan Jr. (Oxford: Oxford University Press, 2007), 185, 189; Roland Greene, "Sir Philip Sidney's Psalms, the Sixteenth-Century Psalter, and the Nature of Lyric," *Studies in English Literature, 1500–1900* 30, no. 1 (1990): 23; Katherine R. Larson, "From Inward

Conversation to Public Praise: Mary Sidney Herbert's Psalmes," *Sidney Journal* 24, no. 1 (2006): 23–24.

10. Calvin, *Psalmes of David and Others*, trans. Golding, 166r–v; Théodore de Bèze, *The Psalmes of David*, trans. Anthony Gilby (London: John Harison and Henrie Middleton, 1580), 96–97. The affective reading is emphasized in the early modern pun on deer as "hart" in both translations.

11. Angelo Politiano, *Magni Athanasii opusculum in Psalmos* (London: for Sebastian Gryph of Germany, 1528). Thanks to Dr. Tyler Travillian for help with the Latin translation. On Christ as embodied God and man, prefigured in the Psalms, see Bèze's commentary on Psalm 2, trans. Gilby, 2–3.

12. See Michael Fiedrowicz, introduction to *Augustine's Expositions of the Psalms, 1–32*, ed. John E. Rotelle (New York: New City Press, 2000), 59–60.

13. Dawson and Yachnin, *Culture of Playgoing*, 25.

14. For an exploration of the intra-Protestant dynamics of Eucharistic theology, see Ralph W. Quere, "Changes and Constants: Structure in Luther's Understanding of the Real Presence in the 1520's," *Sixteenth Century Journal* 16, no. 1 (1985): 45–78.

15. Margaret Hannay, *Philip's Phoenix: Mary Sidney, Countess of Pembroke* (Oxford: Oxford University Press, 1990), 86. There are ongoing debates about the Sidneys' religious preferences, which Mary Trull summarizes before arguing that Sidney Herbert has an "independent mind reflecting on the knotty theological problems of her day" ("'Theise Dearest Offrings,'" 38–39). William Ringler notes that Sidney consulted the Geneva Bible and Bèze's work but not necessarily Calvin's (*Poems of Sir Philip Sidney*, ed. William A. Ringler [Oxford: Clarendon Press, 1962], 505–6).

16. Sir Philip Sidney, *The Defense of Poesie*, in *The Major Works*, ed. Katherine Duncan-Jones (Oxford: Oxford University Press, 2002), 215.

17. Anne Lake Prescott, "'King David as a Right Poet': Sidney and the Psalmist,"

English Literary Renaissance 19, no. 2 (1989): 133.

18. Here and elsewhere, I quote Sidney's initial psalm translations from William A. Ringler's edition of *The Poems of Sir Philip Sidney*, in this case pages 274 and 311. On tears, see Hannibal Hamlin, "'The highest matter in the noblest forme': The Influence of the Sidney Psalms," *Sidney Journal* 23, no. 1–2 (2005): 143.

19. Zim, *English Metrical Psalms*, 159.

20. Sidney uses "clayey lodgings" in the *Defense of Poesie* (*Major Works*, 219) and "fleshy darkness" in a May 22, 1580, letter to Edward Denny. See *The Correspondence of Sir Philip Sidney*, ed. Roger Kuin (Oxford: Oxford University Press, 2012), 982. Since some of these lyrics are also prophecies of Christ, whose incarnation is a primary plank of doctrine, the literal nature of the invoked body cannot be completely allegorized; this would verge controversially on docetism.

21. Quoted in Elwood, *Body Broken*, 62.

22. I use Ringler's spelling and content here (*Poems*, 272). See also Gary F. Waller, "The Text and Manuscript Variants of the Countess of Pembroke's Psalms," *Review of English Studies* 26, no. 101 (1975): 9.

23. While the idea of reins can be a commonplace, with Calvin commenting, for example, that "[David] sayeth that even in mennes reynes God hath his judgement seate from whence to execute his jurisdiction" in reference to 139:13 (*Psalmes of David and Others*, trans. Golding, 231r), the idea of "taste" alongside renal judgment emphasizes the physical in a new and deliberate way.

24. Bèze, *Psalmes of David*, 24; Geneva Bible (Rowland Hall, 1560), 237v.

25. For more on faculty psychology, see N. Amos Rothschild's chapter in this volume.

26. Waller discusses this in "Text and Manuscript," 9.

27. Bèze, *Psalmes of David*, 4–5.

28. Margaret Hannay, "'House-Confined Maids': The Presentation of Woman's Role in the Psalmes of the Countess of Pembroke," *English Literary Renaissance* 24, no. 1 (1994): 58–60.

29. Quoted in ibid., 61–62.

30. Ibid., 62–63; Zim, *English Metrical Psalms*, 190–91; Michele Osherow, "Mary Sidney's Embroidered Psalms," *Renaissance Studies* 29, no. 4 (2015): 650, 669.

31. Hooker, *Of the Laws of Ecclesiastical Polity*, 100.

32. Sir Philip Sidney and Mary Sidney Herbert, *The Sidney Psalter*, ed. Hannibal Hamlin, Michael G. Brennan, Margaret P. Hannay, and Noel J. Kinnamon (Oxford: Oxford University Press, 2009), 267.

33. See the exposition on Psalm 13[9]:3 as translated by Maria Boulding, OSB, in *The Works of Saint Augustine: A Translation for the 21st Century*, ed. Boniface Ramsey (New York: New City Press, 2004), 258–59.

34. I am indebted to Nate Sutton for this idea.

35. Geneva Bible, 236r. Calvin emphasizes the hubris of trying to understand God fully in his commentary on this psalm: "Then is there not set downe here [in Psalm 139:14], such a knowledge as may subdue that thynge to our senses, which David hath under the name of wonderfull, confessed too unable to be comprehended" (*Psalmes of David and Others*, 231v).

36. Katherine Eisaman Maus, *Inwardness and Theatre in the English Renaissance* (Chicago: University of Chicago Press, 1995), 10–11.

37. Larson, "Inward Conversation," 22–23.

38. Calvin, *Psalmes of David and Others*, 231v.

39. Ibid. On the bone as representing hidden strength for the psalmist, see Augustine's "Exposition of Psalm 13[9]," in *Works of Saint Augustine*, trans. Maria Boulding, OSB, 272–73.

40. See 139:13 in the Geneva Bible, 265r.

41. Golding, "Epistle dedicatorie," *iiiiv.

42. Augustine, "Exposition of Psalm 13[9]," 270.

43. Bèze, *Psalmes of David*, 378. Calvin echoes this sentiment in his analysis (*Psalmes of David and Others*, 232r).

44. Quoted in Zim, *English Metrical Psalms*, 31.

45. Hannay, *Philip's Phoenix*, 85. Anthony Gilby also recommends daily psalm use in his dedicatory letter to the Countess of Huntingdon, for purposes of encouraging repentance and soliciting mercy. Gilby, "Epistle dedicatorie," in Bèze, *Psalmes of David*, iiiir.

46. Hamlin, *Psalm Culture*, 21–23; Beth Quitslund, "'Teaching Us How to Sing?': The Peculiarity of the Sidney Psalter," *Sidney Journal* 23, no. 1–2 (2005): 97. On the seventeenth-century manuscript of Sidney Psalms 51 and 130, arranged for "soprano voice and lute," see Margaret Hannay, "Re-revealing the Psalms: Mary Sidney, Countess of Pembroke, and Her Early Modern Readers," in *Psalms in the Early Modern World*, ed. Linda Phyllis Austern, David Orvis, and Kari Boyd McBride (Farnham, U.K.: Ashgate, 2011), 24–25.

47. Waller, "Text and Manuscript," 2, and P. Sidney, *Poems*, 502.

Part II

SLEEP, ETHICS, AND EMBODIED FORM IN EARLY MODERN DRAMA

CHAPTER 4

Making the Moor

Torture, Sleep Deprivation, and Race in Othello

TIMOTHY A. TURNER

"The benefit of sleepe, or the necessitie rather needeth no proofe, for that without it no living creature may long endure."[1] So states Thomas Cogan's *The Haven of Health*, a popular Tudor treatise on medicine written as a kind of advice manual for university students but reprinted several times in the second half of the sixteenth century. Cogan's comment, derived directly from Aristotle's well-known *De somno et vigilia*, speaks, of course, to the necessity of sleep—but it also hints at the dangers of sleep deprivation, the subject of this chapter. The essays gathered in the present volume collectively argue that stages of consciousness are bioculturally inflected, exploring, in various ways, "What happens to us when we sleep?" This essay seeks to augment that conversation by pursuing a different, but related, question—"What happens to us when we *don't* sleep?" In particular, and drawing on an eclectic range of sources, it examines episodes of deliberate sleep deprivation as they appear in two of Shakespeare's plays—*The Taming of the Shrew* and *Othello*—in order to explore some of the ways in which the early modern stage presents the dangers of going without sleep. The embodied nature of the early modern stage, in which actors "figure forth" the lived experiences of fictional characters, provides an opportunity for vividly staging the psychological and physiological effects of sleep deprivation. As I hope to show, early modern playwrights were able to use this affordance of theater—the stage's ability to foreground consciousness as well as the susceptibility of the human body to suffering—to show audiences the particular capacity biopower has for *un*ethical *re*definitions of what it means to be human.

In this essay, like Cogan and Aristotle, I take sleep to be one of the "bare needs of life." In doing so, however, I also aim to show how sleep deprivation can become a tool for refashioning subjects in the interests of (forms of) sovereign biopower—the Foucauldian name for a form of sovereignty both predicated on and directed at the biological life of the human species.[2] Foucault introduced the concept in *The History of Sexuality*, volume 1: "It was the taking charge of life, more than the threat of death, that gave power its access even to the body. . . . One would have to speak of *bio-power* to designate what brought life and its mechanisms into the realm of explicit calculations and made knowledge-power an agent of transformation of human life."[3] More recently, the Italian political philosopher Giorgio Agamben has taken up Foucault's work on biopower to argue that the susceptibility of the human body to suffering is in fact a hallmark of modern politics: "It is not the free man and his statutes and prerogatives, nor even simply *homo*, but rather *corpus* that is the new subject of politics. . . . Nascent European democracy thereby placed at the center of its battle against absolutism not *bios*, the qualified life of the citizen, but *zoē*—the bare, anonymous life . . . taken into the sovereign ban."[4] Agamben's work on biopower draws on the Aristotelian distinction between *zoē* (the "bare needs of life" referenced above) and *bios* (Aristotle's "a good life"), both central concepts in the *Politics*.[5] He describes the difference between them as that between the biological needs of human life—like sleep—and the qualified life of the citizen.[6]

Recently, trends in critical analyses of biopower have tended to stress its exercise at the level of the individual and the citizen, as in Agamben's perspective (as opposed to at the level of the population, as in Foucault's). In particular, several scholars and critics writing about the modern era have described torture as an exercise of biopower.[7] These forms of torture, it has been argued, can be seen not merely as the exercise of repressive sovereign power but as a form of technology used to "[constitute] . . . identities" in relation to "power regimes."[8] One such power regime, in this analysis, might include the heteronormative and patriarchal society to which Katherina is made to conform in *Shrew*. As I hope to show, however, whereas in that play Petruchio exercises biopower primarily as a form of torture in service of patriarchy, in *Othello*, Iago exercises it in terms of another vexed and, in the period, still emergent category of identity: race.[9] Ultimately, both *Shrew* and *Othello* represent sleep deprivation in ways that comport with these contemporary descriptions of torture as a form of biopower—a "corporeal technology" aimed at constituting identities and enforcing social hierarchies.[10]

In the early modern period, English interrogators employed both physical and nonphysical methods of torture, usually (but not exclusively) on Jesuit missionary priests. These men were regarded as enemies of the state because they were implicated in plots to overthrow Elizabeth in favor of Mary, Queen of Scots.[11] While interrogatory torture as an assault on the body was usually carried out on the rack, the English did employ other, less direct methods, such as displaying the instruments of torture to frighten victims into preemptive confessions, parading recent victims by the cells of priests awaiting interrogation to terrify them with abject examples of their fate, or starving prisoners in order to coerce confessions.[12] While no one in *Othello* starves, and no rack appears onstage for torturing its characters, Iago arguably subjects the Moor to another form of torture known and used in the period, one that blurs supposed distinctions between physical and psychological techniques: sleep deprivation.[13]

In 1615 the technique of sleep deprivation was used in Scotland on a Jesuit missionary priest named John Ogilvie: "It being remembered, that in the tryal of some criminal persons, it was found that nothing helped more to find out the trueth of the faults wherewith they were charged, then the with-holding of their naturall rest: it was aduised, that [Ogilvie] should bee kept without sleepe for some nights, which was accordingly done: and during which time it was perceived, that hee remitted much of his former obstinacie."[14] Another account of the same episode is more forthright about the effects of sleep deprivation: "The Jesuit in the meyne tyme was convoyit to Edinburgh, and ther keapit in strait waird, and a gaird of men be the space of eight dayis, with small sustenatioun; and compellit and withhaldin perforce from sleap, to the great perturbatioun of his brayne, and to compel him *ad delirium*."[15] Depriving the victim of both food and sleep was understood to make it easier to compel him to act in accordance with the torturers' demands. Indeed, these techniques remain part of the torturer's arsenal today.[16]

92 | SLEEP, ETHICS, AND EMBODIED FORM

This essay augments and extends earlier accounts of torture in both *Shrew* and *Othello* by offering a humoral account of Othello's tortured transformation through sleep deprivation. As Gail Kern Paster argues, "Change of humor in *Othello* . . . occurs in a bodily register that is indistinguishably physical, psychological, and emotional."[17] Like Paster, I posit the "psychosomatic" nature of Othello's transformation. I also see "the work of physiology rather than metaphor" in the play's references to sleep and sleeplessness, and I agree with her that "early modern physiological discourse . . . undergird[s] the play's construction of gender, racial, and ethnic differences," because "it is the discourse in which [the play's characters] necessarily think about the psychological sources of . . . behavior."[18] Shakespeare's interest in the potential of sleep deprivation for the coercive refashioning of human subjectivity dates from early in his career, along with his interest in the humors. Accordingly, in what follows, I sketch an account of sleep deprivations and their humoral effects in the earlier play, *Shrew*, before turning to *Othello* to show how Shakespeare adapts his representation of the practice for a much different context and with very different effects.

Drawing attention to the earlier play demonstrates the playwright's apparent long-term interest in the use and effects of specific torture techniques. I also, however, aim to explore how racial identity appears in *Othello* as the product of a method of torture described here as an exercise of biopower. In doing so, I adopt a historicized approach to the biopolitical valences of Shakespeare's plays. Rather than drawing on modern understandings of biology or race to explain the play, I address these issues by examining them through the lens of early modern humoral theory, with its attendant accounts of human physiology *and* psychology.[19] Thus, although I aim primarily to offer a unique reading of an underappreciated aspect of *Othello* by showing how it fits into an overall pattern in Shakespeare's writing—interest in coercive torture techniques—I do so with another goal in mind. That is, I seek to reconcile the seemingly anachronistic concepts of race, biology, and biopower with a historical approach to forms of knowledge about the living body widely and readily available to early moderns.

1

Shakespeare's career unfolded in the course of what the legal historian John H. Langbein has called the "century of torture," the period in English history when such practices were used more than any other.[20] With the exception of the blinding of Gloucester in *King Lear*, however, overt representations of torture are rare in his plays, though his work repeatedly shows a fascination with torture as a form of mental and physical coercion (even if he typically transposes these activities into apolitical contexts). *Shrew*, an early and useful case study in this vein, demonstrates an obvious interest in coercive refashioning and can be productively examined through the historical lens of torture itself. It is, for example, something of a critical commonplace to note, as Jean Howard does in her introduction to the play in the *Norton Shakespeare*, that Petruchio's pedagogy is "akin to modern methods of torture and brainwashing."[21] But his methods are also akin to *early* modern physical and psychological torture, as the preceding discussion shows, including coercion through starvation and sleep deprivation.[22] The appearance of these techniques in the play therefore makes it particularly appropriate for comparison to *Othello* because both texts represent the exercise of biopower as a tool for "the constitution of hegemonic identities" in certain "power regimes."[23]

Petruchio explicitly describes the usefulness of such techniques for altering behavior in the famous passage that begins, "Thus have I politicly begun my reign." Here, he uses the language of falconry to describe how he plans to tame Katherina by means of sleep deprivation and starvation—an assault thus aimed at two of the fundamental "bare needs of life" described by Agamben and Aristotle:

> My falcon now is sharp and passing empty,
> And till she stoop, she must not be full-gorg'd,
> For then she never looks upon her lure.
> Another way I have to man my haggard,
> To make her come, and know her keeper's call,
> That is, to watch her, as we watch these kites
> That bate and beat and will not be obedient.
> She eat no meat to-day, nor none shall eat;
> Last night she slept not, nor to-night she shall not.[24]

In this case, according to the *OED*, "watch, v." means "to be or remain awake" (sense 1.1a)—or, in this particular instance, "to keep awake intentionally" (sense 1.1b), a technique employed in falconry "to prevent (a hawk) from

94 | SLEEP, ETHICS, AND EMBODIED FORM

sleeping, in order to tame it" (sense 2.16).[25] Katherina testifies to the effectiveness of these techniques when she later describes herself as "starv'd for meat, *giddy* for lack of sleep, / With oaths kept waking, and with brawling fed" (4.3.9–10; emphasis added). Her description of herself as "giddy" underscores the resonance with established torture techniques in early modernity, which were utilized to induce the altered state of consciousness that results in the subject's compliance. "Giddy" seems to be used here primarily to mean "having a confused sensation of swimming or whirling in the head, with proneness to fall; affected with vertigo, dizzy" (*OED*, "giddy, adj.," sense 2a). According to Hernan Reyes, "Even short-lived sleep deprivation causes hallucinations, paranoia and disorientation and can have deleterious psychological effects on an individual."[26] When the play is considered in relation to such psychological effects, including the starvation and sleep deprivation designed to "perturb[e]" the brains of captured early modern Jesuits, then Katherina's taming links more clearly to the historical appearance of torture in this period, and indeed may have been recognized by early modern audiences in this context.[27] It also appears as the exercise of biopower as that term is defined here: an assault on the bare needs of biological life, intended in this case to remake the identity of the person victimized by these methods.

The scene later in *Shrew* when Petruchio forces Katherina to call the sun the moon, for example, can be interpreted in light of these torturous techniques. As a result of her time at her husband's "taming school," she is broken to the extent that she concludes, "What you will have it nam'd, even that it is, / And so it shall be so for Katharina"—prompting Hortensio to declare that Petruchio has finally "won" the contest with his new bride (5.1.21–23). Katherina's transformation is portrayed to ostensibly comic effect. But when it is considered in light of Petruchio's torturous techniques, the cognitive alteration that makes her more pliable can be understood to derive from a physical process whereby sleep deprivation and starvation render her "giddy." Just as, through forced sleeplessness, the Jesuit Ogilvie "remitted much of his former obstinacie," Katherina remits as a result of her husband's coercive, torturous refashioning and literally begins to speak his language.[28]

Indeed, when Katherina is forced to call the sun the moon, one does not have to believe that she is *actually* brainwashed to see Petruchio's coercion of her as insidious. After all, the most common criticism of torture is that it simply forces its victims to say whatever the torturer wants to hear. As Aristotle notes, "We may say what is true of torture of every kind alike, that people under its compulsion tell lies quite as often as they tell the truth, sometimes recklessly making a false charge in order to be let off sooner."[29] The quintessential Shakespearean expression of this view can be found in *The Merchant of Venice*, where Portia declares to Bassanio, "Ay, but I fear you speak upon the rack, / Where men enforced do speak any thing" (3.2.32–33). Elaine Scarry, in a foundational study, argues that the central fact about torture is not its supposed usefulness for information gathering but rather its coercive function—making the victim speak with the torturer's voice. In answering, according to Scarry, "the prisoner is now speaking [the torturer's] words."[30] In these terms, Katherina speaks with Petruchio's words when she calls the sun the moon, or addresses old Vincentio as a "virgin" (4.5.37). She also does this more substantially in the famous final speech in which she espouses the orthodox patriarchal views expected of a "tamed" wife (5.2.136–79). For Scarry, it does not necessarily matter how one interprets the affect of this speech, at least when considering it in light of the coercive methods that have compelled Katherina to speak it at all. Sincere or sardonic, pained or playful, it arises primarily as the result of Petruchio's coercive techniques.

The play's suggestiveness of torture is amplified in that Petruchio had announced his intention to starve and sleep deprive his new bride precisely in political terms: "Thus," he says, "have I *politicly* begun my *reign*" (4.1.188, emphasis added). He situates the exercise of his domestic taming power in the realm of politics and rule—a fact that has, of course, elicited significant commentary, in particular with regard to his exercise of patriarchal power.[31] Petruchio's techniques have also been examined through the lens of political-philosophical work on biopower—bringing "life and its mechanisms into the realm of explicit calculations and [making] knowledge-power an agent of transformation of human life," in Foucault's formulation.[32] Julia Reinhard Lupton, for example, describes "Petruchio's farmhouse outside the city [as] a restraining or reeducation camp, enclosing a kind of violent biopolitical pastoral."[33] Building on this idea, Shakespeare's representation of Kate's treatment may draw on his knowledge of real, contemporary torture techniques used on Jesuits, witches, scolds, and others in early modernity.[34] These negative forms of biopower entail isolating and assaulting the biological processes of life in order to bring into being vulnerable human bodies as both ground and object of the exercise of sovereignty. Shakespeare's examination of these subjects suggests the extent to which his plays can be read in relation to the emergence in early modernity of the modern biopolitical paradigm of sovereign power, and in relation to the role torture itself played in this emergence as a mechanism that deploys knowledge-power to transform human life.

Shrew offers an appropriate starting point for such work precisely because, in the first volume of *The History of Sexuality*, Foucault traces the origins of biopower in terms of patriarchy: "For a long time, one of the characteristic privileges of sovereign power was the right to decide life and death ... derived no doubt from the ancient *patria potestas* that granted the father of the Roman family the right to 'dispose' of the life of his children and his slaves."[35] In terms of the play, Petruchio's torturous techniques culminate in the articulation of the patriarchal ideology espoused, sincerely or not, in Katherina's final speech. Here, she instructs her fellow wives, for example, to "dart not scornful glances from those eyes, / To wound *thy lord, thy king, thy governor*" (5.2.137–38; emphasis added). To demonstrate her submission to her husband, Katherina ends the speech by placing her hand on the ground so that Petruchio may, if he chooses, step on it. Her act should absolutely be understood as a biopolitical gesture because what she is offering is the susceptibility of her body to pain, and this susceptibility appears as the basis, object, and proof of Petruchio's patriarchal power over her. The torturous techniques he employs have reconstituted, for Katherina, the hegemonic identity of a submissive wife under patriarchy. The gesture thus serves as a touchstone for the way in which the play can be read in relation to the emergence of the biopolitical paradigm of sovereignty. It also indicates that we should look for traces of this paradigm in Shakespeare's work not only in tragedies and histories—to the blinding of Gloucester in *Lear*, for example, or Othello's sleep deprivation, as I describe it below—but also in comic and domestic plays, where biopower arises not only as a matter of state but also, as Petruchio might put it, as ordinary "household stuff" (3.2.231).

2

In *Othello*, the exercise of biopower is directed at an altogether different subject: race. In this play, Shakespeare's interest in coercive refashioning is conjoined with humoral theory, the form of what Foucault calls "knowledge-power" most commonly associated with the living body in early modernity. This conjunction takes shape through the play's representation of the effects of sleep deprivation. As noted above, this torture technique should be understood in terms of its physiological and psychological effects and, consequently, its implications for the humoral theories of race that are emergent in this period. In this vein, Iago's psychological or cognitive assault on Othello should be examined in tandem with the physiological manipulation of the Moor's humors and the disastrous effects thereof.

The groundwork for Shakespeare's depiction of the humors in *Othello* was laid much earlier, during his work on *Shrew*. In this earlier play, Petruchio deploys an adept knowledge of humoral manipulation. When Petruchio and Katherina first arrive at his home, Petruchio immediately begins to deprive her of food by throwing out some freshly prepared mutton, supposedly for her own good:

> I tell thee, Kate, 'twas burnt and dried away,
> And I expressly am forbid to touch it;
> For it engenders choler, planteth anger,
> And better 'twere that both of us did fast,
> Since of ourselves, ourselves are choleric,
> Than feed it with such overroasted flesh. (4.1.170–75)

This is, presumably, an ironic example of what Petruchio later calls "a way to kill a wife with kindness" (4.1.208)—supposedly protecting the choleric Katherina by keeping her from further heating and drying her humors. In *The Castell of Health*, Sir Thomas Elyot warns cholerics not to partake of foods that are too hot and dry: "For where the meats do much exceede in degree the temperature of the body, they annoy the body in causing distemperaunce. As hoat wynes, pepper, garlike, onions, and salte, be noyfull to them which bee cholericke because they bee in the highest degree of heate and dryeth above the just temperance of mans body in that complexion."[36] Thomas Cogan issues a similar warning about garlic: "But cholericke folks should abstaine from it especially in hot seasons, for it doth inflame and dry much, and engendreth red choler and adust humors."[37] Petruchio cannily deploys his knowledge-power of diet and humoral theory to dominate, control, and transform others.

In *Othello*, such manipulation takes the form of sleep deprivation. Othello experiences many sleepless nights. His wedding night is interrupted by

Iago with a warning about Brabantio's approach, and then he is called before the senate and sent to Cyprus immediately (Act 1). His journey to Cyprus at sea is plagued by storms (between Act 1 and Act 2). On the night of his arrival in Cyprus, a brawl (engineered by Iago) occurs, and he leaves to assist Montano. Othello does not return to bed—"Myself will be your surgeon," he insists—and at that point he also declares that "'tis the soldiers' life / To have their balmy slumbers wak'd with strife" (2.3.254, 257–58). Finally, the murder of Desdemona occurs at night in a restless bed. These disruptions have informed the long-standing debate over whether his marriage is ever consummated, but another way to look at them would be to say that Shakespeare also carefully indicates Othello's lack of sleep over the course of the play.[38] In each case (with the exception of potentially sleepless nights at sea), these interruptions are the product of Iago's machinations. In this light, Othello's sleep deprivation is shown to arise from external rather than internal sources.

These passages suggest that we ought to attach more than metaphoric significance to Iago's pledge to "practic[e] upon [Othello's] peace and quiet / Even to madness" (2.1.310–11). He even enlists Desdemona in this sleep-depriving enterprise (although she is unwittingly complicit in his scheme). Promising to Cassio that she will continually press his case to her husband, she declares,

> My lord shall never rest,
> I'll watch him tame, and talk him out of patience;
> His bed shall seem a school, his board a shrift,
> I'll intermingle every thing he does
> With Cassio's suit. (3.3.22–26)[39]

This passage includes a direct lexical connection to the earlier Shakespearean examination of the use of sleep deprivation for altering behavior, the "taming school" run by Petruchio. Notably, Desdemona proposes to "*watch* [Othello] *tame*" (3.3.23; emphasis added). Like Petruchio, she uses the language of falconry to explain how she will change her spouse's mind by assaulting the bare needs of his life. Later in the same scene, Iago explicitly declares his "practice" a success when, in an aside, he gloats, "Not poppy, nor mandragora, / Nor all the drowsy syrups of the world, / Shall ever medicine [Othello] to that sweet sleep / Which [he] ow'dst yesterday" (3.3.330–33).

The disruption of the general's sleep appears to Iago as a fundamental feature of his success. He achieves this outcome not only by rousing Othello in the night but also by activating a kind of self-reinforcing cycle in which the general's aroused suspicions further cause him to lose sleep, rendering him susceptible to even more suspicion and, ultimately, violence. The vivid tableau Lodovico refers to at the conclusion as "the tragic loading of this bed" may therefore achieve additional symbolic heft insofar as Othello finally obtains the bed rest that eludes him throughout the play, as if the only sleep he is able to achieve comes to him in death (5.2.363).

Much recent scholarship has described the dexterity with which Iago manipulates Othello in cognitive or psychological terms.[40] Examining sleep as a physiological process as it was understood in early modernity, however, also brings to light the ways in which Othello's cognitive transformation may have been understood in terms of the humoral effects of sleep deprivation. Early modern medical treatises frequently mention the risks of "watch," or sleeplessness: "The commodity of moderate sleepe appeareth by this, that natural heate which is occupied about that matter, whereof procedeth nourishment, is comforted in the places of digestion, & so digestion is made better or more perfite by sleepe, the body fatter, the mynde more quiet and clere, the humours temperate, and by much watch all thinges happen contrary."[41] "Watch," in other words, was held to produce a "mynde" that is *less* "quiet and clere" and "temperate." Notably, in *Othello*, the general does bid "farewell the tranquil mind!" (3.3.348). In this reading, the play may therefore be understood to portray both the physical and the psychological effects of going without sleep. These effects include, for example, the famous "trance" into which he falls (4.1.43, stage direction)—especially when that moment is understood in terms of the description of the effects of sleep deprivation in the torture chamber, where it is used to produce a "great perturbatioun of [the] brayne."[42] For Stanley Cavell, who repeatedly describes Othello as being in a "trance," this state is one result of the play's organization, which links the characters' experiences to "witch trials" and a "setting of legal torture."[43] Even prior to his fit, however, when Othello first complains of a headache, or "a pain upon [his] forehead," Desdemona assumes that this pain is the result of sleep deprivation: "That's with *watching*," or going without sleep (3.3.284–85; emphasis added).[44] Of course, this is not to suggest that a good nap would have been enough to forestall Othello's downfall. But the play's portrayal of sleep deprivation and its disastrous effects does demonstrate

Shakespeare's interest in the connections among humoral theory, cognition, and the mind-body connection, as well his awareness for the potential of humoral manipulation as a form of early modern biopower.

It is possible to trace a medical account of Othello's physical deterioration as well as his identity transformation and ensuing behavior as the result of sleep deprivation, at least in part, in terms of these widely circulating early modern understandings of humoral physiology and psychology. Indeed, Shakespeare may well have adapted these views to suit his own purposes in the play. Consider, again, Elyot's *Castell of Health*, which argues that "immoderate watch dryeth too much the body" and that "much drying of the body, eyther with long watch, or with much care and tossing of the mynde . . . all these thinges do annoy them that be greeved with any melancholy."[45] As a melancholic, in this account, Othello would experience especially pernicious effects from sleep deprivation, since "persons having natural melancholy . . . do require very much sleepe, which in them comforteth the powers animal, vital, & natural."[46] Robert Burton's *Anatomy of Melancholy* also emphasizes this need for sleep: "It is a received opinion, that a Melancholy man cannot sleep over-much." Citing the Dutch physician Lemnius, Burton describes the deleterious effects of sleep deprivation on these individuals: "It causeth driness of the brain, frensie, dotage, and makes the body dry, lean, hard, and ugly to behold, as Lemnius hath it. The temperature of the brain is corrupted by it, the humours adust, the eyes made to sink into the head, choler increased, and the whole body inflamed."[47] (Burton uses the term "adust" to denote "any of the humours of the body when considered to be abnormally concentrated and dark in colour, and associated with a pathological state of hotness and dryness of the body" [*OED*, "adust, adj.," 1a].) Thomas Cogan also notes the necessity of sleep as a process of regulating the body's temperature by "cooling." In digestion, he writes, "vapours and fumes ris[e] from the stomacke to the head, where through coldnesse of the braine, they being congealed, do stoppe the conduites and ways of the senses, and procure sleepe."[48] According to these prevailing medical theories, if Othello would normally require more sleep than individuals of other humoral temperaments would, then his sleep deprivation would generate what early modern writers call "unnatural" melancholy—a process of heating caused in part (as Cogan suggests) by preventing the cooling process necessary for the regulation of a healthy temperature.

Elyot also records the conventional view that the "melancholike is cold and drie." Sleep deprivation, however, would have the effect, through the principles of adustion, of rendering Othello's humors less temperate, both hotter and drier, and thus producing the humoral combination, hot and dry, associated with those of choleric temperament, "in whome the fire hath preheminence."[49] In his *A Treatise of Melancholie* (1586), Timothy Bright describes the process this way: "The unnaturall [melancholy] is an humour rising of melancholie before mentioned, or else from bloud or choler, wholly chanunged into an other nature by an unkindly heate, which turneth these humours . . . into a qualitie wholly repugnant, whose substance and vapor giveth such annoyance to all the partes, that . . . maketh strange alterations in our actions, whether they be animal or voluntarie, or naturall not depending upon our will."[50] This passage might just as well describe Othello's transformation in the play from dispassionate melancholic to passionate, jealous choleric.

All of this has implications for portrayals of early modern race in light of humoral theory. As far back as 1930, Lily B. Campbell was stressing the centrality of adustion to early modern understandings of the bodily humors: "Now if for some reason the humours are subjected to excessive heat, there results an unnatural humour that is to be distinguished from the natural humours and from the unnatural excess of a natural humour. This unnatural humour is generally referred to as melancholy adust. Melancholy adust, then, was the unnatural humour that resulted from any one of the humours putrifying or being burnt through excessive heat. And the importance of distinguishing between the natural melancholy humour and the melancholy adust cannot be overstated."[51] Patricia Parker has, more recently, shown that "melancholy 'adust' was . . . part of a developing lexicon of racial terms" in this period that "connected the discourses of melancholia and racial darkness, signaling not only the tanning or scorching by the sun that turned the Ethiope black but [also] a melancholic adustion or burning . . . [and] part of the humoral discourse of melancholia, already associated with blackness and Moors."[52] Humoral adustion is also related to Othello's race because the term *adust* might designate "a dark brown colour, as if scorched; (of a person) dark-skinned, tanned" (*OED*, "adust, adj.," 2b). (John Florio glosses the term as "adust, burnt, scorched, parched, scalded, tanned.")[53] Othello's skin color thus has a humoral-ethnological explanation, understood as the result of an accumulation of black bile and associated with the melancholic temperament characteristically produced by the African climate.

This account suggests that sleep deprivation, as a process, would further heat and dry Othello's race-linked melancholy humor, according to Shakespeare's adaptation of prevailing early modern medical theories. It thus suggests an enriched explanation for, and heretofore unappreciated aspect of, the Moor's transformation, by positing a new explanation for the humoral and physiological basis of his psychological shift. If one accepts the premise that Othello's sleep is disrupted and deprived over the course of the play, as its language and action clearly indicate, then the source of his natural melancholy, his ordinary black bile, is, through lack of sleep, "burn[ed] like the mines of sulphur" (3.3.329) and turned into "blacke choller" adust—that is, scorched black bile "having in it violence to kill, with a dangerous disposition."[54] The ethnological and humoral basis of this transformation has previously been described by Mary Floyd-Wilson. As she puts it, "Iago's manipulation of Othello does not awaken the Moor's repressed passions or provoke his innate savagery: it utterly transforms the Moor's humors."[55] In Floyd-Wilson's account, this manipulation takes the form of "Iago aim[ing] first to poison Othello's mind with incommensurable conceits. Those conceits will then simmer, before burning the Moor's blood and *producing* heated passions."[56] Though in his testimony before the Venetian senate Othello seems to insist on his innate coolness because his "heat" is "defunct," over the course of the play, humoral language does suggest the heating of his temperament (1.3.263, 264). After his ire has been raised, for example, he declares to Desdemona that he "should make very forges of [his] cheeks, / That would to cinders burn up modesty, / Did [he] but speak [her] deeds" (4.2.74–75). He exclaims, "Fire and brimstone!" (4.1.234), and Emilia later tells him he is "rash as fire" to accuse Desdemona of infidelity (5.2.134). Ultimately, when he begins to regret the murder in the final scene, he imagines himself in hell, "roast[ed] . . . in sulphur" and "wash[ed] . . . in steep-down gulfs of liquid fire" (5.2.279–80). Early in the play, the military crisis that eventually sends the characters to Cyprus had been described by Cassio as "a business of some heat" (1.2.40)—an utterance that seems, in retrospect, prophetic. Rather than seeing such language as merely metaphorical, I interpret it to contain what Paster might call a "trace of . . . medical discourse."[57] In accordance with prevailing humoral theories of the period, over the course of the play, the sleep deprivation Othello experiences causes a physiological reaction—the heating and adustion of his humors—that also produces a psychological transformation and attendant changes in his behavior.

3

Iago's assertion that "these Moors are changeable in their wills" indicates his desire to seize control of Othello's capacity to act (1.3.346–47).[58] A humoral account of the effects of "watch" in the play suggests that Iago may do so in part by "practicing" upon Othello's "peace and quiet." This is a technique also used by torturers in the period to produce more pliant subjects, to coerce and compel their victims and make them "as tenderly led by th' nose / As asses are" (1.3.401–2). Though Iago's techniques of sleep deprivation do not mirror exactly some techniques of early modern torturers—stress positions and loud noises, for example—they nonetheless seem to produce similar cognitive effects.

Such a reading, however, also has consequences for understanding race in the play. If older critical approaches "quibbled over how quickly Othello yields to" his supposedly inherent barbarity, "modern readings of the play . . . evaluat[e] instead how easily Othello falls prey to racial stereotypes."[59] Desdemona gives voice to an older view of temperamentally cool and dispassionate Africans when she speaks of jealousy and claims that Othello is not subject to that vice because "the sun where he was born / Drew all such humors from him (3.4.29–30)."[60] As I have argued here, however, over the course of the play, the melancholic Othello, naturally cool and dry in temperament, is transformed by sleep deprivation, a form of torture that, through humoral manipulation, effects physiological and psychological changes that render him more susceptible to Iago's continued manipulation. In this way, Iago is not so much inventing race as *making* it, in the double sense of the term—not only *creating* but also *coercing* it into being. The word is offered by Iago himself, as in his pledge to "*Make* the moor thank [him], love [him], and reward [him]" (2.1.308; emphasis added).

Rather than merely representing the emergence of a racial stereotype, then, *Othello* might well be understood to present a theory of racialization. Through Iago's humoral manipulation, understood here as an exercise of biopower, Othello is made to speak with his torturer's (racist) voice. Othello's use of the word "wrought" in his dying speech ("Then must you speak /

Of one not easily jealous, but being wrought, / Perplexed in the extreme") can mean both emotionally distraught and made or created (5.2.344–46).[61] Iago, drawing on his physiological and psychological knowledge of the bodily humors, thus (re)makes the Moor—conforming the general to his ensign's own, more derogatory racial theories.

It is in this sense, then, that I describe Iago's torturous technique as an exercise of biopower—that is, as a mechanism that utilizes his knowledge-power of the bodily humors to transform (a) human life. Iago uses torture to constitute, for Othello and for those who view or read of his transformation, a new kind of "hegemonic identit[y]"[62] and enforce "a political hierarchy based on invented biological demarcations."[63] Though far from a "biological" account of race in any modern sense, my reading of *Othello* examines an early modern text in light of Shakespeare's adaptation of one early modern conceptual model for understanding the physiology and mechanics of the living body: humoral theory. Furthermore, considering torture—a coercive technique grounded in the body's susceptibility to physical and psychological disruption—in relation to biopower suggests that the practice should be understood not merely as an exercise of the disciplinary, sovereign power to let live or to cause to die. Sovereignty, too, should be examined in terms of its production not only of docile *bodies* but also of docile *minds*—that is, through its deployment of knowledge-power over cognition and psychology to transform life by assaulting both body and mind. Doing so entails paying closer attention to these coercive techniques as they have appeared not only in the torture chamber itself but also in its theatrical transfiguration into Petruchio's country estate or the distant shores of Cyprus.

Thinking historically about Renaissance biopower and its exercise also necessitates taking into account the ways in which early modern humoral theorists themselves address the mind-body connection, or what Bright, in 1586, calls "the familiaritie . . . betwixt mind and bodie: howe it affecteth it, and how it is affected of it againe."[64] And because, as it turns out, race has become the most frequent object of the exercise of biopower in the modern era, *Othello* appears as a seminal text in the history of how and why that came to be: the history of the invention of a "biological" and "natural" (though actually cultural and fictional) account of race that governed, and in fact continues to govern, the exercise of sovereign power in modernity.[65] The play binds an exploration of torture as a coercive technique together with humoral theory and links them both to the invention of an embodied, if not quite biological, conception of race. Such binding occurs, not incidentally, in tandem with the birth of the racist stereotype of the violent black man, one that turns out to have early modern biopolitical (which is to say humoral) origins. The play thus stages the racialized "birth of biopolitics," to borrow yet another Foucauldian formulation—though, as usual, Shakespeare both anticipates Foucault and expresses himself with more poetic flair: "Hell and night / Must bring this monstrous birth to the world's light" (1.3.403–4).

NOTES

1. See Thomas Cogan, *The Haven of Health* (London, 1596), 232.

2. For a reading of biopower and sleep in Spenser's *Faerie Queene*, see Benjamin Parris's essay in this volume.

3. Michel Foucault, *The History of Sexuality*, vol. 1, *An Introduction*, trans. Robert Hurley (New York: Vintage Books, 1990), 143.

4. Giorgio Agamben, *Homo Sacer: Sovereign Power and Bare Life*, trans. Daniel Heller-Roazen (Stanford: Stanford University Press, 1998), 124.

5. Aristotle, *The Politics and the Constitution of Athens*, trans. Benjamin Jowett, ed. Stephen Everson (Cambridge: Cambridge University Press, 1996), 13.

6. Agamben, *Homo Sacer*, 1.

7. Patricia Cahill, *Unto the Breach: Martial Formations, Historical Trauma, and the Early Modern Stage* (Oxford: Oxford University Press, 2008), for example, includes a sustained discussion of biopower in relation to military praxis. She makes the useful distinction that "the exercise of discipline has to do with the desire to control individual bodies" and "the exercise of biopower aims to control life itself" (106).

8. "Biopower . . . allows us to conceptualise torture as a specific kind of corporeal technology that, while intensively preoccupied with the imprinting of power on bodies . . . is not solely about the repression of enemy bodies. Rather, torture constitutes an integral element of a . . . regime in which torture mediates both the constitution of hegemonic identities and their location within national and transnational power regimes." See Teresa Macias, "'Tortured Bodies': The Biopolitics of Torture and Truth in Chile," *International Journal of Human Rights* 17, no. 1 (2013): 116.

9. Dorothy Roberts describes torture as "a particularly effective technology for enforcing the racial order: race is a system of governance that classifies human beings into a political hierarchy based on invented biological demarcations." See "Torture and the Biopolitics of Race," *University of Miami Law Review* 62, no. 2 (2008): 229. On race and biopower, see Ladelle McWhorter, "Sex, Race, and Biopower: A Foucauldian Genealogy," *Hypatia* 19, no. 3 (2004): e.g., 48, and David Macey, "Rethinking Biopolitics, Race, and Power in the Wake of Foucault," *Theory, Culture, and Society* 26, no. 6 (2009): 186–205.

10. Macias, "'Tortured Bodies,'" 116.

11. See Timothy A. Turner, "Othello on the Rack," *Journal for Early Modern Cultural Studies* 15, no. 3 (2015): 102–36; Elizabeth Hanson, *Discovering the Subject in Renaissance England* (Cambridge: Cambridge University Press, 1998); James Heath, *Torture and English Law: An Administrative and Legal History from the Plantagenets to the Stuarts* (Westport, Conn.: Greenwood Press, 1982); and John H. Langbein, *Torture and the Law of Proof: Europe and England in the Ancién Regime* (Chicago: University of Chicago Press, 1977).

12. Heath, *Torture and English Law*, 212; Robert N. Kingdon, ed., *The Execution of Justice in England*, by William Cecil, and *A*

True, Sincere, and Modest Defense of English Catholics, by William Allen (Ithaca: Cornell University Press, 1965), 76; Thomas Norton, *A Declaration of the Favourable Dealing of Her Maiesties Commissioners Appointed for the Examination of Certaine Traitours, and of Tortures Unjustly Reported to be Done on them for Matters of Religion* (London: C. Barker, 1583), sig. A.a.iiir.

13. Sleep deprivation was often used in Scotland to interrogate suspected witches as well as Jesuit priests. See Brian P. Levack, *The Witch-Hunt in Early Modern Europe* (Abingdon, U.K.: Routledge, 2006), 86; Gail Kern Paster, *The Body Embarrassed: Drama and the Disciplines of Shame in Early Modern England* (Ithaca: Cornell University Press, 1993), 254; Robert M. Schuler, "Bewitching *The Shrew*," *Texas Studies in Language and Literature* 46, no. 4 (2004): 387–431; and Darius Rejali, *Torture and Democracy* (Princeton: Princeton University Press, 2009), 290–91.

14. *A True Relation, of the Proceedings Against John Ogilvie, a Jesuit* (Edinburgh: Printed by Andro Hart, 1615), 12–13.

15. *The Historie and Life of King James the Sext* (Edinburgh: James Ballantyne, 1825), 387. These passages are briefly discussed and quoted by George Ryley Scott, *The History of Torture Throughout the Ages* (London: Luxor Press, 1959), 90.

16. See, e.g., Hernán Reyes, "The Worst Scars Are in the Mind: Psychological Torture," *International Review of the Red Cross* 89, no. 867 (2007): 591–617.

17. Gail Kern Paster, *Humoring the Body: Emotions and the Shakespearean Stage* (Chicago: University of Chicago Press, 2004), 63.

18. Ibid., 63, 64, 75.

19. See, for example, McWhorter's brief sketch of the history of the concept of race ("Sex, Race, and Biopower," 47–54), as well as her comments on the emergence of the field of biology—a term not coined, as she notes, until 1802 ("Sex, Race, and Biopower," 50, and see her note 20).

20. Langbein, *Torture and the Law of Proof*, 71.

21. See *The Norton Shakespeare*, 2nd ed., ed. Stephen Greenblatt et al. (New York: W. W. Norton, 2008), 139.

22. See Lynda E. Boose, "Scolding Brides and Bridling Scolds: Taming the Woman's Unruly Member," *Shakespeare Quarterly* 42, no. 2 (1991): 179–213, and Emily Detmer, "Civilizing Subordination: Domestic Violence and *The Taming of the Shrew*," *Shakespeare Quarterly* 48, no. 3 (1997): 273–94.

23. Macias, "'Tortured Bodies,'" 116.

24. *The Taming of the Shrew*, 4.1.188–98. All quotations of Shakespeare in this chapter are from *The Riverside Shakespeare*, ed. G. Blakemore Evans (Boston: Houghton Mifflin, 1997). Subsequent references will be made parenthetically. The spelling of names from the play in this chapter derive from this edition.

25. See the chapter "Howe you shall manne a Falcon" in George Tuberville's *The Book of Falconrie or Hauking, for the Onely Delight and Pleasure of all Noblemen & Gentlemen: Collected out of the Best Aucthors as well Italians as Frenchmen, and some English practices Withall Concerning Faulconrie* (London: Christopher Barker, 1575), 101.

26. Reyes, "Worst Scars," 609.

27. *Historie and Life of King James*, 387.

28. *True Relation*, 12–13.

29. Aristotle, *Rhetoric*, trans. John Henry Freese, Loeb Classical Library 193 (Cambridge, Mass.: Harvard University Press, 1939), 1.15.8 [1376b–1377a].

30. Elaine Scarry, *The Body in Pain: The Making and Unmaking of the World* (New York: Oxford University Press, 1985), 36.

31. See, for example, Boose, "Scolding Brides"; Detmer, "Civilizing Subordination"; Dustin Gish, "Taming the Shrew: Shakespeare, Machiavelli, and Political Philosophy," in *Shakespeare and the Body Politic*, ed. Bernard J. Dobski and Dustin Gish (Lanham, Md.: Lexington Books, 2013), 197–220.

32. Foucault, *History of Sexuality*, 1:143.

33. Julia Reinhard Lupton, "Animal Husbands in *The Taming of the Shrew*," in *Thinking with Shakespeare: Essays on Politics and Life* (Chicago: University of Chicago Press, 2011), 49. Lupton ultimately reads the play in terms of "both the negative and the positive faces of biopower" to highlight "an affirmative biopolitics [that] might

find some fodder in early modern husbandry's mobile network of persons, animals, and things" (50, 53). Meanwhile, Nichole E. Miller connects the play more firmly to the destructive exercise of biopower of the sort that I describe here. See Miller, "The Sexual Politics of Pain: Hannah Arendt Meets Shakespeare's Shrew," *Journal for Cultural and Religious Theory* 7, no. 2 (2006): 30.

34. Like Boose ("Scolding Brides"), Detmer ("Civilizing Subordination"), and Schuler ("Bewitching *The Shrew*"), I connect the play to these destructive practices even as they are adapted in a comedy.

35. Foucault, *History of Sexuality*, 1:135. Agamben, one of this passage's most important recent commentators, also discusses the history of the *patria potestas* and sees in it "a kind of genealogical myth of sovereign power: the magistrate's *imperium* is nothing but the father's *vitae necisque potestas* extended to all citizens" (*Homo Sacer*, 55–56). For a representative sample of divergent views of the *patria potestas* among classicists, see Antti Arjava, "Paternal Power in Late Antiquity," *Journal of Roman Studies* 88 (1998): 147–65; Raymond Westbrook, "*Vitae necisque potestas*," *Historia: Zeitschrift für Alte Geschichte* 48, no. 2 (1999): 203–23; Brent Shaw, "Raising and Killing Children: Two Roman Myths," *Mnemosyne* 54, no. 1 (2001): 31–77.

36. Sir Thomas Elyot, *The Castell of Health* (London, 1595), 25.

37. Cogan, *Haven of Health* (1636), 67.

38. See T. G. A. Nelson and Charles Haines, "Othello's Unconsummated Marriage," *Essays in Criticism: A Quarterly Journal of Literary Criticism* 33, no. 1 (1983): 1–18, as well as David Schalkwyk, "Othello's Consummation," in *Othello: The State of Play*, ed. Lena Cowen Orlin (London: Bloomsbury, 2014), 203–33.

39. A short study of disordered sleep in *Othello* mentions Desdemona's plan but does not address or suggest the concerted effort made by Iago and described here; see Joel E. Dimsdale, "Sleep in *Othello*," *Journal of Clinical Sleep Medicine* 5, no. 3 (2009): 280–81. See also LaRue Love Sloan, "'I'll watch him tame, and talk him out of patience': The Curtain Lecture and

Shakespeare's *Othello*," in *Oral Traditions and Gender in Early Modern Literary Texts*, ed. Mary Ellen Lamb and Karen Bemford (Aldershot, U.K.: Ashgate, 2008), 85–99, on Desdemona's "watching" and oral traditions surrounding the wakefulness caused by a wife's "curtain lecture" to her husband.

40. See Paul Cefalu, "The Burdens of Mind Reading in Shakespeare's *Othello*: A Cognitive and Psychoanalytic Approach," *Shakespeare Quarterly* 64, no. 3 (2013): 265–94; Mary Floyd-Wilson, *English Ethnicity and Race in Early Modern Drama* (Cambridge: Cambridge University Press, 2003); Daniel Juan Gil, *Shakespeare's Anti-Politics: Sovereign Power and the Life of the Flesh* (Basingstoke, U.K.: Palgrave Macmillan, 2013); and Turner, "Othello on the Rack."

41. Elyot, *Castell of Health* (1595), 70.

42. *Historie and Life of King James*, 387. Elyot (ibid., 48r) actually connects the falling sickness not with too little sleep but with too much: "Immoderate sleepe maketh the Bodye apt unto palsies, apoplexies, falling sicknesse," while "immoderate watch . . . maketh the Body apte to consumption." On links between sleep, epilepsy, and melancholy, see Roberto Lo Presti, "'For sleep, in some way, is an epileptic seizure' (*somn. vig.* 3, 457a9–10)," in *The Frontiers of Ancient Science: Essays in Honor of Heinrich von Staden*, ed. Brooke Holmes and Klaus-Dietrich Fischer (Berlin: Walter de Gruyter, 2015), 339–96; Floyd-Wilson, *English Ethnicity and Race*, 154; and Patricia Parker, "Black *Hamlet*: Battening on the Moor," *Shakespeare Studies* 31 (2003): 127–64. Daniel Vitkus, "Turning Turk in *Othello*: The Conversion and Damnation of the Moor," *Shakespeare Quarterly* 48, no. 2 (1997): 145–76, also discusses epilepsy in terms of its association with Islam and the Prophet Mohammed (155).

43. Stanley Cavell, "Epistemology and Tragedy: A Reading of *Othello*," *Daedalus* 103, no. 3 (1979): 34, 38, 39, 43, 42.

44. There is, of course, also irony here in that Othello becomes more watchful, or observant, in light of his aroused suspicions regarding Desdemona's (imagined) infidelity, or that the "pain" in question may refer to a cuckold's horns.

45. Elyot, *Castell of Health* (1595), 48r, 76r.

46. Ibid., 48r.

47. Robert Burton, *The Anatomy of Melancholy* (Oxford, 1621), H4a. See the original passage in Levinus Lemnius, *The Touchstone of Complexions, Generallye Appliable, Expedient and Profitable for all Such, as be Desirous & Carefull of Their Bodylye health: Contayning Most Easie Rules & Ready Tokens, Whereby Every One May Perfectly Try, And Throughly Know, as Well the Exacte State, Habite, Disposition, and Constitution, of his owne Body Outwardly: As also the Inclinations, Affections, Motions, & Desires of his Mynd Inwardly*, trans. Thomas Newton (London: Thomas Marsh, 1576), 59r. For more on how Burton's text represents sleep, see Cassie Miura's essay in this volume.

48. Cogan, *Haven of Health* (1596), 232. In accordance with the theory that seizures also are caused by rising vapors that affected the brain, then evaporation—resulting from the drying out caused by sleep deprivation—could be thought to cause Othello's epileptic fit.

49. Elyot, *Castell of Health* (1595), 3v, 3r.

50. Timothy Bright, *A Treatise of Melancholie* (London: Thomas Vautrollier, 1586), A2r–v. On Shakespeare's use of Bright, see F. David Hoeniger, *Medicine and Shakespeare in the English Renaissance* (Newark: University of Delaware Press, 1992), 50: "From Bright's book, Shakespeare could have learned much not only about different types of melancholy but also about other humors, both in their natural and their 'burnt' or 'adust' states." Hoeniger cites several discussions by previous editors of *Hamlet* to conclude that Shakespeare probably knew Bright's text; see Hoeniger's notes 36 and 38.

51. See Lily B. Campbell, *Shakespeare's Tragic Heroes: Slaves of Passion* (Cambridge: Cambridge University Press, 1930), 75.

52. Parker, "Black *Hamlet*," 139.

53. John Florio, *A worlde of wordes, or Most copious, and exact dictionarie in Italian and English, collected by John Florio* (London: Arnold Hatfield for Edward Blount, 1598), 8.

54. Elyot, *Castell of Health* (1595), 9v.

55. Floyd-Wilson, *English Ethnicity and Race*, 147. See also John E. Curran Jr., "'Duke Byron Flows with Adust and Melancholy Choler': General and Special Character in Chapman's 'Byron' Plays," *Studies in Philology* 108, no. 3 (2011): 364.

56. Floyd-Wilson, *English Ethnicity and Race*, 151, emphasis in the original.

57. Paster, *Humoring the Body*, 64.

58. See Floyd-Wilson, *English Ethnicity and Race*, 151.

59. Ibid., 146; as Floyd-Wilson is at pains to show, neither the older nor the newer readings "seriously [dispute] associations between savagery, blackness, and jealousy," and thus the history of readings of *Othello* has been informed by the supposed truth that Africans were hot tempered because they came from a hot climate. The persistence of this belief is itself an aftereffect of the play, which in fact appears at the moment in history when such stereotypes are coming into being—"a crossroads in the history of etiological ideas"—when older geohumoral views of melancholy Moors as sagacious and spiritual were giving way to newer ideas about their supposedly innate proclivity for lust, jealousy, and rage (ibid., 140).

60. Another passage in the play, 3.3.76–78, spoken after Othello grudgingly assents to the request that he meet with Cassio, seems to suggest that Desdemona assumes the natural coolness of Othello's temperament: "Why, this is not a boon; / 'Tis as I should entreat you *wear your gloves*, / Or feed on nourishing dishes, *or keep you warm*" (emphasis added).

61. Turner, "Othello on the Rack," 127 and n44.

62. Macias, "'Tortured Bodies,'" 116.

63. Roberts, "Torture and the Biopolitics of Race," 229.

64. Bright, *Treatise of Melancholie*, 33–34. Writing in 1930, Campbell concludes, "No modern psychologist has more strenuously insisted upon the fundamental relationship between body and mind or body and soul than did these writers of the sixteenth and seventeenth centuries in England" (*Shakespeare's Tragic Heroes*, 79).

65. On this point see, for example, McWhorter, "Sex, Race, and Biopower," 49.

CHAPTER 5

Sleep, Vulnerability, and Self-Knowledge in *A Midsummer Night's Dream*

JENNIFER LEWIN

> This one fact of sleep—defenceless, recurrent, and prolonged—shows
> the inadequacy of all the theories of adaptation to environment which
> are put forward as explanations of so much that is inexplicable.
> —ELIAS CANETTI, *Crowds and Power*

Sleep is a pervasive phenomenon throughout Shakespearean drama. Plots in all dramatic genres involve characters who seek sleep, fall asleep, and awaken from sleep, describing its benefits and lamenting its perils. Most of these occurrences share the element of vulnerability: sleepers are vulnerable both to their surroundings and to others' interpretations. Genre determines the consequences of this vulnerability, however. Central to sleep's presence in the dramatic genres of history and tragedy is a sense that its famed resemblance to death ("Sleep is the brother of death," according to Greek mythology) exposes the fragility of sleepers' lives to the point of predicting a character's imminent demise. This is similar for disrupted sleep. Examples include Clarence in *Richard III*, the eponymous hero in *2 Henry IV*, and references linking sleep to the kingdom's larger sense of turmoil

SLEEP, ETHICS, AND EMBODIED FORM

throughout *Richard II*. In the tragedies, vulnerability to the threat of death and to fatal misunderstanding are consistently paired with being asleep or preparing for sleep. Consider the murder of Hamlet Sr. during sleep, the circumstances of Desdemona's murder at bedtime near the end of *Othello*, the merely temporary restorative sleep of King Lear as he nears death, sleep's role throughout *Macbeth*, and Romeo's mistaking of Juliet's sleep for death. Tragic sleepers' lives are liminal; these characters either soon die or generate the demise of others.

In the comedies, sleep also consistently signals bodily and mental vulnerability and subjection to others' control, but these effects tend to be temporary, and sleep's restorative properties are ultimately affirmed. The epigraph from Elias Canetti above is suggestive for the workings of sleep here. Despite the dangerous position it places us in, its persistently rejuvenating qualities leave us marveling at our own survival and crafting a narrative of inevitability.[1] Comedy is the ideal genre for this effect. In *Twelfth Night*, to consider a brief illustration of its workings, Malvolio seeks to control Cesario's initial access to Olivia by falsely claiming to her visitor that Olivia is asleep. The failure of his strategy is linked to the inalterable march toward marriage for the lovers and his ultimate rejection and exclusion from this process. In *The Taming of the Shrew*, expressions of the desire to control sleep (by the Lord, Petruchio, Katherine, and Bianca) try to manipulate the sharp distinction between waking experience and sleeping vulnerability, for goal-driven ends. In these and other examples, sleep in a comedy can be an engine of transformation, by first raising tensions and then driving ineluctably toward marital outcomes.[2]

A major exception to these connections between sleep and genre, and to the stark contrast I have been describing between history/tragedy and comedy, is the subject of this essay: the permanent (but invisible) effects of vulnerability to others during sleep in *A Midsummer Night's Dream*. In this comedy, sleep is bizarrely and pervasively involved in asserting the triumph of Oberon's magic, unbeknownst to those he has affected. Largely due to Oberon's machinations, the sleepers awaken with new feelings and attitudes that last and define their choices and identities—but without awareness of the events that created these permanent changes. (Such a lack of knowledge distinguishes the characters in this particular comedy from, say, Christopher Sly or Katherine Minola, who either know who is acting upon them and why, or are returned later to their original state.) The fact that Oberon chooses to manipulate both Titania and Bottom and the four young lovers specifically during moments of their sleep, entirely without their knowledge, should expand our understanding of the myriad ways in which "night is the kingdom of the fairies."[3] The flower juice not only both "allow[s] a third party to influence lovers' eyes and hearts" and defines the "nature of encounters in the woods" but also does so at a juncture in the lovers' bodily and mental experience in which they already are positioned to be particularly vulnerable to influences they are unaware of.[4] Canetti, in a discussion of "lying down and how it relates to power as compared with the other postures of the human body," remarks that this posture "express[es] complete impotence, especially, of course, when it is combined with sleep. . . . A man who lies down gives up all relationship with his fellows and withdraws into himself."[5] Oberon, however, seems fixated on constructing multiple situations in which he successfully challenges the possibility of withdrawal from one's environment and others in it. At the same time, he co-opts others' attempts to withdraw for his own lasting purposes.

The play thereby offers a counternarrative to early modern lyric poetry's idealizations of sleep, emphasizing the way that a narrative genre instrumentalizes slumber for purposes of plot, characterization, and emotional development. Depictions of sleep in early modern lyric instead show its value to emotional life as being first and foremost contained within its closing off of the senses' access to external stimuli—hence, its welcome control over one's environment.[6] In a formulation familiar from treatises on the subject of sleep, the first four lines of Richard Brathwait's "Of Sleepe" turn bodily entrapment into a liberation of the soul: "Sleepe is the Prison that restraines the sense / From due performance of her offices, / Yet th'glorious Soule is of that excellence / It mounts aloft, and scornes such Bonds as these."[7] In sonnet sequences, sleep is able to isolate one from the feelings of vulnerability, alienation, and rejection permeating waking life, and it can provide relief from these and other torturous effects of courtship, desire, and love. The lyric speaker in Samuel Daniel's *Delia* (1592) invokes Somnus's aid in avoiding both the contemplation of daytime problems and the disturbances of Morpheus's productions: "Relieve my languish, and restore the light / With darke forgetting of my cares, returne."[8] Similarly, in Sidney's *Astrophil and Stella* 39 and Shakespeare's sonnet 43, sleep prevents vulnerability to daytime struggles. In post-Petrarchan love, sleep is a powerful means of preserving stability and preventing vulnerability in one's inner life, by isolating one from conflicts with the daytime world (which is beyond one's control) through the soothing forgetfulness of an interior space.

Historical evidence also attests to early modern cultural expectations of sleep's role as providing the conditions for protecting and fostering inner life. According to Sasha Handley, "Sound and restorative sleep had always been prized as an essential support to life but it became more highly valued than ever before for safeguarding the faculties of human reason."[9] These faculties were tied to a new understanding of the self, as sleep began to be considered "an area of life which we call 'private life' and which we separate from the rest of our activities that we think of as our public or social life."[10] But the violability of embodied sleep in drama challenges both the lyric idea of a self-contained, retreating subject and the historical idea of a self with a private life. In Shakespeare's *A Midsummer Night's Dream*, inner, private life cannot be protected during sleep—and, moreover, those who experience exposure while slumbering do not even know they have experienced it. More broadly, then, this essay shows the contribution of sleep in this Shakespearean comedy to, as Richard Meek and Erin Sullivan have put it, "the diversity and even mystery of early modern emotional experience, particularly as it related to the understanding of the self."[11] In the play, emotional experience is shaped mysteriously by what happens during sleep, through transformations that one does not realize one is undergoing. Yet self-understanding proceeds and shifts accordingly.

For the following study of sleep in *A Midsummer Night's Dream*, a third consequence follows: sleep allows us to reconsider how moral agency and consciousness work in literature. Until now, examining the mental lives of literary characters has by and large assumed the characters' wakefulness. A new rubric is needed for understanding how what happens to characters during sleep constitutes a special category worth attending to. Michael Bristol, for example, has argued that "Shakespeare's characters inhabit a contingent world where they are faced with novel, unpredictable, and unprecedented situations that require evaluation and judgment" and that "the plays make us care about such decision-making in a way that engages our own concern."[12] Given the circumstances of sleep in *A Midsummer Night's Dream*, how do we understand the processes of "evaluation and judgment"? How does sleep alter what we mean by "decision-making"?

As I have been stating, and as the analysis of the play that begins in the next section of this essay will demonstrate, manipulation and vulnerability are crucial to the role of sleep in the play. This feature causes sleep to differ sharply from dreaming, which is a process where some form of individual thought—or, perhaps, even choice making—might be possible. Insofar as nocturnal experience in the play has been addressed, it has pertained to dreaming rather than sleeping, with topics including the meaning of the play's title, Bottom's report of his vision, and Hermia's description of a nightmare.[13] In his introduction to the Oxford edition, Peter Holland distinguishes between vision and dream: "If we have responded to the play fully, we will share with Bottom the sense of vision, of something revealed from out there, from the world of fairy, not the false or trivial world of dream but a revelation of another reality." Although Holland later claims that the play "also makes of sleep the mark of a series of crucial transitions," and Harold F. Brooks writes that sleep is "one of the main means by which the play is unified," neither editor analyzes sleep itself in any detail.[14] Oberon and Puck's application of the flower juice stresses a major difference between dreaming and sleeping, however: the fairies intentionally use sleep in order to manipulate their oblivious targets' beliefs, emotions, and actions. Sleepers are unaware upon waking that they have been manipulated, while the play's dreamers know that they have dreamed and describe their memories of those dreams. Furthermore, dreamers such as Bottom and Hermia famously analyze their experiences as having had a profound impact. By contrast, sleepers are never told that these events transpired, so they are unable to register them as such, let alone evaluate them. They are ignorant of their vulnerability, what happened during their sleep, and hence how nocturnal activity has shaped their present selves. This condition of exclusion from knowledge makes sleep differ radically from the play's experience of dreams. Sleepers are permanently transformed, but the final word about the success of this process is not their own.

KNOWLEDGE AND CONTROL

Oberon's obsession with his victims' sleep is part of a larger pattern of his desire for control and power—not only over others' emotions and commitments but also over the comedic narrative itself. By his own account, Oberon's plan originates from a desire to seize the changeling boy from Titania's possession. But this plan of action recasts storytelling in general in the play, making it a weapon for dividing and conquering more broadly. As

114 | SLEEP, ETHICS, AND EMBODIED FORM

Louis Montrose famously has argued, Oberon "attempt[s] to take the boy from an infantilizing mother and to make a man of him" with the love plot, highlighting especially the play's penchant for "enact[ing] a male disruption of an intimate bond between women." Sleep enables the advancement of Oberon's "claims for a spiritual kinship among men that is unmediated by women," in ways only he and Puck and we are aware of.[15] This ideologically driven narrative structure prevents sleep from providing a space to sustain one's personal vision of respite, as it does in the lyric tradition. Instead, sleep yokes individual characters to outcomes determined by Oberon's misogynistic designs. Manipulation is gendered, and genders all the characters he commands as female.

Oberon's explanation of how the sleep-inducing flower came to have its magical properties, ironically, is instead quite reverential toward female power. It is framed in terms of Cupid's being vanquished by the "fair vestal" or "imperial votaress" whose mark he misses (2.1.164, 169). Oberon thereby indicates the female ruler's immunity to the love god's influence—but one should remember that his magic rewrites Cupid's powerlessness into his own fearless co-optation of the product of this event. As Stephen Orgel puts it, "If magic liberates lovers from the tyranny of paternal authority, it is also the instrument of a much larger patriarchal order, not at all liberating but ultimately controlling."[16] The vestal virgin may have eluded Cupid's arrow, but Oberon is able to harvest and use the resource resulting from the missed encounter.

Furthermore, his interest in sleep permits Oberon to divide and conquer others, in ways that go beyond what he initially tells Puck. First, he emphasizes to Puck that they are engaging in powerfully secretive communication sealed off from others—except, of course, the audience, whose awareness and complicity develop in ways that isolate us from the unaware lovers in these scenes. Puck is the only fairy with knowledge of Oberon's plans and background, and Oberon consolidates his allegiance by playing on the distinction between ignorance and knowledge. This move shows his control over Puck, just as he will control the lovers. Next, Oberon asks if Puck remembers an earlier part of the event of discovering the herb—the moment that a mermaid seemed to tame the "rude sea" (2.1.152). When Puck says he does, Oberon goes on to divide the experience into smaller parts by further specifying that "that very time I saw, but thou couldst not" what Cupid did afterward (2.1.155). Oberon's constant awareness of who knows (and saw) what (and when) is the prerequisite for his isolation of those on whom he uses the herb.

After describing how the shaft's contact with the flower occurred, Oberon describes to Puck how they will use the juice that the flower produces:

> Fetch me that flower; the herb I shew'd thee once:
> The juice of it on sleeping eye-lids laid
> Will make or man or woman madly dote
> Upon the next live creature that it sees.
> Fetch me this herb; and be thou here again
> Ere the leviathan can swim a league. (2.1.169–74)

Oberon emphasizes the exclusivity of his relationship with Puck when he starts giving his command, reminding Puck to seek "the herb I shew'd thee once." He is also insistent on control over Puck, as indicated by the repetition of the command "Fetch me" at the starts of two lines. Significantly, Oberon at this juncture does not specifically let Puck know on whom he intends to use the herb or why.

Still, Oberon does immediately share this information—with the audience. And he shares it in a way that differs from what he tells Puck, making us appreciate the differences he generates between the groups who are learning and being affected by his plans. Although he himself knows that this herb will "unite the couples" and "harmonize sexuality,"[17] his obsession with privately shaping others' emotions and beliefs via sleep makes it hardly surprising that the instructions to Puck discussed above are only one version of his stated intentions. Just after Puck dashes off to "fetch" the love-in-idleness, Oberon tells the audience:

> Having once this juice,
> I'll watch Titania when she is asleep,
> And drop the liquor of it in her eyes.
> The next thing then she waking looks upon,
> Be it on lion, bear, or wolf, or bull,
> On meddling monkey, or on busy ape,
> She shall pursue it with the soul of love:
> And ere I take this charm from off her sight,
> As I can take it with another herb,

116 | SLEEP, ETHICS, AND EMBODIED FORM

I'll make her render up her page to me.
But who comes here? I am invisible;
And I will overhear their conference. (2.1.176–87)

This time, Oberon highlights more specifically that he will himself administer the liquor drops, and also adds the presence of "another herb" that will "take this charm from off her sight." The woman he will affect is now identified as Titania, who will fall in love with "the next thing" she sees. He even elaborates on the earlier "creature" designation with the naming of six animals, providing tangible and visualizable details. Finally, he discloses his second intention—excluded from the directive to Puck—that he'll "make her render up her page to me." All of these refinements of his previous description of his intentions are accessible to the audience alone, narrated in a future tense that both outlines and instantiates the comic trajectory. Excluding Puck from these narrative specifics and unfolding them only to the audience compartmentalizes Oberon's instructions and reveals information selectively. Thereby, the audience becomes complicit in his willingness and ability to alter others, in ways they will not be aware of as coming from him.

Lest we forget, however, the main purpose of enchanting Titania is to kidnap the changeling boy. And her rhetoric about this boy likewise highlights the issue of control—but, this time, tied to moral responsibility. Titania has been protecting the boy for personal reasons: she has assumed responsibility for him after his mother's death. Titania's emphatic rhetoric implies that she believes it would be an injustice to do any less: "But she, being mortal, of that boy did die; / And for her sake do I rear up her boy; / And for her sake I will not part with him" (2.1.135–37). Her testimony of resistance to Oberon's demand for the boy is also an aspect of their relationship that has not been addressed sufficiently in scholarship on *A Midsummer Night's Dream*. Its strength comes as something of a shock each time one reads it—making Oberon's plan to seize control of her and the boy while she sleeps all the more startling and all the more logical. (While she is awake and in control of herself and the boy, Oberon would have no chance.) Her territory in the world of the fairies is where she protectively watches over the boy, preventing Oberon from having power to remove him. Yet she is completely unaware that, as she articulates her watchfulness, he could very well be planning his control over her slumber, in order to figure out how best to violate it. And yet this moment marks a similarity between them. Like Oberon whose "I" over and over again tells Puck that he alone controls and alters the release of information, Titania uses her personal memories of her past relationship as a reason for refusing Oberon: she, too, constructs a future narrative trajectory that is rooted in a prior event. Oberon's ability to take this narrative power away from her, to trump her commitment to her votaress as well as her ability to shape the course of narrative events, is both misogynistic and indicative of what sleep is able to provide a cover for. As Northrop Frye puts it, "It seems clear that Titania does not have the authority that she thinks she has."[18]

Part of Oberon's capacity to inflict his own narrative structure on the play involves his intimate knowledge of Titania's environs:

> I know a bank where the wild thyme blows,
> Where oxlips and the nodding violet grows,
> Quite over-canopied with luscious woodbine,
> With sweet musk-roses and with eglantine:
> There sleeps Titania sometime of the night,
> Lull'd in these flowers with dances and delight;
> And there the snake throws her enamell'd skin,
> Weed wide enough to wrap a fairy in:
> And with the juice of this I'll streak her eyes,
> And make her full of hateful fantasies. (2.2.248–58)

This speech echoes Oberon's earlier series of vivid, elaborate, and nostalgic descriptions of how he came to know about the herb. In both, he emphasizes private knowledge of places. As Edward Casey claims in *The Fate of Place*, it is common to have "an active desire for the particularity of place— for what is truly 'local' or 'regional.'"[19] Experiencing this desire for a local place that he is privileged to have known (but is currently unwelcome in), Oberon lavishly details what he previously found and experienced in the bower. By asserting "I know a bank" and continuing with luxuriant floral imagery of Titania's bower and her sleeping practices, Oberon emphasizes his intimacy with the fairy queen, positioning his privileged knowledge as a means to impose his dramatic narrative on others.

From this foundation, he finally discloses to Puck what he plans to do to Titania while she sleeps—exposing intentions that vary from what he told the audience earlier. Instead of repeating the comic list of animals she could fall in love with, he says he will "make her full of hateful fantasies." This effect also differs from the effect that the Athenian men (first Lysander, then Demetrius) will experience. Although they were drugged with the same herb as Titania, the men's outcomes have shifted, from (1) falling in love with the first person they see upon waking, to (2) being "more fond on her than she upon her love." Titania's emotions and affection will be centered on Bottom as an ass soon enough, but her experience of the drug will not have a comparative dimension as it will for the human men. Additionally, it has an element of "hateful" affect that speaks to Oberon's desire for vengeance. By creating disparate outcomes for the same drug, Oberon displays an unusual power to fine-tune his methodologies for managing others' emotions without their knowledge. In the remainder of the essay, we will explore two arenas in which he uses this particularized power. First, sleep creates a condition for manipulation that emphasizes his own whims—and, in the case of Titania, an ability to entertain himself and the audience with the sight of her lovemaking. Second, sleep allows Oberon to compensate for Demetrius's withholding nature by having him not only reciprocate but even go beyond Helena's passion. In these ways, Oberon not only manipulates others in their sleep with permanent consequences but also reforges comedic narratives without the participants' full knowledge or consent.

MANIPULATION AND ITS EFFECTS

Titania starts Act 2, Scene 2 by asking her fairies for "a roundel and a fairy song" and for someone to "sing me now asleep; / Then to your offices and let me rest" (2.2.1, 7–8). She is unaware that she is about to be made to forget herself—and her state of mourning and moral conviction about the changeling boy, a state that she directly formed in association with her relationship to her votaress. Sleep is Oberon's last resort, the only means by which Titania falls to him. Otherwise, in waking moments she fights with him forcefully and he loses the argument. In her bower, as Casey theorizes, her particular place is defined; confined to this sacred space, she appears to be completely unaware of his menacing threat. The irony of her being lulled to sleep by fairies who specifically dispel charms must not be lost on the audience, who knows what Oberon intends. Asleep, Titania loses any semblance of control or power. The fairy magic seems to cooperate with Oberon's own plan to get her into a state of sleep; the fairies do not realize they assist him more than her at this moment.

When she awakens in Act 3 to find Bottom, who has been transformed into an ass, as her new beloved, her address to Bottom makes it clear that she thinks she still is in control, even mentioning sleep as one of the benefits of having the attendants she will provide, who will "sing while thou on pressed flowers dost sleep" (3.1.150). The irony of Titania's linkage of sleeping and control over others is noticeable. Her specific focus on using magic to shape a sleep environment makes her bragging seem at once consistent with Oberon's own habits, unbeknownst to her, and at the same time drastically misplaced. She believes it enables her to show off an ability to enjoy pleasurable manipulation of others' labor. But neither she nor those workers know the limitations that have been placed on this ability and how, for Oberon, sleep is now a facilitator in generating those limitations. Oberon's stronghold over sleep seems to grow even greater in relation to this mistaken assessment of her own powers.

Following this scene with Titania, characters appear whose "conference" Oberon has stated he wants to "overhear." Fleeing from the city of Athens into the forest, the humans Helena and Demetrius are sparring over the dangers of the night, in language highly reminiscent of the lyric Petrarchanism described earlier. A parallel conversation will occur soon after between two other fleeing Athenians, Lysander and Hermia. Before they are separated, Lysander agrees to sleep at a distance from Hermia, who insists on their bodies not being close to one another. In the other pairing, Demetrius is the insistent one, warning Helena of impropriety and the risks to women of being outdoors in the dark. Helena, instead, treats darkness as a means to the familiar end of positioning the lovers to appreciate each other in a more concentrated way, as it does in sonnets such as Shakespeare's sonnet 43. But this time the sentiment is given to a female rather than a male lover and speaker:

> Your virtue is my privilege: for that
> It is not night when I do see your face,
> Therefore I think I am not in the night;
> Nor doth this wood lack worlds of company,
> For you in my respect are all the world:
> Then how can it be said I am alone,
> When all the world is here to look on me? (2.1.220–26)

As in the love lyrics of John Donne, here the "world" is him. She need fear no threats to their relationship from within or without, because they categorically do not exist. Still, the unrequited nature of Helena's love for Demetrius exacerbates the tension between her vision of harmony—between sleep and love—and his, between sleep and existential and sexual danger. Oberon watches this and seems to decide before our eyes that his love juice would do well to aid these soon-to-be sleepers too. In shaping the narrative of these human characters, once again, Oberon is imposing a patriarchal comic narrative arc on the plot: this time, one that leads directly to marriage, by means of manipulating the unconscious experiences of his unwitting subordinates.

Returning with the flower, Puck has a task designed to resolve the strife Oberon has witnessed: he must find this "very Athenian" man Demetrius and put the juice on his eyes. The next thing the man sees will be Helena, whom then he will love. Oberon specifies that the herb not only will cause the man to love the woman but also that he will love her more than she loves him (2.2.265–66)—again augmenting and altering his original description of the transformation process, without acknowledging the fact of this variation. (It is unclear why this is an important effect for him, but it emphasizes the relative powerfulness of the herb and what can happen under its spell.) Oberon seeks to penetrate into the emotional lives of Demetrius and Helena, not merely by making the resistant party cooperative but also by providing a surfeit, or an imbalance, that manipulates them beyond what he had promised. The lovers would never know that the source of this affection is not their own hearts but the love juice, administered during sleep. His strategy precludes the revelation of its workings.

Oberon means to have Puck anoint Demetrius with the love juice— but, as we know, Puck mistakes Lysander for Demetrius in practice. (This is because he does not know that two Athenian men are gallivanting about in the woods and then sleeping in close proximity to each other). Puck applies the juice in a brief moment at the end of Act 2, immediately after Oberon visits Titania, and just before the start of Act 3, in which our next glimpse of Titania will be her awakening and seeing Bottom. Structurally, this juxtaposition allows the characters (and their circumstances) to act as foils for one another, facilitating comparisons of different moments when sleepers are manipulated. First, Puck's mistake exposes another unusual gap in the play, between what we think a character knows and what he says. When Puck sees Lysander and Hermia lying apart, he praises Hermia for making this decision—for reasons that we, in the audience, know not to be her own: "She durst not lie / Near this lack-love, this kill-courtesy" (2.2.82–83). How does Puck know this? We have not seen Oberon tell him about Helena and Demetrius, nor do we have evidence that he has seen them. Here again, sleep in the play is connected with inconsistencies in what characters know and think about each other, with the tensions between human knowledge and fairy knowledge only exacerbating these discrepancies. And the sleep-linked inconsistencies continue. The juice-anointed Lysander, after seeing Helena and expressing love for her, uses Hermia's sleep to protect himself and Helena from Hermia's potential discovery of the present situation: "She sees not Hermia. Hermia, sleep thou there: / And never mayst thou come Lysander near!" (2.2.142–43). Acting under the drug's influence, Lysander has switched allegiances. Now, his shifts in knowledge and perception have led him to try to manipulate the sleep of others in his own right, in order to advance his own (revised) narrative of how the comedy should pair lovers for marriage.

Lastly, Helena's mode of waking Lysander returns us to the distinctions between sleep in tragedy and history plays on the one hand and comedy on the other, with this play occupying an uneasy space in the middle. Sleep highlights the similarity between the look of the sleeping and the dead—and, thus, how easy it is to mistake one state for the other. Helena asks if Lysander is sleeping or dead, and that is the excuse for waking him up. Linking to the tragic overtones of this moment, in Act 3, Puck is telling Oberon about his success with the love juice and transforming Bottom into an ass when, suddenly, Hermia and Demetrius appear before them. Hermia accuses Demetrius of murdering Lysander while both she and Lysander slept. Moreover, part of Hermia's evidence of Lysander's virtue is his not having "stolen away" while she sleeps, and she later will accuse Demetrius of being even more traitorous because killing someone who is asleep and thus unable to defend himself is dishonorable. With all of these allusions to death, honor, and especially to killing the sleeper, Shakespeare highlights the generically ambidexterous status of sleep in *Midsummer*. It is a means of inflecting a dramatic narrative toward a particular trajectory, but it can also reinflect or refract seemingly tragic or comic events, as a means to develop both generic and affective nuances.

If sleep can bring out cross-generic nuances, though, it can also act to resolve a plot, in a more straightforwardly instrumental way. In a strange and humorous twist of events, Demetrius himself immediately falls asleep, just in time for Oberon to instruct Puck to bring Helena to him to set the couples right. But Oberon then witnesses all four of the lovers sparring in a chaotic way, and he devises a more elaborate solution: to have Puck cause them to fall asleep from emotional exhaustion after fighting extensively. At that point, he will "crush this herb into Lysander's eye; / Whose liquor hath this virtuous property, / To take from thence all error with his might / And make his eyeballs roll with wonted sight" (3.2.366–69). This is an extreme solution, because Puck is asked to manipulate the weather for the first time in the play. (The weather earlier in the opening of Act 2 had been described by Titania and Oberon as reacting to, and not being controlled by, the fairy rulers' quarrel.) Here the male rulers fully are in control of the weather. And one assumes the "herb" is the same love juice, but again its qualities have expanded yet once more: now it removes "error." Able to command both natural elements and the particular efficacies of an herbal remedy, Oberon has gained new tools in his quest for authority over the narrative trajectory—and these tools facilitate a correction to his previous course.

Of course, Oberon has another cognitive solution to the problem of the mortals' memories. After all, if characters such as Demetrius (or even Bottom) remember the present turmoil, they will continue to be affected by it—and their memories would not lead to a tidy plot outcome. Instead, Oberon will turn their experiences into "a dream and fruitless vision" (3.2.371). This language foreshadows and allows Bottom's "rare vision" to rewrite the language of dreams and visions and contrast it with what happens in sleep. (In other words, Bottom is offered the memory of the experience without the knowledge of how it came about.) In this way, sleep's manipulations are not memorable to anyone—except Bottom, in the realm of fantasy. Instead, they are silently absorbed into the identities and self-knowledge of the characters, without the possibility for reflection or reason-driven synthesis.

Finally, to tie all of the strands of the plot together, Oberon's culminating projects are to obtain the changeling boy and to restore Titania's former perceptions—both in the service of his larger patriarchal goals. As Act 4 begins, we first see Titania and Bottom in her bower. At this point, Oberon decides to "undo / This hateful imperfection of her eyes," echoing the language of "hate" that he previously employed. She hardly believes what has transpired and asks Oberon for an explanation: "Tell me how it came this night / That I sleeping here was found / With these mortals on the ground" (4.1.99–101). At this point, sleep—as the instrument of Oberon's control over others—shifts to the more elevated language of wonder and dream: Titania, in wonderment, requests a narrative from her husband that will make sense of puzzling events. Then, the waking lovers and Bottom offer explanations of their experiences that emphasize their feelings of confusion and amazement—in other words, filtering their ideas through the language of wonder, since the language of sleep and external manipulation is not available to them. As they start to make sense of their states as permanent, and as the play's comic ending codifies these states in marriage ceremonies, the characters are unaware of Oberon's ability to shape their feelings and Puck's ability to mislead them. From this moment on, however, they do register an awareness that their emotional lives have transformed—even if the origins of the metamorphoses remain obscured.

Stanley Cavell observes that the play "is built from the idea that the public world of day cannot resolve its conflicts apart from the resolutions in the private forces of night. For us mortals, fools of finitude, this therapy must occur by way of remembering something, awakening to something, and by forgetting something, awakening from something."[20] What he calls "this therapy" happens fairly frequently, starting in the play's second act— but we would be remiss not to remember that it would not occur were it not for Oberon's deliberate plans. It is really Oberon's therapy. In it, Oberon prevents the characters explicitly from knowing that they are awakening to feelings and forgetting other feelings according to his own will, which does not necessarily match theirs. And this dynamic applies not only to "us mortals" within the play. In Act 1, Titania delivers a deliberate, assertive speech, in which she displays a remarkable certainty of purpose and a memory of past experience that knows its scope and details. After Oberon's intervention—which she does not consciously participate in—she is powerless to sustain the influence or the memory of these ideas while under the spell of the love juice, experiencing this "therapy" without realizing it. What is the price of "forgetting" when one character forces it upon several others, both mortal and immortal? The "resolutions" Cavell writes of are Oberon's, their origins less mysterious or obfuscated than Cavell would have them be, though they remain so to the lovers.

As Katharine A. Craik and Tanya Pollard observe, "Late sixteenth- and early seventeenth-century writers not only identified emotional experience firmly with the body, but also privileged the sensations aroused by imaginative literature."[21] Sleep's close association with these phenomena, along with its indispensability as a plot and stage device in comedy, illustrate its relevance to this discussion. In *A Midsummer Night's Dream*, slumber has created the means and the (literal) place for changing the minds of those who are otherwise recalcitrant, especially Titania regarding the boy and Demetrius regarding Helena. They shift their views without hesitation, moral qualms, or realization of the source of these transformations. Titania and the lovers may never find out what happened. Unlike the lovers, though, Titania knows with some degree of confidence that Oberon knows, and so does the audience. Puck's final speech asks us to participate in the duplicity; in ways I hope I have shown, the audience already has, more than even he may realize.

If, according to Sasha Handley, sleep "was a process over which [early modern people] could and did exercise partial control," in this play, Shakespeare leaves that control in the hands not of people but of fairies. In her work, Handley describes a "common concern to sleep in 'safety' and 'security'—two concepts that stimulated efforts to attain physical, psychological and spiritual protection during the hours of sleep."[22] These ideas certainly are expressed by Hermia at one point during her successful effort to avoid the potentially damaging consequences, both public and bodily, of sleeping alongside Lysander. But she in that moment stands as an exception to the rule in *A Midsummer Night's Dream*—a play whose characters, subjected to outside influence while they sleep, will never know how little control they were able to assert over their self-knowledge, affections, friendships, marriages, and comic narratives.

NOTES

1. Elias Canetti, *Crowds and Power*, trans. Carol Stewart (Harmondsworth, U.K.: Penguin, 1973), 391.

2. For an alternative reading of the manipulation of sleep in *The Taming of the Shrew* as a form of early modern torture, see Timothy Turner's essay in this volume.

3. Anne Paolucci, "The Lost Days in *A Midsummer Night's Dream*," *Shakespeare Quarterly* 28, no. 3 (1977): 318.

4. Susan Wiseman, *Writing Metamorphosis in the English Renaissance, 1500–1700*

(Cambridge: Cambridge University Press, 2013), 19, 20.

5. Canetti, *Crowds and Power*, 391.

6. For more on sleep in lyric, see Giulio Pertile's essay in this volume.

7. Richard Brathwait, "Of Sleepe," in *A New Spring Shadowed in Sundry Pithie Poems* (London: G. Eld, 1619), D2r.

8. Samuel Daniel, *Poems and "A Defence of Ryme,"* ed. Arthur Colby Sprague (Cambridge, Mass.: Harvard University Press, 1930), 75.

9. Sasha Handley, *Sleep in Early Modern England* (New Haven: Yale University Press, 2016), 5.

10. Christopher Hamilton, *Living Philosophy: Reflections on Life, Meaning and Morality* (Edinburgh: Edinburgh University Press, 2001), 150.

11. Richard Meek and Erin Sullivan, introduction to *The Renaissance of Emotion: Understanding Affect in Shakespeare and His Contemporaries*, ed. Richard Meek and Erin Sullivan (Manchester: Manchester University Press, 2015), 2.

12. Michael Bristol, ed., *Shakespeare and Moral Agency* (New York: Continuum, 2010), 5. On how Shakespearean characters experience consciousness and self-consciousness, see the introduction to Paul Budra and Clifford Werier, eds., *Shakespeare and Consciousness* (New York: Palgrave Macmillan, 2016), 1–12.

13. See, for example, David Young, *Something of Great Constancy* (New Haven: Yale University Press, 1966), 115–26; Leon Guilhamet, "*A Midsummer-Night's Dream* as the Imitation of an Action," *Studies in English Literature, 1500–1900* 15, no. 2 (1975): 266–71; Florence Falk, "Dream and Ritual Process in *A Midsummer Night's Dream*," *Comparative Drama* 14, no. 3 (1980): 263–79; Eleanor Cook, "'Methought' as Dream Formula in Shakespeare, Milton, Wordsworth, Keats, and Others," *English Language Notes* 32, no. 4 (1995): 34–46; Peter Holland's introduction to his edition of *A Midsummer Night's Dream* (Oxford: Oxford University Press, 1995); and Peter Brown, ed., *Reading Dreams: The Interpretation of Dreams from Chaucer to Shakespeare*

(Oxford: Oxford University Press, 1999). Subsequent citations of *Midsummer* will be made parenthetically from the Holland edition.

14. Holland, introduction, 21 and 108; Harold Brooks, introduction to *A Midsummer Night's Dream*, ed. Harold Brooks (London: Thomson Learning, 2006), xc. See also Brooks, introduction, li.

15. Louis Adrian Montrose, "'Shaping Fantasies': Figurations of Gender and Power in Elizabethan Culture," *Representations* 2 (Spring 1983): 69.

16. Stephen Orgel, *Imagining Shakespeare: A History of Texts and Visions* (New York: Palgrave Macmillan, 2003), 89.

17. David Mikics, "Poetry and Politics in *A Midsummer Night's Dream*," *Raritan* 18, no. 2 (1998), 115.

18. *Northrop Frye on Shakespeare*, ed. Robert Sandler (New Haven: Yale University Press, 1986), 46.

19. Edward Casey, *The Fate of Place: A Philosophical History* (Oakland: University of California Press, 1997), xiii.

20. Stanley Cavell, *Pursuits of Happiness: The Hollywood Comedy of Remarriage* (Cambridge, Mass.: Harvard University Press, 1981), 142.

21. Katharine A. Craik and Tanya Pollard, eds., *Shakespearean Sensations: Experiencing Literature in Early Modern England* (Cambridge: Cambridge University Press, 2013), 3. See also Meek and Sullivan, introduction to *Renaissance of Emotion*, 1–24.

22. Handley, *Sleep in Early Modern England*, 6–7.

CHAPTER 6

"The Heaviness of Sleep"

Monarchical Exhaustion in King Lear

BRIAN CHALK

In a lively interview, Sir Ian McKellen calls the experience of playing King Lear "one of the most tiring jobs you can possibly get." From the moment Lear comes onstage, McKellen avers, "he's going through dreadful physical and mental decline, essentially going mad in front of the audience." The task of playing Lear is, in other words, exhausting. Even to an experienced Shakespearean actor, who has succeeded in nearly every major role the playwright created over the course of his career, sustaining the "constant level of high emotion, anger, and regret, and bewilderment" that the part requires takes its toll. For Lear, unlike Shakespeare's other monarchs, this "anger, and regret, and bewilderment" relate directly to the deterioration associated with the aging process. Reflecting on aspects of the role that will form the focus of this essay, McKellen notes that the one element of relief an actor can count on going into a performance is that, after roughly an hour and a half of strenuously emotional behavior, Lear succumbs to sleep. Collapsing the needs of the king with the needs of the actor who plays him, McKellen concludes that "Shakespeare very kindly gives" Lear—and, by extension, the actor—"a rest."[1]

Shuttling from the world of knighted actors to the sleeping habits of Shakespeare's monarchs, this essay explores how King Lear's relationship with sleep connects and differentiates him from a succession of earlier Shakespearean kings who suffer from insomnia. In 2 *Henry IV*, King Henry famously encapsulates this insomniac condition when, remarking on his troubled sleep, he concludes, "Uneasy lies the head that wears a crown" (3.1.31).[2] For Henry, Garrett Sullivan Jr. has remarked, "Insomnia marks the king *as* king."[3] Although the illness that afflicts Henry also relates to his age, the play implies that his insomnia and eventual death connect fundamentally with the experience of being king.[4] For Henry IV, the inability to sleep is a necessary attribute of the monarch, with the divide between sleeping and waking doubling for the ontological barrier that separates the ruler from his subjects.

Later in his career, Shakespeare begins to expand his stance on what Sullivan refers to as "monarchical wakefulness." For King Hamlet and King Duncan, who are murdered while sleeping, rest leaves the monarch in a state of vulnerability that realizes the anxieties to which Henry IV has already given voice. In an article exploring the role of "sovereign sleep" in *Hamlet* and *Macbeth*, Benjamin Parris considers the dangerous relationship between wakeful kings and sleeping subjects with reference to the theory of the "King's Two Bodies," which insists that the king possesses "a natural body common to all humans, as well as a mystical 'superbody' that perpetuates the life of the state and lends an aura of divine perfection to the sovereign."[5] Given the mutually constitutive but ontologically separate nature of these two dimensions of identity, the suspension of activity of either would seem to throw both into crisis. "What *does* happen to the body politic," Parris therefore wonders, "when the sovereign body natural sleeps?"[6]

Sleep creates an image of human imperfection in the sovereign body natural: bodily life in sleep resembles death, and so the king's mortality resurfaces, even though his body natural's flaws are supposedly taken up and wiped away by the presence of the body politic. The tragic dissolution of sovereignty in both *Hamlet* and *Macbeth* suggests that sovereign sleep and insomnia not only impinge upon the monarch's ability to maintain watchful rule but also radically alter the metaphysical bonds between bodies natural and politic.[7]

In Parris's astute analysis, the murders of King Hamlet and King Duncan realize the consequences of setting aside the wakeful vigilance that Henry IV insists is fundamental to the monarch. As Rebecca Totaro has demonstrated in a study of *Hamlet*, the tradition and importance of maintaining "watchful rule" to protect the sleeping had long-standing relevance in English culture. "Shakespeare's choice to open *Hamlet* with a night watch that is fortified at once against sleep, foolishness, and trickery," Totaro points out, "gave audiences an example of a watch that was vigilant and yet human."[8] With *King Lear*, I suggest, Shakespeare expands the scope of the issues that these studies address. Showing signs of decreased vigilance from the moment he enters the stage, Lear yields willingly what King Hamlet and King Duncan surrender only in death. What happens, the play asks, when the sovereign attempts to surrender the body politic prior to the death of the body natural?

In contrast with Shakespeare's earlier kings, Lear allows the playwright to explore the consequences of closing rather than widening the gap between king and subject, by examining his need for sleep. As early modern health manuals make clear, questions surrounding the value of sleep were of interest well beyond the world of monarchs. In Thomas Cogan's popular *The Haven of Health*, for instance, Cogan agrees that sleep inevitably places the subject in a vulnerable position. "In sleepe," Cogan observes, "the senses be unable to execute their office, as the eye to see, the eare to heare, the nose to smell, the mouth to tast, and all sinewy parts to feele."[9] Sleep, then, disables the senses, detaches sleepers from the waking world, and renders subjects defenseless in a manner that recalls Shakespeare's murdered kings. And yet, Cogan concedes, "the benefit of sleepe, or the necessitie rather needeth no proofe, for that without it no living creature may long endure." The wide-ranging benefits he goes on to list read like a panacea for much of what troubles Lear: "For sleep helpeth the digestion and maketh it perfect, it recovereth strength, it refresheth the bodie, it reviveth the minde, it pacifieth anger, it driveth away sorrowe, and finally, if it be moderate it bringeth the whole man to good state and temperature."[10] In *King Lear*, the king's need for sleep marks the deterioration of the monarch, but it also recognizes the status of his body natural, in need of physical restoration. The anger, sorrow, and sickness that Lear experiences in the play emerge as concerns that, he acknowledges, affect subjects as well as kings. Ultimately, only the healing powers of sleep emphasized by Cogan can briefly restore Lear's body natural, allowing him the clarity to recognize his daughter Cordelia.

This restoration of Lear's body natural, however, does not correspond with a reinvigoration of his body politic—distancing him further from kingship in the mode of Henry IV. Even after he awakens, Lear seems to exist in a euphoric, dreamlike state that dislodges him from the reality of the action

130 | SLEEP, ETHICS, AND EMBODIED FORM

onstage, rendering him susceptible to the plots of characters that seek his demise. At various points in the play, Shakespeare explores Lear's need for sleep in relation to the loss of his monarchy, the deterioration of his psyche, and the regressive nature of the aging process. Finally, consolidating sleep's thematic relevance to the play's design on both a literal and a figurative level, the tragedy culminates with Shakespeare's most devastating use of the standard early modern metaphor linking sleep and death. In *King Lear*, Shakespeare intensifies this resemblance by putting it onstage, and making the audience hope along with Lear that Cordelia is merely asleep when he emerges howling with her dead in his arms in Act 5.

THE INFIRMITY OF AGE

Sullivan's work on sleep and Shakespeare's kings deals primarily with *2 Henry IV* and *Henry V*, perhaps the scripts where Shakespeare explores the topic most directly. Throughout the course of these two plays, we see Henry IV pass down his insomnia to Prince Hal, his formerly slumbering son, along with the crown. Indeed, Hal's transition from "unthrifty son" to Henry V, in Sullivan's view, parallels a progression from the idle sleep characteristic of Falstaff to the "wakeful vigilance" of the "warlike Harry": "The implication is that while the 'happy low' can sleep, that ability confirms their status as low, as incapable of a vigilance that can only be maintained by the monarch."[11] This pressure on the monarch to sustain a state of wakefulness, Sullivan suggests, is at the thematic center of these history plays and leads both kings to reflect memorably on the subject in some of their most famous respective speeches.

The following lines from *2 Henry IV*, which I quoted partially above, are key for Sullivan's analysis. They also emphasize aspects of Henry's perspective on sleep that, I suggest, differ from Lear's:

> Canst thou, O partial sleep, give thy repose
> To the wet sea-boy in an hour so rude,
> And in the calmest and most stillest night,
> With all appliances and means to boot,
> Deny it to a King? Then happy low, lie down!
> Uneasy lies the head that wears a crown. (3.1.26–31)

For Henry, the divide between waking and sleep is analogous to that of the unbridgeable chasm between monarch and subject. The "happy low," represented by the "wet sea-boy," enjoy the benefits of rest, while the king is suspended in a state of "uneasy" consciousness. When Henry IV's son Henry V compares himself to his subjects in a similar speech, moreover, Sullivan observes that "Henry's thesis is that all that separates king from peasant is 'ceremony,' but he develops it in a way that suggests precisely the opposite. ... In other words, it is wakefulness, not ceremony, that generates an almost metaphysical barrier between ruler and ruled; it is in wakefulness that the crown finds its true authorization."[12] A king, then, holds himself up to what is ultimately an impossible standard for all who are subject to biological imperatives. For Henry IV and Henry V, the issue is not merely that the king *should* refrain from sleep but that the responsibilities of the body politic ought to keep him awake, regardless of what the body natural requires.

One difference between Shakespeare's earlier kings and his later ones such as Lear is that insomnia begins to connect later kings more directly with the theatrical world of the play and its other characters, rather than separating him from them.[13] In other words, later in Shakespeare's career, the dividing line between monarch and subject—and, I suggest, sleeping and waking—becomes more porous. Shakespeare puts this ambiguity to dramatic use. For the most part, in *King Lear*, rather than announcing his thematic interest in sleep through a speech or soliloquy, Shakespeare assimilates allusions to sleeping and dreaming into the framework of the play. Lear's need of sleep forms a consistent undercurrent in the opening acts that sets him apart from previous Shakespearean kings, and the relationship between his exhaustion and his deteriorating sense of reality becomes increasingly important as the plot progresses.

Beginning with his erratic behavior in the opening scene, the question of Lear's wakefulness is at issue almost immediately after the play begins—both to Lear himself and to the characters around him. The perspective of Lear's daughters reminds the audience to understand him as an aging father as well as a retiring king. Associating her father's mental deterioration with his station in life, Goneril encourages Regan to observe "how full of changes his age is" and notes that the "infirmity of his age" has intensified the reality that Lear has "ever but slenderly known himself" (1.2.283; 288–89). From the perspective of two of his daughters, the aging process exacerbates qualities already nascent in his personality. After banishing Cordelia, the only daughter who is sympathetic to his plight, Lear seeks to restore his former sense of his identity by surrounding himself with knights and summoning the Fool, characters that remind him of his former self.

The Fool in particular consistently exposes Lear's tendency to project his mental lassitude onto others rather than acknowledging its consequences. When the Fool fails to appear immediately, Lear tellingly concludes that "the world's asleep" (1.4.42). From the old king's perspective, it is "the world's" lack of wakefulness, rather than his own, that prevents Lear from being Lear:

> Doth any here know me? This is not Lear.
> Doth Lear walk thus? Speak thus? Where are his eyes?
> Either his notion weakens, his discernings
> Are lethargied—Ha! Waking? 'Tis not so.
> Who is it that can tell me who I am? (1.4.200–205)

The Fool's reply—"Lear's shadow"—brings the nature of Lear's questions into focus.[14] The former king's incredulity at the way the world responds to him inspires him to question both his intellectual and sensory capacities and suggests the extent to which his sense of self depends upon that sense being mirrored in the actions of others. When the external world fails to capitulate to his monarchical imperatives, Lear experiences his disorientation as a form of exhaustion.

Lear's questions also emphasize the discrepancy he experiences between inner and outer reality in a manner that conveys the extent of his deterioration. Moving from a pointed use of the third to the first person, Lear uses embodied language to ask if his "notion" and "discernings," or intellect and comprehension, have been reduced to a "lethargied" state. "In early modern English," as Giulio J. Pertile has recently pointed out in an essay on *King Lear*, commenting on this same passage, lethargy "could refer to a precise medical disorder, a kind of coma or catatonic state."[15] At least according to the characters that surround him, this description seems analogous to the "catatonic" stupor in which Lear finds himself, and anticipates the coma-like sleep that he will experience in Act 4. Lear's issue, as the Fool notices, is not that the "world's asleep" but that Lear seems to exist at a remove from the reality of his surroundings. From Lear's perspective, this remove relates to the gap between monarch and subject that he hopes to sustain—but his questions still anticipate the more advanced state of confused exhaustion he experiences later in the play. After he awakens to reunite with Cordelia, we shall see, he poses similar questions in a manner that evacuates them of irony. In both instances, his mental lethargy inspires him to question whether he is sleeping or "waking."

Representatives of the younger generation confirm Lear's anxieties about his decreased status by consistently connecting the need for sleep with the mental lethargy of elders or of those under elders' control. Edmund serves as spokesman for this position when he describes sleeping as a mode of existence that the old encourage in the "legitimate" to prevent them from prematurely claiming their inheritance. Unlike this "tribe of fops," produced within a series of "dull, stale, tired bed[s]" and "got 'tween a sleep and wake," Edmund is a product of the "lusty stealth of nature" (1.2.1–15). When his father appears onstage, Edmund uses this same metaphor to incriminate his legitimate brother in a letter he claims Edgar wrote to him. "If our father would sleep till I waked him," the false letter promises, "you should enjoy half his revenue for ever, and live the beloved of your brother, Edgar" (1.2.50–52). Among other literal and thematic similarities, Gloucester's reaction to this threat makes clear that he shares Lear's fear that he lacks the liveliness to contend with the ferocious vitality of his heirs. Edmund's lines suggest the extent to which the play equates wakefulness with youthful vigor, ambition, and power.

This hostility toward sleep aligns Edmund with Goneril and Regan, both of whom express contempt for their father's "dotage" and eventually die competing for Edmund's hand in marriage. Early in the play, all three have the potential to inspire sympathy in the audience, precisely because of how oblivious their fathers are to their perspectives. In the following, Goneril describes her father's behavior in terms that emphasize his dreamlike capriciousness:

> 'Tis politic and safe to let him keep
> At point a hundred knights? Yes, that on every dream,
> Each buzz, each fancy, each complaint, dislike,
> He may enguard his dotage with their powers,
> And hold our lives in mercy. (1.4.301–5)

Subordinated to his superfluous knights, Lear's daughters live at the mercy of every "dream" or "fancy" that allows him to sustain the illusion that he

134 | SLEEP, ETHICS, AND EMBODIED FORM

possesses his former authority. The more obvious the fictional nature of this belief becomes, according to Goneril, the more intensely Lear "enguards" himself within his "dotage," as if his faltering cognition is somehow safeguarded behind the knights with which he surrounds himself. Instead of framing insomnia as a necessary condition of one in power, Goneril and Regan read Lear's half-awake dreams and fancies to suggest exhaustion and deterioration.

Shakespeare most commonly uses the word *dotage* when referring to the overwhelming and potentially debilitating effects of love. In *Antony and Cleopatra*, to take an example closely contemporaneous with *King Lear*, Philo begins the play by noting that Antony's "dotage" on Cleopatra "o'erflows the measure" and has "transformed" him into a "strumpet's fool" (1.1.1–2; 14–15). The *OED* informs us that *dotage* can also refer to one whose intellect has been "impaired through age," and "whose feebleness or incapacity of mind" leads to a sort of "second childhood" ("dotage, n.," def. 1a). Lear's need for Cordelia, as distinct from his demands of Goneril and Regan, combines these registers of meaning. The deterioration of his mind intensifies his need for Cordelia and alienates her sisters. Ironically, of course, it is Cordelia's refusal to participate in the fanciful performance he demands in Act 1 that results in her banishment.

Kent and the Fool are characters that Shakespeare associates with Cordelia. Occupying a middling area in the play's generational divide, they criticize Lear's "dotage" as they try to alert him to the danger of his decisions. The Fool, whose criticisms are more oblique and potentially more stinging, sings that

> The man that makes his toe
> What he his heart should make
> Shall of a corn cry woe,
> And turn his sleep to wake. (3.2.30–33)

As the editor of the Arden *King Lear* points out, the song varies a common proverb that promises "pain and sleeplessness" to a man who kicks away someone deserving of love (in this case, likely Cordelia).[16] Despite Goneril's distaste for the "all licensed fool," no character is more consistently critical of Lear's "dotage," although the Fool aligns himself with characters that seek to cure the king of his ailments rather than those who seek to exploit or punish him for them.

Kent, who assures Lear that "he will not sleep" until he has delivered Lear's letter to Regan and Cornwall (1.5.5), seems specifically attuned to and protective of Lear's need for rest, just as Cordelia is. Indeed, at various points in the play, Kent comes across as a sort of self-appointed guardian of Lear's sleep. Prior to the king's sleep after the storm, however, Kent seems to experience Lear's fatigue after Cornwall puts him in the stocks by using the time to sleep onstage. "All weary and o'er-watched," Kent reasons, "Take vantage" (2.3.158–59). The decision to sleep seems strikingly out of character for the industrious Kent until we connect his behavior with that of his master, the only other character to sleep onstage.[17] In addition to looking after the similarly "o'erwatched" king's need for sleep, Kent sets a theatrical precedent that allows Lear to slumber in front of an audience.

UNACCOMMODATED SLEEP

In *King Lear*, Shakespeare places a monarch in a situation that gradually effaces the barriers between monarch and subject we saw Henry IV describe above, to the point where the ruler actually seeks to understand himself as indistinguishable from the ruled. Rather than considering what separates the king from his subjects, when facing the storm, Lear laments his lack of effort to help the nameless rabble and then places himself among them:

> O, I have ta'en
> Too little care of this! Take physic, pomp;
> Expose thyself to feel what wretches feel,
> That thou mayst shake the superflux to them,
> And show the heavens more just. (3.4.33–37)

Instead of war, Lear faces the leveling effects of nature. Before taking shelter, his thoughts turn toward what connects him to the "poor naked wretches" that "bide the pelting of this pitiless storm" (3.4.29–30). Far from dichotomizing his identity in terms of the body politic and body natural, Lear focuses solely on the sensory nature of his experiences. As we saw above, Henry IV imagines the "happy low" of his kingdom enjoying their repose, occasionally at the expense of their duties, during a "calm," "still" evening in which the monarch remains awake. Lear, in contrast, endures nature at its most

136 | SLEEP, ETHICS, AND EMBODIED FORM

vicious—and the experience inspires him to think of those subjects habituated to such conditions out of necessity.

Throughout Act 3 in particular, Shakespeare sustains the connection between Lear's compromised state and the necessity of sleep, with the conditions of others in mind. Subordinating his needs to those of a subject, Lear instructs the Fool to enter the hovel before he does. "In, boy; go first," Lear insists. "You houseless poverty / Nay, get thee in. I'll pray, and then I'll sleep" (3.4.27–28).[18] Whereas Henry V and his father before him consider sleep a luxury a king cannot afford, the need for sleep aligns Lear with the poverty-stricken subjects he realizes he has hitherto ignored. What inspires this interest is the newfound *similarity* he discerns between his condition and theirs, rather than the difference. For Lear, the need for sleep closes the divide between the king and his subjects rather than widening it.

Shakespeare interweaves references to Lear's need for sleep throughout Act 3, where the attitudes that characters take toward the needs of others increasingly serve as a dividing line between good and evil in the play. Furious at their treatment of his servant, Lear arrives at Regan's castle demanding that Regan and Cornwall "come forth and hear" him, "or at their chamber-door I'll beat the drum / 'Till it cry sleep to death" (2.4.112–13). Then, however, sounding like a servant himself, Lear leaves after begging on his knees that Goneril and Regan "vouchsafe" him "raiment, bed, and food" (2.4.149). Considering Lear's explicit demands for the material conditions of monarchical sleep in conjunction with the social dimensions surrounding the same in Jacobean England further suggests how alienated Lear has become from what he earlier described as "th'addition[s] of a king," which he insists he will retain after dividing his kingdom (1.1.133). In James's court, the "Gentlemen of the Chamber" represented the king's inner circle. Populated primarily by Scots, their duties included dressing the king and sleeping in the same room.[19] Implicit in such a role is the responsibility of sustaining the king's aura while also caring for him during his most intimate and vulnerable moments. When Goneril and Regan deny Lear shelter and a place to sleep, they make a point of targeting this aspect of his kingly identity by purging his retinue. "What need you five-and-twenty [. . .]," Goneril asks pointedly, "To follow in a house where twice so many / Have a command to tend you?" (2.4.256–58). Raising the stakes on her sister, as she frequently does, Regan wonders, "What need one?" (2.4.259). The change in the conditions of the monarch's repose represents a concurrent downward shift in his status.

The devaluation of Lear's entourage changes the subject of the conversation with his daughters from what the king merits by virtue of his position to what he needs to sustain himself as a human being. It also, I suggest, represents a conceptual shift in the play, from understanding sleep as something the king does—literally or figuratively, ceremoniously or in the company of his retainers—to something that the person Lear does humbly, on his own. In the scenes immediately following his expulsion from Regan's castle, outcast characters such as the disguised Kent, the Fool, and Gloucester serve as a sort of de facto version of Lear's "Gentlemen of the Chamber." This descent culminates with the addition of Edgar disguised as Poor Tom, whose semicoherent ramblings seem to align with Lear's reflections as he emerges: "Away, the foul fiend follows me! Through the sharp hawthorn blow the winds. Hum, go to thy bed and warm thee" (3.4.45–46). Assuming Edgar's sufferings must mirror his own, Lear insists that Edgar also gave "all" to his daughters and "entertains" him for one of his former hundred knights (3.6.36–37). Failing to recognize his discarded son, Gloucester comments specifically on the unsuitability of Lear's attendant: "What, hath your grace no better company?" (3.4.127). Far from advertising his prestige, Lear's retinue after his conflict with Goneril and Regan represents the extent of his deterioration.

Lear's famous assessment of Edgar as "the thing itself, unaccommodated man" tellingly follows directly upon Regan's refusal to offer him accommodations, and once again raises the king's capacity to sleep as an issue (3.4.96–97). In several different ways, the early modern word *accommodate* connotes the needs and privileges associated with sleep. To "accommodate" suggests the ability to "adapt oneself (to); to adjust to new or different conditions," or "to provide or equip [a person] with something necessary or convenient" (*OED*, "accommodate, v.," defs. 2c and 3b). Lear's inability to adapt to increasingly adverse conditions—and, more specifically, to reconcile these changes with his sense of identity—are at the center of his mental descent. Increasingly, as the play continues, sleep tropes the unaccommodated state that Edgar epitomizes for Lear.

When Lear finally takes shelter, his erratic behavior gives evidence of the sleep deprivation that his companions seek to remedy. In a hallucinatory variation of the opening scene of the play, Lear's sense of reality escapes him as he recruits the Fool and Edgar to help him "arraign" his daughters for their treatment of him:

138 | SLEEP, ETHICS, AND EMBODIED FORM

LEAR: Arraign her first: 'tis Goneril, I here take my oath before this
honorable assembly, kicked the poor King her father.
FOOL: Come hither, mistress. Is your name Goneril?
LEAR: She cannot deny it.
FOOL: Cry you mercy, I took you for a joint-stool.
LEAR: And here's another whose warped looks proclaim
What store her heart is made on. (15.29–36)[20]

Increasingly, the incoherence of the old king renders even the Fool and Edgar straight men to his performance. The latter breaks character with asides that comment on Lear's condition: "Bless thy five wits . . . My tears begin to take his part so much / They mar my counterfeiting" (3.6.16; 19–20). Edgar's lines remind the audience that his performance of insanity provides Lear with a distorted mirror of his own actual deterioration.

Lear's visions in this scene, in which he also sees and hears his daughters' dogs barking at him, come across as a sort of waking nightmare that continues in Act 4 when he encounters the blinded Gloucester. According to the Swiss theologian Ludwig Lavater's *Of Ghostes and Spirites Walking by Nyght* (1572), a *visum*, or waking dream, "signifieth an imagination or a certayne shewe, which men being in sleep, yea, and waking also, seeme in their judgemente to behold."[21] Capturing another dimension of Lear's experience, the definition that Timothy Bright offers in his *A Treatise of Melancholie* (1586) notes that objects perceived as part of a dream could appear "as if [they] were represented unto us brode awake," and that dreams were capable of making the past and the future seem as though they were the present.[22] Key to both descriptions is the disorientation induced by the subject's inability to separate sleeping from waking. In the moments before he succumbs to sleep, Lear's warped perceptions convert a "joint stool" into Goneril and Edgar into one of his erstwhile hundred knights. Whereas a king's retinue traditionally reinforces the king's sense of himself, Lear's companions participate in his delusional scenarios in the hope of inspiring him to rest.

Lear's sleeplessness exacerbates the symptoms of madness that intensify as the play progresses, culminating with him falling asleep onstage at the conclusion of Act 3. Far from the ceremonious overtures associated with sleeping kings, Kent and the Fool coax Lear into repose in a manner that acknowledges his tenuous grasp on sanity. Kent, who had himself slept onstage earlier, ministers to Lear's needs by encouraging his master to do the same: "How do you, sir? Stand you not so amazed: / Will you lie down and rest upon the cushions?" (3.6.30–31). The noisiest, most frenetically paced act in the play culminates with Lear succumbing to sleep:

> KENT: Now, good my lord, lie here and rest awhile.
> LEAR: Make no noise, make no noise. Draw the curtains, so,
> So, We'll go to supper i'th'morning.
> FOOL: And I'll go to bed at noon. (3.6.39–42)

Lear's final, hypnagogic requests anticipate the childlike wonder and confusion with which he will later greet Cordelia. Anticipating this reunion, Kent describes sleep in terms of its potential curative benefits: "Oppressed nature sleeps: / This rest might yet have balmed thy broken sinews, / Which, if convenience will not allow, / Stand in hard cure" (3.6.90–93). The recovery Kent hopes for emphasizes the body natural rather than any sense of royal dignity. Lear's attempts to act like a king in the scene highlight his tenuous grasp of reality rather than representing a monarchical form he can restore. "Accommodated" in an outbuilding on Gloucester's estate, in the company of two banished men and the Fool, Lear submits to his exhaustion.

CORDELIA'S "KIND NURSERY"

While Lear's behavior leading to his initial sleep in the play damages his monarchical grandeur, his need for sleep humanizes him in a manner unique among Shakespeare's kings. Among other purposes, it rehabilitates the negative impression he makes on the audience with his egregious behavior in Act 1 and lays the foundation for the return of Cordelia. Lear's reunion with his youngest daughter in Act 4 further complicates the play's interest in the relationship between sleep and death, and brings the relevance of sleep to the surface more prominently than any other scene in the play. Beginning with the opening scene, Lear associates Cordelia with every aspect of sleep that the play explores in the acts leading to their reunion, most especially the relationship between sleep deprivation and the regressive nature of aging.

"I loved her most," Lear admits even in his anger after disowning Cordelia, "and thought to set my rest / On her kind nursery" (1.1.120–21). Ranging back to the fourteenth century, the word *nursery* has been used to describe a place where children specifically sleep (*OED*, "nursery, n. and adj.," def. 1a). When it comes to Cordelia, Lear seems to embrace the infantilization that he objects to from his other daughters. The conditions that he describes also give us a sense of the accommodations that he envisioned her supplying, and that Goneril and Regan refused him. The denial of the restful nursery that Cordelia represents provokes the anger that leads to his madness.

After Lear's dreamlike interlude with the blinded Gloucester, during which his tenuous grasp on reality shows signs of his sleep deprivation, Lear falls asleep in the custody of Cordelia's entourage, further distancing himself from his former royal identity by replacing the English attendants of his own court with French ones.[23] "What can man's wisdom," Cordelia asks before she reencounters her sleeping father, "In the restoring of his bereaved sense?" (4.4.9–10). The doctor's answer matches Kent's sympathetic diagnosis of the exhausted king:[24]

> There is means, madam.
> Our foster-nurse of nature is repose,
> The which he lacks. That to provoke in him
> Are many simples operative whose power
> Will close the eye of anguish. (4.4.12–16)

Describing sleep as the "foster-nurse of nature," the doctor echoes Lear's description of the "kind nursery" he envisioned under Cordelia's care. This answer, moreover, which prescribes sleep literally and metaphorically, is consistent not only with the play's thematic interest in repose but also with contemporary guides on the importance of rest to sustaining mental and physical health. The "simples" the doctor alludes to suggest that Lear's sleep has been aided by a drug of some sort and therefore is not entirely natural.[25] Cordelia, who earlier had provoked her father's fury, here must enable a "foster-nurse" to "close the eye of anguish."

Significant for my purposes here, both of Lear's periods of slumber could be seen as unbecoming of a monarch, because they take place during key battles between the British and French armies. Whereas, for previous Shakespearean kings, war provokes insomnia that they define as intrinsic to the identity of a monarch Lear is marginalized from the military operations that take place in his play and appears blissfully unaware of the stakes until Cordelia falls victim to the consequences of losing. In his brief essay

"On Sleep," though, Montaigne provides a useful counterexample of military leaders who sleep peacefully until battle calls them into wakefulness: "I have therefore mark't it as a rare thing, to see great personages sometimes, even in their weightiest enterprises, and most important affaires, hold themselves so resolutely-assured in their state, that they doe not so much as breake their sleepe for them. *Alexander* the great, on the day appointed for that furious-bloudy battle against *Darius*, slept so soundly and so long that morning, that *Parmenion* was faine to enter his chamber, and approaching neere unto his bed, twice or thrice to call him by his name, to awaken him, the houre of the battle against being at hand."[26] For leaders such as Alexander and Darius, "resolutely-assured" confidence in their military operations induces a sense of calm that transfers to those fighting for them. The more "weighty" the enterprise they undertake, the sounder the sleep they experience. To take a Shakespearean example, we might compare Richmond's sleep on the eve of battle with that of Richard III. The two men seem to share a dream in which Richard's victims chastise the sleeping king and then travel across the stage to encourage his successor. Whereas Richard awakes with a start, anticipating his violent death, Richmond, sleeping soundly as Darius, reassures the men who wake him that he has experienced "the sweetest sleep and fairest-boding dreams / That ever entered in a drowsy head" (5.3.225–26). For Lear, in contrast, the physical and mental rehabilitation that sleep engenders ironically parallel his political diminishment while also humanizing him in a manner that provokes sympathy.

Early modern commentators also distinguished among various types of sleep based on depth as well as duration. Deep, sustained sleep was desirable, but, according to Philip Barrough's treatise on medical care, allowing even the sick to sleep too long could be harmful. In a condition that he calls "coma sleep," which he distinguishes from the less harmful "dead sleepe," the patient is inclined to "speake they wot not what, and they lie with their whole body out of order, and they have partly such signes as appeare in the frenesie, and partly such as in lethargie."[27] When the doctor informs Cordelia that Lear "hath slept long," and asks that she wake him, he seems intent on gauging whether Lear's condition has improved based on the type of sleep he was experiencing (4.7.18).

Lear's initial sleep in the play at the conclusion of Act 3 apparently does not provide the curative function that early modern manuals describe. In Act 4, his interactions with Gloucester demonstrate that he still retains the

142 | SLEEP, ETHICS, AND EMBODIED FORM

same symptoms. As Cordelia's conversation with the doctor reveals, Lear's next period of slumber seems deeper and more sustained:

> CORDELIA: How does the king?
> DOCTOR: Madam, sleeps still.
> CORDELIA: O you kind gods,
> Cure this great breach in this abused nature!
> The unturned and jarring senses, O, wind up
> Of this child-changed father! (4.7.12–18)

Although Cordelia first identifies Lear as "the king," the "breach" in his "abused nature" makes him appear "child-changed," a description that strips Lear of any remaining monarchical grandeur. This assessment equates the need for sleep with dotage, while once again recalling Lear's desire to find repose in Cordelia's "nursery." Lear, in this way, represents what Henry IV— and, to a lesser extent, Henry V—fear they will become, although it's not clear they have the capacity to imagine the extent of Lear's deterioration.

The doctor stipulates that Lear remains "in the heaviness of sleep" when he arrives onstage, emphasizing the depth of his slumber. The stage directions tell us that he is *in a chair carried by servants*. The chair, likely the same stage prop used as the throne in the play's opening scene, visually reinstates him to his former role while practically sustaining his compromised state. Lear's awakening, in Marjorie Garber's view, is not so much a dream as a "waking vision."[28] In either case, Lear's behavior after he revives demonstrates a clear change from his earlier, tempestuous demeanor. Addressing the vulnerability of sleep, Lear confesses that he is "not in his perfect mind" and that he does not know where he did "lodge last night," once again connecting Lear's need to sleep with his lack of suitable accommodations (4.7.60, 65).

As other early modern commentators emphasize, the restorative value of sleep was also contingent on the time of the day that it took place. Thomas Elyot's *The Castel of Helthe* (1539), for instance, warns against the health risks of sleeping during the afternoon: "And therefore whosoever waketh in the tyme of sleep, or slepe when he ought to wake, he perverteth, and hurteth not only hys memorie, but also manye tymes shal engender apostemes, catarres, reumes, agues, palsyes, and many other grevous and naughty diseases of the body."[29] Whereas Falstaff, perhaps Shakespeare's most notable napper, cheerfully ignores these warnings even after experiencing many of the symptoms Elyot describes, kings were not in a position to allow their bodies to deteriorate so casually. Relating Elyot's mandate to Shakespeare's kings, Totaro points out that "sleeping during the day was a bad sign showing a weak body; pair this weakness with a lax watch over that body, as in King Hamlet's case . . . and the consequences are grave."[30] In a fleeting moment of lucidity, Lear seems to acknowledge his own weakness as he expresses surprise at the vulnerability of his body. "They told me I was everything," he remarks, ruefully. "'Tis a lie. I am not ague proof" (4.6.104–5). The illusion of kingly invincibility to which Lear was encouraged to subscribe reveals itself as faulty only when exhaustion distances the king from reality.

When Lear awakes, unaware of the time of day, his questions further our impression of his ambiguous mental status while also reframing the questions about his identity that he posed rhetorically earlier in the play: "Where have I been? Where am I? Fair Daylight? / I am mightily abused" (4.7.53–54).[31] The doctor's remark, that "he's scarce awake" and should be let "alone awhile," again suggests that Lear is hovering on the border between sleeping and consciousness. Lear's disorientation mirrors the conceptual confusion regarding his status. Building on Parris's analysis of *Hamlet* and *Macbeth*, we can connect the liminal state Lear occupies to the ambiguous status of the body politic, which also seems to hover uncertainly in this play with no assurance of locating a suitable heir. Lear's confusion as to whether he is alive or dead furthers this sense of uncertainty. "You do me wrong to take me out o'the grave," he tells Cordelia, equating his "dead" sleep with actual death. "Thou art a soul in bliss" (4.7.41–42).

As the play concludes, Lear's confusion evolves into a metatheatrical exploration of the relationship between sleeping and death. Sleep appears frequently in early modern literature in general (and Shakespeare's works in particular) as a standard anticipatory metaphor for death. Sir Thomas Browne, for instance, found sleep and death so alike that he dared not submit to the former without saying his prayers, just in case the latter took him unawares.[32] Sonnet 73, in which "Death's Second Self . . . seals up all in rest," provides one of many well-known Shakespearean examples (line 8). With *King Lear*, Shakespeare intensifies the comparison of sleep and death by inciting the audience to experience the confusion. Entering the stage with Cordelia dead in his arms, Lear himself dies attempting to collapse the difference between the world that his reality forces him to inhabit and that of his dreams. As Stephen Greenblatt reminds us, none of the sources Shakespeare seems to have consulted while writing the play end with this unrelentingly tragic turn of events.[33] Shakespeare's original audience as well as the characters would therefore have shared the hope that Cordelia might awaken onstage.

The metatheatrical dimensions of the scene, moreover, heighten its intensity. When a character dies onstage, the audience knows that the actor is alive and presumably conscious. In this case, however, they must discern along with Lear whether the actor playing Cordelia is feigning sleep or death. Lear's initial assessment sounds as if he is addressing this question directly and putting it to rest: "She's gone forever. / I know when one is dead and when one lives; / She's dead as earth" (5.3.233–35). Similar to his stance earlier in the play, however, Lear's self-conscious insistence on clarity only confirms his confusion. With his dying words, Lear for the last time urges the audience to indulge his illusions: "Do you see this? Look on her! Look, her lips. / Look there. Look there" (5.3.286–87). Lear paradoxically intensifies the moment by calling attention to the artificiality of the performance. The actor's lips *are* moving, but Cordelia is dead. Immediately afterward, the same confusion applies to Lear himself.

As I have tried to demonstrate in this essay, monarchical wakefulness in this play transforms into a gradual evacuation of agency through exhaustion and a final return of the king to nature, in a position among—not above— his subjects. The heaviness of the desire to succumb to death parallels the desire for sleep in Act 3. Arriving onstage shortly before Lear, Kent says he comes in the hope of bidding his "king and master aye good night," collapsing sleep and death before Lear enters the stage (5.3.209–10). Similar to Lear's earlier sleep, moreover, Kent encourages Lear to cross the divide: "Vex not his ghost. O let him pass! He hates him much / That would upon the rack of this rough world / Stretch him out longer" (5.3.313–15). Earlier, Kent oversees Lear's sleep; here, in a version of the same function, he confirms his death. In this play, to quote Edgar's concluding lines, "the weight" of the "sad time" envelops the characters onstage (5.3.299). The audience, if the performance is successful, wishfully occupies this same realm as Lear, a theatrical world in which Cordelia awakes as if from sleep and Lear is free to rest in her "kind nursery," and to atone for his sins against her.

NOTES

1. *WTF with Marc Maron*, episode 621: "Sir Ian McKellen," July 20, 2015, podcast, produced by Brendan McDonald, http://www.wtfpod.com/podcast/episodes/episode_621_-_sir_ian_mckellen.

2. *The Norton Shakespeare*, ed. Stephen Greenblatt et al., 3rd ed. (New York: W. W. Norton, 2016). Unless otherwise noted, all subsequent quotes in this chapter from Shakespeare's plays and poems are taken from this edition and will be cited parenthetically.

3. Garrett Sullivan Jr., *Sleep, Romance, and Human Embodiment: Vitality from Spenser to Milton* (Cambridge: Cambridge University Press, 2012), 92.

4. For Hal, who tellingly assumes the king is dead when he sees him sleeping, the crown represents both the source of his father's insomnia and the illness that ends his life. "This golden rigol," in Hal's words, induces an alternative form of sleep "that hath divorced so many English kings" from life (4.3.167–68).

5. Benjamin Parris, "'The body is with the King, but the King is not with the body': Sovereign Sleep in *Hamlet* and *Macbeth*," *Shakespeare Studies* 40 (2012): 101.

6. Ibid.

7. Ibid., 102.

8. Rebecca Totaro, "Securing Sleep in *Hamlet*," *Studies in English Literature, 1500–1900* 50, no. 2 (2010): 410.

9. Thomas Cogan, *The Haven of Health, Chiefly gathered for the comfort of students, and consequently of all those that have a care of their health, amplified upon five words of Hippocrates, written Epid. 6. Labour, cibus, potio, somnus, Venus* (London: Henry Middleton for William Norton, 1584), 236.

10. Ibid., 237.

11. Sullivan, *Sleep, Romance, and Human Embodiment*, 91–92.

12. Ibid., 94–95. Sullivan also does more to distinguish between Henry IV and Henry V than I have in this section.

13. This is true of the early King Richard III, who alienates the audience as well as his few companions and suffers "fitful sleep" after he achieves his goal of securing the crown.

14. The quarto version of the play assigns the Fool's reply to Lear himself in the form of a question, perhaps making him more conscious of his deterioration.

15. Giulio J. Pertile, "*King Lear* and the Uses of Mortification," *Shakespeare*

Quarterly 67, no. 3 (Fall 2016): 336. As Claude Fretz points out, moreover, Lear's use of the word *lethargy* "echoes the early modern understanding of sleep as a deactivation, impotence, or death of the senses": Fretz, "'Either his notion weakens, or his discernings / Are lethargied': Sleeplessness and Waking Dreams as Tragedy in *Julius Caesar* and *King Lear*," *Études Épistémè* 30 (2016): 29.

16. William Shakespeare, *King Lear*, ed. R. A. Foakes (London: Bloomsbury Arden Shakespeare, 2013), 265nn31–34.

17. "Kent's sleeping on stage," David Bevington observes, creates "an extraordinary metatheatrical moment" that "allows him to be inactive and 'not there' as the previous scene ends" while also presaging "Lear's sleep in an outbuilding on Gloucester's estate" ("Asleep Onstage," in *From Page to Performance: Essays in Early English Drama*, ed. John A. Alford [East Lansing: Michigan State University Press, 1995], 70–71).

18. "Lear's madness," Claude Fretz has recently argued, "is a central part of Shakespeare's representation of human suffering in this tragedy, and it is suggested that the king's madness is exacerbated by his sleep deprivation" ("'Either his notion weakens,'" 24.)

19. Michael B. Young, *King James and the History of Homosexuality* (New York: New York University Press, 2000), 26.

20. This episode occurs only in the quarto version of the play.

21. Ludwig Lavater, *Of Ghostes and Spirites Walking by Nyght and of Strange Noyses, Crackes, and Sundry Forewarnynges, Whiche Commonly Happen Before the Death of Menne, Great Slaughters, [and] Alterations of Kyngdomes* (London: Henry Benneyman for Richard Watkins, 1572), 11.

22. Quoted in Fretz, "'Either his notion weakens,'" 22.

23. Nancy Simpson-Younger has pointed out that in early modern Europe "the process of watching a sleeper was a part of everyday life, because sleep always took place in a community context"; see Simpson-Younger, "Watching the Sleeper in *Macbeth*," *Shakespeare* 12, no. 3 (2016):

260. The sight of a sleeping body places ethical demands on watchers to sustain the slumbering individual's "community-based form of identity" and ensure that he or she was not exploited. Cordelia claims this role from Kent during Lear's second onstage slumber.

24. The Folio identifies the doctor as a "gentleman."

25. I am grateful to the anonymous reviewer of this essay who made me aware of this allusion.

26. *The Essayes of Montaigne: John Florio's Translation*, ed. Bennett A. Cerf and Donald S. Klopfer (New York: Modern Library, 1933), 234.

27. Philip Barrough, *The Method of Phisick, Conteyning the Causes, Signes, and Cures of Inward Diseases in Mans Body* (London: Printed by Richard Field, 1601), 31.

28. Marjorie Garber, *Dream in Shakespeare: From Metaphor to Metamorphosis* (New Haven: Yale University Press, 1974), 124. "The awakening of Lear," Garber continues, "reaches out to unify more than inner man and outer world—for a moment it unifies time itself, obliterating the differences between death and life, this world and the next" (124).

29. Thomas Elyot, *The Castel of Helthe gathered and made by Syr Thomas Elyot knyghte, out of the chiefe authors of physyke, wherby euery manne may knowe the state of his owne body, the preseruatio[n] of helthe, and how to instructe welle his physytion in syckenes that he be Not deceyued* (London: Thomas Berthelet, 1539), sig. 47r.

30. Totaro, "Securing Sleep in *Hamlet*," 414.

31. By similarity and contrast, the comparison of 2 *Henry IV* once again proves useful. The play also features a scene in which a child of the king watches the monarch sleep. As Hal observes his father, he is struck by how little difference there is between sleep and death:

By his gates of breath
There lies a downy feather which stirs not;
Did he suspire, that light and weightless down
Perforce must move.—My gracious lord, my father!
This sleep is sound indeed; this is a sleep
That from this golden rigol hath divorced
So many English kings. (4.3.162–68)

Ultimately, the only sleep permissible to the monarch is the sleep of death that transfers the body politic to his heir. Although Hal has mistaken his father's sleep for death, his decision to take the crown from his pillow, Sullivan points out, implicitly solves the problem of "monarchical sleep" in the play in that his actions, however hasty, confirm that he is ready to assume the state of "perpetual wakefulness" that his father must abandon in death. *King Lear*, in several respects, reverses the dynamics of this scene while engaging with many of its same themes. In Act 4, the king awakes thinking both he *and* his child are dead rather than the other way around.

32. Sir Thomas Browne, *Religio Medici*, in *The Major Works*, ed. C. A. Patrides (London: Penguin, 1977), 155.

33. See *Norton Shakespeare*, 3rd ed., 2321.

Part III

SLEEP AND PERSONHOOD IN THE EARLY MODERN VERSE EPIC AND PROSE TREATISE

CHAPTER 7

Life and Labor in the House of Care

Spenserian Ethics and the Aesthetics of Insomnia

BENJAMIN PARRIS

More than a few readers—including Harry Berger Jr., Deborah Shuger, William Oram, Garrett Sullivan Jr., Giulio Pertile, and Russ Leo—have offered compelling accounts of Edmund Spenser's interest in bodily states of shock, swoon, trance, stound, and paralysis.[1] In turn, many of these critics note that representations of sleep in *The Faerie Queene* foreground sleep's similarly stultifying effects on consciousness and sensation, making it a useful poetic figure for carelessness, idleness, and the "impulse to deny the demands of work in the world."[2] The affective extremes of sleeping life and related states of stupor and inaction have thus received thoughtful and due attention from some of Spenser's most insightful readers. But critics have given much less attention to the poet's representations of insomnia, especially as they relate to the "vitall powres" (2.7.65) and productive efforts of embodied life—powers whose successful maintenance is a toilsome affair that so often vexes Spenser's allegorical heroes.

In the following pages, I grapple with an underappreciated scene of sleepless suffering that is also a reflection on the vital powers of life and labor: Sir Scudamor's visit to the House of Care in Book 4 of *The Faerie Queene*. My argument draws on two areas of inquiry not often brought together by critics of early modern literature—Marxist theory and biopolitics. Like Marx, Spenser shows a deep interest in the laboring capacities of the living human body and in the physiological cycles and processes that repair it through sleep. These concerns emerge clearly in his allegorical figuration of Scudamor's insomnia as a team of laboring blacksmiths in the House of Care. Scudamor's care takes the form of fiery, self-consuming jealousy that forces him to become the involuntary watcher of an endless production of care, in turn alienating him from the recovery of his bodily life and vitality through the restorative virtues of sleep. Moreover, Spenser personifies Care as a master craftsman who watches over, controls, and profits from the productive efforts of the laboring smiths. This calls for a Marxist reading of the process by which Scudamor's physical vitality is involuntarily constrained and eroded by a nocturnal care that will not let him sleep.

At the same time, insofar as Scudamor's bout with Care represents the full-blown eruption of a jealous wound to his heart and soul (originating from Ate's slanders in Canto 1), any reading of the scene must attend carefully to the role played by Scudamor's physical life and passions leading up to this moment. I argue that Scudamor's care and its allegorical capture by the master blacksmith has biopolitical significance, much in the sense that Julia Reinhard Lupton attributes to the life of "animal virtues" that are tapped and tamed by the art of husbandry, and that form the fabric of intimacy between Petruchio and Kate in Shakespeare's *The Taming of the Shrew*.[3] Lupton's biopolitical analysis of husbandry and its gathering of vital powers—which she reads simultaneously as an art of cultivating domestic virtues and a brutal technique of domination—provides a suggestive framework for assessing Spenser's allegory of care. The work of the blacksmiths both harnesses Scudamor's vitality and alienates him from it, by tapping the hero's psychosomatic generation of care and transforming it into a scene of endless production that keeps him from sleep. This process unfolds at an imagined threshold between the *oikos* and the workshop of the master craftsman, where what should be a private experience of restorative virtue for Scudamor instead becomes a socialized scene of nocturnal labor and insomnia. In this way, Spenser's allegory is part of the genealogy of biopower and capital—two enterprises that subject the body to a regime of disciplined productivity and whose ongoing social reproduction depends upon sleep as an essential source of restoration. But it is also important to see that for Spenser, the tools of allegorical epic are well suited to the elaboration of his point concerning the susceptibility of human care and vitality to historically particular forms of capture and exploitation. Allegorical personification is the means by which Spenser's epic draws biological life and human consciousness into a structure of meaning that in turn conveys to his readers a form of ethical knowledge concerning the vital powers and virtues of physical life. In the House of Care, ethical care is a quilting point for early modern discourses concerning the biology of sleep, phenomenal self-understanding, and allegorical form.

As several critics have shown, the predominant theories of sleep in Spenser's world draw on Aristotelian natural philosophy in viewing sleep as a psychosomatic process that actualizes the powers of the nutritive soul while suspending its animal and human capacities.[4] The nutritive powers of the soul are responsible for the living being's growth and sustenance. It is therefore a virtue that makes possible the exercise of any virtue whatsoever, by safeguarding the self-reproductive powers of life.[5] In this way, early modern sleep itself actualizes a form of biopower, or an immanent and autopoetic capacity of the living body.[6] Yet sleep by its very nature also resists the sort of willed agency and instrumentalization of the body that are necessary features of biopolitical control and production alike. The actualization of this virtue thus requires, somewhat paradoxically, that the self must abandon all its conscious cares and animal sensations. In other words, sleep temporarily halts the harnessing and sharpening of all virtues, save that of life's unconscious regeneration and recovery. And this point is key to understanding why Spenser depicts Scudamor's overly vigilant attunement to care as an experience of insomnia: while the restorative virtues of sleep might salve the wound in Scudamor's heart by calming his soul, that vital power is instead occluded by the anxious, animal care that grips his being. Scudamor's care forces him to embody an involuntary form of sleepless watch that estranges him from the self-healing virtues of psychosomatic recovery that inhere within. Care and his team of workers thus figure Scudamor's sleepless care as the forced reshaping of his soul's immanent and vital power in ways that do not hone or perfect its capacity for self-restoration but instead subject it to a transformative process of production that only generates more care.

Ultimately, I argue that Scudamor's insomnia serves as the vehicle of a critique that Spenser launches against the endless biopolitical sharpening and instrumentalization of virtues across various forms of life embodied by the human being. An important vein of Spenser's allegory of care thus

152 | SLEEP AND PERSONHOOD

implies that the immanent physiological norms structuring organic human life—including the restorative virtue of sleep—can be radically transformed and even threatened by the demands of care that make up the social world. Marx conveys a similar insight regarding the vitality of the worker in the struggle over the limits of the working day, and he likewise underscores the centrality of sleep in the campaign to establish an acceptably healthy norm against the dictates of capital.[7] Clearly, the sources of Spenser's worry are the potential harms of worldly care and the cultivation of virtue, in their tendency to inflame the soul with a manic vigilance. Yet his allegorical rendering of that threat also prefigures the biopolitical fate of human vitality and its appearance as labor power under the rule of capital, which insists upon the endless production and extraction of surplus value even as it erodes the material and biological foundation of that process. It is perhaps in this sense that Scudamor's experience in the House of Care is most pertinent to the prehistories of biopower and capital, because it provides us with an early modern view of biological vitality in tension with a social scene of production, just before the rise of the sciences of life and political economy.[8]

1

The ethical stakes of Scudamor's trip to the House of Care—as well as the logic behind Spenser's choice of insomnia as the vehicle for his biopolitical critique of virtue—can be drawn out by an appeal to the conceptual and historical foundations of Marx's account of the working day in volume 1 of *Capital*. According to Marx, the advent of English capitalist manufacture in the seventeenth century is "merely an enlargement of the workshop of the master craftsman of the guilds," one that represents a key moment in the history of the division of labor and, as it turns out, the history of human sleep (439). Marx views the development of capitalism in part as a process by which the worker's life is increasingly brought under the reign of capital. He provides a theoretically sophisticated account of how work becomes a site of invisible or latent domination, as workers are forced to increase the amount of time that they labor for the capitalist master while decreasing the amount of labor time devoted to reproducing their own life and well-being. And, for Marx, sleep—or the lack thereof—has a central role to play in this process, as the working day is steadily expanded and the worker's vitality conversely eroded by a lack of physical nourishment and rest.

Marx tracks the history of the struggle over the length of the working day by citing numerous firsthand accounts of physicians, factory inspectors, and political economists during England's industrial revolution. This matter is of decisive importance in the ongoing battle between capitalists and the working class, Marx argues, whose respective rights to purchase and sell labor power on the market of exchange he characterizes in the following terms: "There is here therefore an antinomy, of right against right, both equally bearing the seal of the law of exchange. Between equal rights, force decides. Hence, in the history of capitalist production, the establishment of a norm for the working day presents itself as a struggle over the limits of that day, a struggle between collective capital, i.e., the class of capitalists, and collective labour, i.e., the working class" (344). At stake in this tug-of-war to establish a norm for the working day is the amount of time allotted to each worker for the reproduction of their life—time for the eating, socializing, gaming, and (most important to my purposes here) the sleeping that is essential to preserving human vitality. From the perspective of capital, there is a constant push to establish an ever-shrinking minimum of what it must pay out so that the worker can reproduce their labor-power and return the next day, only to sell this labor anew for an hourly wage. The less that capital must expend on the worker's reproduction of life, the better. At the same time, capital's tendency to push toward a minimum expenditure inevitably encounters a limit in the form of the natural norm that every worker embodies as the "physical limits to labour-power." As Marx writes,

> Within the 24 hours of the natural day a man can only expend a certain quantity of his vital force. . . . During part of the day the vital force must rest, sleep; during another part the man has to satisfy other physical needs, to feed, wash and clothe himself. . . . The worker [also] needs time in which to satisfy his intellectual and social requirements, and the extent and number of these requirements is conditioned by the general level of civilization. The length of the working day therefore fluctuates within boundaries both physical and social. But these limiting conditions are of a very elastic nature, and allow a tremendous amount of latitude. (341)

In these passages Marx establishes a framework for analyzing the working day through the concept of the norm. Bodily life and its vital powers posit immanent, biological norms that dictate the natural limits of physical work as well as the food and rest that is necessary for the continued reproduction of life. But these physiological norms are reciprocally shaped by the social norms of human life, which Marx describes with his characteristically grim wit as "moral obstacles" to capital's "werewolf-like hunger for surplus labour" (353). This hunger in turn causes capitalist industry to push for increasingly longer working days, "ranging from 12 to 14 or 15 hours," as well as a "night-labour, irregular meal-times, and meals mostly taken in the workrooms themselves, pestilent with phosophorus" (356). All of this leads Marx to declare that "Dante himself would have found the worst horrors in his *Inferno* surpassed in this industry" (356).[9]

At this stage in his argument, Marx's analysis of industrial capitalism lays bare a key contradiction. As a result of capital's insatiable appetite for the valorization of value, it treats workers as nothing more than labor-power waiting to be instrumentalized, and thus constantly oversteps the physical limits of the working day. The result is that capital inevitably erodes the health of the populations upon which it entirely depends. It "usurps the time for growth, development and healthy maintenance of the body. . . . It reduces the sound sleep needed for the restoration, renewal and refreshment of the vital forces to the exact amount of torpor essential to the revival of an absolutely exhausted organism. It is not the normal maintenance of labour-power that determines the limits of the working day here, but rather the greatest possible daily expenditure of labour-power, no matter how diseased, compulsory and painful it may be, which determines the limits of the worker's period of rest" (376). For Marx, the worker's sleep is thus a biological norm whose boundaries under capitalism fluctuate sharply according to both internally posited requirements and those imposed on the life of the worker by capital. For life under capital, a persistent lack of rest resulting in exhaustion becomes the new norm.

As Georges Canguilhem argues, this sort of dialectical movement between immanent biological norms and the social milieu is a defining aspect of Western societies that are increasingly shaped by scientific knowledge and practices in the wake of the Enlightenment. When combined strategically with the vital power exuded by the natural life of the species, scientific technology and force can reshape the organic life of humankind and even entirely subvert the standing order of that life: "Human will and human technology can turn night into day not only in the environment where human activity unfolds, but also in the organism itself whose activity confronts the environment."[10] Canguilhem's work on the pliability and power of norms in the human sciences and society is crucial to the work of his student Michel Foucault, who draws on Canguilhem's ideas in linking the normalizing thrust of biopolitics to the advent of capitalism. In the first volume of *The History of Sexuality*, Foucault argues that industrial capitalism "would not have been possible without the controlled insertion of bodies into the machinery of production and the adjustment of the phenomena of population to economic processes," all of which is strategically orchestrated through the concept of the norm.[11] As I have already shown in my discussion of Marx's account of the working day, the determination of this norm involves the natural, organic life of workers and the vital means of its reproduction, struggling within a socially constituted environment of wage-labor under capitalism. The normativity of sleep is where the biopolitical and Marxist frameworks meet, as sleep is an essential (if not the most essential) terrain on which this struggle unfolds.

In other words, sleep constitutes an immanent biological normativity—or, in the parlance of Spenser's Aristotelian worldview, a psychosomatic virtue of self-restoration. The poet treats this virtue as an ethical norm for the life of his heroes, even as they struggle to maintain that norm in light of the demands of an ever-vigilant sharpening of virtue and the endless work of self-care. The daily toil of virtue must be temporarily suspended, since even the mightiest of heroes must sleep. But, as any insomniac knows, the turn from hypervigilance to somnolence is rarely easy. This is the dynamic that fuels Scudamor's insomnia in the House of Care and that leads Spenser to figure the hero's surplus of harmful care as the endless hammering of a team of blacksmiths whose work is not for their own benefit but rather serves primarily to inflate the status of their master, Care.

2

In typical Spenserian fashion, it is somewhat unclear whether the discord that seizes hold of Scudamor and leads to his travails in the House of Care is the direct result of Ate's slanderous account of Amoret's infidelity with Britomart, or if we should trace its origins even further backward in the poem. Such a reading would return us to the conclusion of Book 3, and to Spenser's emendation of the original ending of the 1590 edition of the poem. In that version, after Britomart rescues Amoret from Busyrane, Book 3 concludes with an image of Scudamor and Amoret reunited in a gushy embrace that melts their senses and gives the impression that the two have fused into one: "Had ye them seene, ye would have surely thought, / That they had been that faire *Hermaphrodite* . . . So seemd those two, as growne together quite."[12] If, as William Oram argues, "the heroes of Book Three attempt to achieve a fruitful social relationship, a loving harmony of dissimilar selves," then the 1590 ending to Book 3 seems to threaten its own core premise.[13] The harmony between persons that Spenser suggests is necessary to friendship and social benefit cannot occur without some separation, of course, since harmonious relations between entities imply that those entities are to some extent autonomous.

Later, in Book 4, Spenser will represent the work that consumes the denizens of the House of Care as the forging of "yron wedges" that "carefull minds invade" (4.5.35), perhaps suggesting that the wedge of care is what first drives Scuadamor and Amoret asunder, becoming the engine of production to the poem's ongoing narrative. Spenser's allegory of friendship thus begins with a poetic revision that quite literally splits the 1590 union of Amoret and Scudamor. The revised Book 3 concludes with a scene of Scudamor's downtrodden spirit and ruined hopes at the gates of Busirane's castle, where "his expectation to despaire did turne, / Misdeeming sure that her those flames did burne" (3.12.45). Britomart of course successfully rescues Amoret and returns safely from the perils of Busirane's palace, but Scudamor has already fallen victim to his dread and abandoned the scene, taking Amoret's nurse Glauce with him.

It is possible that we are meant to read the fires of Care's forge as Scudamor's internalization of the dreadful flames that envelope Busirane's palace, to which Ate's accusations serve as a slanderous bellows. Scudamor's lack of faith, first in Britomart's rescue effort and second in both Britomart's and Amoret's fidelity, results in an enflamed heart and physical distemper that erupts in the first canto and continues to smolder across Book 4. This illustrates both the virtuous potential of the physical body and its susceptibility to affective extremes. As Giulio Pertile has argued, Spenser's allegory is driven in the early books by moments that foreground the unconscious biological and somatic processes of private life, over and above the perceptual or intellective experience of characters (Guyon's swoon in Book 2 is one key example). It is precisely when deadening the senses and temporarily freezing the activity of the hero's "vital spirits," he suggests, that the poem's allegorical figuration turns to the invisible motions of embodied life and their role in promoting or dismantling virtue.[14]

Something similar is at work in the case of Scudamor's psychosomatic inflammation and symptomatic bout of insomnia. At the same time, its poetic rendering as a form of heightened sensorial captivation and furious activity among workers in the forge suggests that in Book 4 we are moving toward a greater concern with the social repercussions of virtue in its more public incarnations—and the notion that pursuing public virtue and heroism can overexert and exhaust the self.[15] That is not to say that Spenser's interest in the physiological foundation and vital processes of life does not continue in Book 4. Clearly it does, as in his initial description of Ate, whose nature is nothing but the drive to sever and unseat both private and public forms of integrity. Spenser connects this drive with the realms "below" that harbor "damned sprights":

> Her name was *Ate*, mother of debate,
> And all dissention, which doth dayly grow,
> Amongst fraile men, that many a publike state
> And many a private ofte doth overthrow.
> Her false *Duessa* who full well did know,
> To be most fit to trouble noble knights,
> Which hunt for honor, raised from below,
> Out of the dwellings of the damned sprights,
> Where she in darknes wastes her cursed daies & nights. (4.1.19)

"Dissention" is a term worth lingering upon, in that it implies a severing or separation that divides the root *sens* against itself. Ate's divisive power is a kind of negative virtue that topples mighty men and empires alike. Spenser seems to attribute her capacity to do so to her dark and obscure origins. In fact, I would suggest that Spenser's slightly imprecise diction intentionally conflates the "noble knights" who hunt for honor with Ate's origins "from below," suggesting that the "damned sprights" are those excitable animal spirits attributed in early modern moral psychology and medical science to the physiological life of that "rational animal" also known as the human.[16] The obscure depths of the human body and its interwoven physiological and spiritual processes were objects of great philosophical, theological, and scientific concern in Spenser's world, even if these vital spirits were also ultimately an invisible power that eluded the empirical senses. In the case of Spenser's "noble knights, / Which hunt for honor," the risk seems to be that they may unearth something invisible yet "damned" that lurks within their own psychosomatic beings. A further implication would be that Ate potentially dwells in the dark and personal depths of all humankind, waiting to be stirred from her slumber.

Whether or not Ate's influence over Scudamor begins before her official appearance in Canto 1, he keeps the fires of jealousy smoldering inside him over the course of Book 4, since the House of Care takes physical form as a blacksmith's forge in Canto 5. When Scudamor first approaches Care's ramshackle cottage with Glauce, the two hear hammering from inside that alerts them to the fact that "some blacksmith dwelt in that desert ground" (4.5.33). Spenser's figurations of Scudamor's care as a vital fire that animates his body, yet risks being hijacked and bellowed into full-blown wrath and fury, makes the blacksmith's forge and its master, Care, an ideal allegorical scene of personification. When Glauce and Scudamor step into Care's workshop, they

> found the goodman selfe,
> Full busily unto his worke ybent;
> Who was to weet a wretched wearish elfe,
> With hollow eyes and rawbone cheeks forspent,
> As if he had in prison long bene pent:
> Full blacke and griesely did his face appeare,
> Besmeared with smoke that nigh his eye-sight blent;
> With rugged beard, and hoarie shagged heare,
> The which he never wont to combe, or comely sheare. (4.5.34)

The immediate description of Care as a "goodman selfe," whose devotion to his work is so complete that Spenser figures it as an active bending, suggests that Scudamor's practice of self-care is likewise painfully strained, if not entirely bent off course. What ought to be a natural ethical orientation toward the good, one that flourishes with the proper care of his soul, has instead become a source of crippling and self-consuming consternation. Care's physical appearance marks the extent to which Scudamor's care is eating away at his vitality rather than preserving it. At the same time, the vaguely ascetic markers—Care looks as if he has been wasting away in a prison cell, "pent" up much like monks doing deep penance in isolation from the world—simultaneously indicate Scudamor's failed *askesis* and his undue devotion to the jealous "smart" that consumes him. The blacksmith Care has been fully dedicated to his work, as is evident from not only his unkempt hair and beard but also his soot-stained skin and compromised eyesight. These details also indicate that Care's diligent attention to his forge has, somewhat paradoxically, given rise to a form of carelessness and inattention to his own bodily life and physical appearance, just as Scudamor has imperiled his life by cultivating an unhealthy attachment to jealousy that stems from Ate's falsehood.

Scudamor's initial impression of Care soon gives way to a view of Care's six minions, "about the Andvile standing evermore, / With huge great hammers, that did never rest / From heaping stroakes, which theron soused sore" (4.5.36). John Steadman was the first to recognize that Spenser's image of these "six strong groomes" and their discordant hammering creatively reshapes the legend of Pythagoras's discovery of the science of harmony. According to the tale, Pythagoras serendipitously uncovered the secret while walking by a blacksmith's forge and hearing the harmonic resonance of differently sized hammers striking the anvils. "Transformed into a figure of discord," Steadman argues, "the Pythagorean forge becomes an image of Scudamor's alienation from Amoret and Britomart through Ate's slanders. It is a broken harmony, the emblem of a broken friendship."[17] That seems true enough, but I would also argue that the alienation depicted in this scene involves a form of personal discord as self-estrangement, which stems from Ate's nefarious influence on Scudamor's physical life and its vital processes as much as his social relations with others. For Spenser, these enterprises are intimately connected, and the life of the personal body both shapes and is shaped by its social situation and the forms of care demanded of it.[18] Care is both a burdensome obligation and a source of the world's sadness, but also a vital relation of benefit and support between living beings—one that they can turn back upon themselves by cultivating the psychosomatic powers and virtues that define them. This point is a familiarly stoic one found in writings by Seneca and Cicero, who assert respectively that the labors of care [*cura*] are what perfects the good in human life and that the "mental anguish . . . which often must be felt on a friend's account, has no more power to banish friendship from life than it has to cause us to reject

160 | SLEEP AND PERSONHOOD

virtue because virtue entails certain cares and annoyances [*curas et molestias*]."[19] Readers have long cited Cicero's essay on friendship as an important source for Spenser in Book 4, but they have not fully appreciated the ways that Spenser draws on and responds to Cicero—and indeed the broader tradition of the stoic ethics of care—by further emphasizing the need to care for the vital processes of life that are grounded in physical and finite embodiment, which he places in direct tension with traditional obligations of the ethical and spiritual care of souls.[20] Spenser's human is divided across forms of life and forms of care that split the self in its orientations toward the world and toward its own capacities as a living, sensing, and thinking being.

Appropriately, then, Scudamor first encounters his care as a personification in the figure of the blacksmith, which then splits into the six grooms who labor together under his watch, forming a scene of collective union-in-division. On the one hand, the sound of their hammers, "like belles in greatnesse orderly succeed[ing]," produces an effect of rising sonic amplification by way of an ordered progression (4.5.36.8). But the poet also remarks upon the fact that the grooms' order is disordered by the fact that they are all six strapping, "strong groomes, but one then other more; / For by degrees they all were disagreed" (4.5.36.5–6). The physical differences are visible in both their bodies and the size of the hammers they bear, as well as the discordant racket they make "from heaping strokes, which thereon soused sore" (4.5.36.4). Still, their laboring energies find unity in the overall effect of an amplification or excess that characterizes their work: "That he which was the last, the first did far exceede" (4.5.36.9).

But what exactly is that work? Based on the following stanza, it looks as if the excess produced by the laboring smiths serves only to inflate the status and appearance of their master himself. Care no longer appears as a "wretched wearish elfe" with sunken cheeks, but now "he like a monstrous Gyant seem'd in sight . . . So dreadfully did he the andvile beat, / That seem'd to dust he shortly would it drive: / So huge his hammer and so fierce his heat, / That seem'd a rocke of Diamond it could rive, / And rend a sunder quite, if he thereto list strive" (4.5.37.1, 5–9). Since we have already been told that the work of Care's forge is the production of "yron wedges" of "unquiet thoughts, that carefull minds invade" (4.5.35.8–9), Care's inflated being and his concomitant increase in the power to divide should be read as figurations of Scudamor's care, in its propensity to swell and increase simply by virtue of the belabored attention he bestows upon it. This is why Scudamor, upon stepping further into the cabin, finds himself immediately drawn into the visual spectacle of the work performed by Care's minions:

> Sir *Scudamor* there entring, much admired
> The manner of their worke and wearie paine;
> And having long beheld, at last enquired
> The cause and end thereof: but all in vaine;
> For they for nought would from their worke refraine,
> Ne let his speeches come unto their eare.
> And eke the breathfull bellowes blew amaine,
> Like to the Northern winde, that none could heare:
> Those *Pensifnesse* did move; and *Sighes* the bellows weare. (4.5.38.1–9)

Scudamor's care has been transfigured into an incessant work of "wearie paine" that is nonetheless entirely captivating. His vision of the laboring smiths elicits an admiration and curiosity that leads him to enquire the "cause and end" of their work, but the smiths remain silent, their attention fully consumed by the work they perform. Solely devoted to the singular task of hammering away at Care's anvils, the workers' heightened focus and productivity conduce solely to the generation of more care, thereby inflating their master in his very being.

At this point in my reading of the scene, a central connection with Marxist thought is no doubt apparent. Just as the capitalist extracts surplus value from the workers laboring under his watch and for the sake of his own profit, Care extracts an excess or surplus of care from the smiths that directly feeds his largeness. Spenser's depiction of a team of blacksmiths laboring under the watchful gaze of Care thus resonates with Marx's account of the thoroughgoing transformations of the worker's vital powers and capacities under the ruling power of capital. More precisely, the poet's allegorical figuration of Scudamor's care as a scene of nocturnal production imagines a surplus of care being garnished for the benefit of the master blacksmith, at the direct expense of Scudamor's vital capacity to restore his bodily life through sleep—a capacity personified by the disordered union of the laboring grooms, who work not for themselves but instead for the benefit of Care himself. Such a reading implies that both Scudamor and the workers of the forge, who present to him an allegorical rendering of his own vital

162 | SLEEP AND PERSONHOOD

powers in disarray, are working to produce an endless supply of care that only increases the power and allegorical being of their master.

Scudamor's inability to discover the "cause and end" to this diligent work of the blacksmiths also perfectly captures the futility of a heart and mind so obsessed with a particular affective burden—in this case, jealous care—that it enters a new zone of careless inattention to the world and its demands, including even the most basic of bodily needs. Hence, when he perceives that Care's workers will not heed his queries, Scudamor lays "his wearie limbs" upon the floor (4.5.39.3), hoping to restore his vital powers in sleep. Instead, he finds himself craving a release that will not come:

> There lay Sir *Scudamor* long while expecting,
> When gentle sleep his heavie eyes would close;
> Oft chaunging sides, and oft new place electing,
> Where better seem'd he mote himselfe repose;
> And oft in wrath he thence againe uprose;
> And oft in wrath he layd him downe againe,
> But wheresoever he did himselfe dispose
> He by no meanes could wished ease obtaine:
> So every place seem'd painefull, and ech changing vaine. (4.5.40.1–9)

Scudamor's psychosomatic inflammation persists and once again grows into a state of wrath. The visual and sonic stimulation provided by the spectacle of Care's workers looks at once to be the result of, and the driving force behind, his fury. Scudamor's insomnia is simultaneously the cause and effect of an enflamed care that involves both his bodily sensations and his psychic faculties. The discordant note first stuck by Ate has now escalated into a chorus of hammers whose "sound his senses did molest," while "the bellowes noyse disturb'd his quiet rest, / Ne suffred sleepe to settle in his brest" (4.5.41.4–5). Adding yet more fuel to the fire, the surrounding wildlife joins in the fun, as "dogs did barke and howle / About the house, at s[c]ent of stranger guest: / And now the crowing Cocke, and now the Owle / Lowde shriking him afflicted to the very sowle" (4.5.41.6–9). Scudamor's sensorial agitation seizes and tortures that part of the soul that he shares with animal life, a point that Spenser slyly underscores by making Scudamor's environmental surroundings teem with animal activity that mirrors the endless productions of Care's forge. Care forces Scudamor's "animal virtues" to appear and captivate his soul in a nefarious form, in turn blocking him from actualizing the nutritive, plantlike virtue of restoration in sleep that he desperately needs.

The excessive and self-erasing nature of Scuadmor's care is further indicated by its figuration as the ongoing "smart" of his wounded heart, a pain that continues even beyond the scene of hammering and focused production by Care's team of blacksmiths. Care, the "wicked carle the maister Smith," sneakily nips Scudamor's flesh with a "paire of redwhot yron tongs" just as he finally manages to fall asleep despite the racket of the workshop (4.5.44.2). But when the hero looks for the source of this aggravation, Care is nowhere to be found: "Yet looking round about him none could see; / Yet did the smart remaine, though he himselfe did flee" (4.5.44.9). Certainly, Care flees the scene, but Spenser's ambivalent pronouns also leave us with the feeling that this painful "smart" is so all-consuming that it causes Sir Scudamor's own sense of self to vanish as well. Spenser has already conceived the effects of this smarting wound as an erasure of the human self, which becomes clear when we read the painful smart of Canto 5 in light of the smart that Scudamor experiences in the first canto, when he hears Ate's slanders against Amoret and Britomart. There, the hero's heart is pierced "with inward griefe, as when in chace / The Parthian strikes a stag with shivering dart, / The beast astonisht stands in middest of his smart" (4.1.49.7–9). The wound that Scudamor experiences in the earlier passage not only arrests his senses and leaves him in a state of shock; it also achieves these ends through a kind of animalization of his being that emphasizes his susceptibility to forces not entirely human but that nevertheless animate him. The "smart" in both cantos 1 and 5 conveys a vital, animal power that undoes the fundamental ground of Scudamor's sense of self and makes the sensation of suffering into a new basis of his ontological bearing. And it is precisely because Scudamor's life takes this form in the House of Care that the master smith and his minions are able to extract from it a surplus that feeds them in their productive efforts and allegorical beings alike—all at the expense of Scudamor's ability to restore his bodily life through its immanent virtue of self-recovery.

As the vital benefit of sleep eludes the jealousy-stricken Scudamor, the poem reveals that the hero's amplification of a misguided notion of care is both a refusal to care for his own physical life and an ethical failure, only exacerbating the fact that he has made a mess of his spiritual and ethical duties by falling prey to Ate's slanders. In this way Scudamor's life, like the lives of many Spenserian heroes, is unavoidably split between the physical and spiritual demands of care. Indeed, the wedge of care's most fundamental division may be the division between forms of life that pertain in the early modern world to political theology and *physis*, exposing a form of life that is merely living and yet capable of becoming an object of care. As ethical value in Spenser's world is beginning, ever so slowly, to separate itself from an exclusive attachment to the Christian theology of virtue, a new kind of value emerges, one that pertains to the core physical life and vitality of the body.[21] The poet's interest in insomnia and his depiction of it as a threat to the vital powers of the body thus point to the material, unconscious processes of life and their centrality to the well-being of the laboring human. These ideas make Spenser's epic poem an important site of discovery for the early modern world's mounting fascination with the vital power of living beings, and their approaching future as objects of scientific and political economic concern. Sir Scudamor's strife in the House of Care is thus a prescient figure for the biopolitical struggles around life and labor that will come to define our world, in its many vacillations between carelessness and care.

NOTES

1. Harry Berger Jr., *The Allegorical Temper* (New Haven: Yale University Press, 1957); Deborah Shuger, "'Gums of Glutinous Heat' and the Stream of Consciousness: The Theology of Milton's Maske," *Representations* 60 (1997): 1–21; William A. Oram, "Spenserian Paralysis," *Studies in English Literature, 1500–1900* 41, no. 1 (2001): 49–70; Garrett Sullivan Jr., *Sleep, Romance, and Human Embodiment: Vitality From Spenser to Milton* (Cambridge: Cambridge University Press, 2012), 29–46; Giulio Pertile, "'And all his senses stound': The Physiology of Stupefaction in Spenser's *Faerie Queene*," *English Literary Renaissance* 44, no. 3 (2014): 420–51; Russ Leo, "Medievalism Without Nostalgia: Guyon's Swoon and the English Reformation *Descensus ad Inferos*," *Spenser Studies* 39 (2014): 105–47.

2. This is how Oram reads the Cave of Morpheus in Book 1 ("Spenserian Paralysis," 55). See also Benjamin Parris, "'Watching to banish Care': Sleep and

Insomnia in Book 1 of *The Faerie Queene*," *Modern Philology* 113, no. 2 (2015): 151–53, on "deadly sleep," and Berger, *Allegorical Temper*, 23–25, on perversion of "raw materials of life" in Mammon's Cave.

3. Julia Reinhard Lupton, "Animal Husbands," in *Thinking with Shakespeare: Essays on Politics and Life* (Chicago: University of Chicago Press, 2011), 25–67. For more on *The Taming of the Shrew*, sleep, and husbandry, see Timothy Turner's essay in this volume.

4. See Sullivan, *Sleep, Romance, and Human Embodiment*, 24–25; Pertile, "'And all his senses stound,'" 420–51; Parris, "'Watching to banish Care,'" 151–77.

5. See Aristotle's claim in *De anima* 2.4 (trans. J. A. Smith [Oxford: Clarendon, 1931], 416b 14–20) that the nutritive virtue of the soul preserves its possessor, or his claim in *Nicomachean Ethics* 1.13 (trans. Sarah Broadie and Christopher Rowe [Oxford: Oxford University Press,

2002], 1102b5) that the human soul's nutritive virtue is most visible during sleep.

6. For another reading of biopower in early modern drama, see Tim Turner's essay in this volume.

7. Karl Marx, *Capital* (New York: Penguin Classics, 1990), 340–42, 375–76. Subsequent references to this edition will be made parenthetically.

8. On Labor and Life as two of the three "knowledge-transcendentals" that shore up the modern episteme, making possible the consolidation of the life sciences and political economy, see Michel Foucault, *The Order of Things: An Archaeology of the Human Sciences* (New York: Random House, 1970).

9. For an ingenious reading of Marx's *Capital* as a text subtly modeled on Dante's *Inferno*, with Marx playing the role of Virgil's ghost to the proletariat, see William Clare Roberts, *Marx's Inferno: The Political Theory of "Capital"* (Princeton: Princeton University Press, 2016).

10. Georges Canguilhem, "The Normal and the Pathological," in *A Vital Rationalist: Selected Writings from Georges Canguilhem*, ed. Francois Delaporte (New York: Zone Books, 1994), 177.

11. Michel Foucault, *The History of Sexuality*, vol. 1, *An Introduction* (New York: Vintage Books, 1990), 141.

12. Edmund Spenser, *The Faerie Queene*, ed. Thomas P. Roche (New York: Penguin Classics, 1987), 3.12.46a. Subsequent references in this chapter to this edition will be made parenthetically.

13. Oram, "Spenserian Paralysis," 57.

14. See Pertile, "'And all his senses stound,'" especially 428–30.

15. For the claim that we are moving into slightly more secular concerns in the later books, see Oram, "Spenserian Paralysis," 56.

16. As Richard Sugg describes the pervasive "spiritual physiology" of the early modern period, "Spirits could move back and forth with surprising ease between the material and the immaterial, the mental and the physical sides of human life" (*The Smoke of the Soul: Medicine, Physiology and Religion in Early Modern England* [New York: Palgrave Macmillan, 2013], 47).

17. John M. Steadman, "The 'Inharmonious Blacksmith': Spenser and the Pythagoras Legend," *Publications of the Modern Language Association* 79, no. 5 (1964): 664–65, quotation on 665.

18. For an account of Spenser's legend of Friendship that emphasizes a dialectic between boundaries erected through disciplined self-control and a selfhood defined by its open vulnerability to the social, see James Kuzner, *Open Subjects: English Renaissance Republicans, Modern Selfhoods and the Virtue of Vulnerability* (Edinburgh: Edinburgh University Press, 2012), 39–83.

19. Seneca claims that rational care perfects the human good in letter 124.11–15. See *Letters on Ethics*, trans. Margaret Long and A. A. Graver (Chicago: University of Chicago Press, 2015), 499–500. The Cicero quotation is from *Cicero: On Old Age; On Friendship; On Divination*, trans. W. A. Falconer, Loeb Classical Library 154 (Cambridge, Mass.: Harvard University Press, 1923), 159–61.

20. Redcrosse Knight's struggles with sleep and insomnia across Book 1, for instance, underscore sleep's power to replenish and care for his bodily life, while also temporarily annulling the relations of care to which he is obligated in his concern for Una and his allegorical duties as an emblem of holiness. See Parris, "'Watching to banish Care,'" 151–77.

21. Jeff Dolven makes a similar point regarding care and physical life in *The Faerie Queene*. See the conclusion of his essay "Besides Good and Evil," *Studies in English Literature, 1500–1900* 57, no. 1 (Winter 2017): 1–22.

CHAPTER 8

"Sweet Moistning Sleepe"

*Perturbations of the Mind and Rest for the Body
in Robert Burton's* Anatomy of Melancholy

CASSIE M. MIURA

In the *Anatomy of Melancholy*, an expansive three-part work that dissects one of the most fashionable and widespread afflictions of the early modern period, Robert Burton devotes ample space to the subject of sleep. This discourse is recursive in nature and emerges especially in subsections dedicated to the imagination, perturbations of mind, and fearful dreams. Observing that "waking overmuch, is both a symptome and an ordinary cause" of melancholy, Burton surveys a variety of methods for procuring sleep and reports on extraordinary cases such as Hercules de Saxoniâ's mother, who "slept not for seaven months together," or another individual whom, Trincavellius claims, "waked 50 dayes" (1.246, 1.383).[1] As one of the six Galenic nonnaturals, sleep enables Burton to interrogate the limitations of prevailing medical epistemologies of the period and to blend the medical treatise with emerging prose genres such as the skeptical essay.[2] Given its association with fantasy, diabolical encounters, and unknown states such as death, I argue that sleep reveals Burton's reluctance to prescribe medicinal remedies and informs his larger critique of spiritual enthusiasm. While Sasha Handley has made a compelling case for the intersection of the history of sleep and spiritual hygiene during the latter part of the seventeenth century, the *Anatomy*, first printed in 1621, adopts a strikingly secular approach to the subject.[3] Burton never questions the existence of God or the devil, but he is careful to frame his approach to sleep as an inquiry into natural rather than supernatural causes. Since Burton ultimately posits a tranquil mind as the requisite for a good night's sleep, we can observe that, in many respects, the *Anatomy* shares a greater affinity with the philosophical essay, especially in the style of Seneca or Montaigne, than with the early modern medical or theological treatise. Indeed, the frequently satirical mode and skeptical outlook of the *Anatomy*, as well as Burton's parodic use of authorities, suggest that neither the sleeping body nor the unconscious mind can be rationally dissected through the subgenre of the anatomy. In place of rigid prescriptions, Burton instead offers the sleepless and melancholy reader commonsense advice to dispel perturbations of mind and procure rest for the body.

Most medical texts of the period treat melancholia as an innate disposition or biologically determined state—but the six Galenic nonnaturals account for those factors that are subject to change and therefore within an individual's control. This ability, however limited, to alter one's humoral balance lends more agency to the embodied early modern subject than new historicist scholarship in recent years has traditionally allowed. With such practical adjustments in mind, Burton focuses on some of the most rudimentary and material conditions that might affect sleep, such as one's bedtime and sleeping position, the need for clean sheets and quiet, as well as the benefits of relaxing music or pleasant reading in the evening (2.97). When he moves to medicinal remedies, however, Burton's material is as copious as it is contradictory, ranging from popular remedies such as nutmeg, vinegar, or poppy to more obscure recommendations to "annoint the face with Hare's blood" or "use horseleeches behinde the eares" (2.258, 2.256). Rather than offering practical advice that readers might implement in their own lives, Burton here highlights the diversity of opinions pertaining to sleep, framing sleep hygiene as a culturally and historically contingent set of customs. The few recipes that he does provide in the subsection on "Correctors of Accidents to procure Sleepe. Against fearefull Dreames, Rednesse &c" serve as a form of ethnographic survey. Concerning opium as a remedy for sleeplessness, for example, Burton notes that "the Turkes [use] the same quantity for a cordiall, and at *Goa* in the *Indies*, the *dose* 40 or 50 graines" (2.256). Instead of focusing on scientifically "objective" or "universal" characteristics, Burton uses the problem of sleeplessness as an invitation to imagine non-Western prescriptions and alternative courses of treatment.

While Burton's treatment of sleep highlights the delicate relationship between the humoral body and its surrounding environment, he also emphasizes the mutually dependent relationship between the body and the soul. Since, for example, nightmares and other perturbations of mind often disrupt sleep, Burton offers an extended discussion of fantasy and philosophical tranquility as part of his remedy for waking overmuch. Sleep, much more than other Galenic nonnaturals such as diet or exercise, forces Burton to extend his inquiry well beyond the traditional parameters of medical discourse in order to account for both the physical and the metaphysical dimensions of a liminal state. In many ways privileging moral and philosophical modes of therapy above medicinal remedies, Burton's treatment of sleep challenges conventional understandings of the early modern medical treatise and offers new ways of understanding the *Anatomy* as an exemplar of seventeenth-century prose.

1

Two unexpected attitudes toward sleep emerge in the first partition of the *Anatomy* that both underscore epistemological uncertainty and highlight the apparent limitations of the medical treatise as Burton's chosen form. The first is the idea that humoral balance may, in some cases, be restored through excess and indulgence rather than through moderation or restraint. The second is that conceptual distinctions between cause, symptom, and cure are radically unstable in the humoral body.[4] Burton writes, "Nothing better than moderate sleepe, nothing worse then it, if it be in extreames or unseasonably used. It is a receaved opinion, that a melancholy man cannot sleepe overmuch; *Somnus supra modum prodest* [extra sleep is beneficial], as an only Antidote, and nothing offends them more, or causeth this malady sooner, then waking, yet in some cases Sleep may do more harme than good" (1.245). While melancholy individuals may require more sleep than others, too much sleep can exacerbate their condition by increasing the likelihood of nightmares and other disruptive sleep phenomena. Here, Burton complicates the viability of prescribing a specific nighttime regimen because he regards sleep as both a common cause and cure of melancholy.

Burton's inability to determine, even from a physiological perspective, whether sleep ultimately benefits the body is especially evident in his delightful comparisons of melancholy individuals to dormice. The dormouse, a particular species of rodent, takes its name from the Latin word *dormire*, meaning "to sleep," because it hibernates during the long and cold winter. Despite the diminutive appeal of this sleepy creature, Burton first uses it to disparage melancholics who sleep too much. He argues that sleep "dulls the Spirits, if overmuch, and senses; fills the head full of grosse humours; causeth distillations, rheums, great store of excrements in the braine, and all the other parts, as *Fuchsius* speaks of them, that sleepe like so many Dormice" (1.246). Here, Burton suggests that humans and animals share enough biology in common to warrant such a comparison, but he nevertheless cautions readers from sleeping excessively lest their brains and bodies become too sedentary.

When he returns to this same comparison in a later section, however, Burton takes an entirely different tack, this time offering the dormouse as a model to be emulated and going even so far as to extoll the virtues of sloth. He writes, "As Waking that hurts, by all means must bee avoided, so sleepe, which so much helps, by like waies, *must be procured, by nature or art, inward or outward medicines, and be protracted longer than ordinary, if it may be, as being an especiall helpe.* It moistens and fattens the body, concocts, and helps digestion (as we see in Dormice, and those *Alpine* Mice that sleepe all winter), which *Gesner* speaks of, when they are so found sleeping under the snow in the dead of Winter, as fat as butter" (2.96). These two representations of the dormouse reveal contrasting attitudes toward sleep that coexist during the early modern period. While sleeping too much may make the body more susceptible to illness, sleeping "longer than ordinary" is necessary to counterbalance the extreme dryness caused by melancholy humors. For an individual whose humoral disposition approaches equilibrium, moderation in all nonnatural things helps to maintain the body in an already healthy state. For a melancholy individual, however, Burton suggests that excess should be met with excess. The dormouse is not just fat, it is "fat as butter" and, in a later section, Burton even relays advice "*to annoint the soles of the feet with the fat of a dormouse*" in order to procure sleep (2.256). Sleep not only regulates the temperatures of the body but also moistens the brain, which easily becomes dry because of adust humors or waking overmuch. Common moral associations of sleep with gluttony or sloth are here transformed into a practical remedy.

Burton's insistence on the material and physiological conditions of sleep becomes all the more important once he turns to address the supernatural phenomena that are often the subject, if not the cause, of bad dreams. In order "to procure this sweet moistning sleepe," we learn that different medical authorities have argued that one should go to bed two to three hours after supper and rest for seven to eight hours (2.97). Similarly, one should begin sleeping on the right side in order to aid digestion and then switch to the left side between the first and second sleep (2.96). Burton also includes recommendations to "lie in cleane linnen," to listen to "*sweet Musicke*" or the sound of "*lene sonantis aquae* [gently trickling water]," and "*to read some pleasant Author till he be asleepe*" (2.97). If it becomes "usual to toss and tumble, and not sleep," he adds that "Ranzovius would have them if it be in warme weather, to rise and walke three or four turnes (till they be cold) about the chamber, and then goe to bed againe" (2.98). The only advice that Burton himself adds to this collection of conventional wisdom is the comment, "I say, a nutmeg and ale, or a good drought of muscadine, with a tost and nutmeg or a posset of the same, which many use in a morning, but, mee thinkes, for such as have dry braines, are much more proper at night" (2.98). (Despite here offering only commonsense advice, Burton still feels compelled to cite Ranzovius along with Jobertus, Ficinus, Bernardinus Tilesius, Piso, Andrew Borde, and Rhasis, among other authorities.) Even today, nutmeg and alcohol are popular home remedies for insomnia—but Burton's attention to natural means of procuring sleep is worthy of note, since we are far less likely to attribute waking overmuch to supernatural phenomena.

Throughout the *Anatomy*, Burton insists that no matter how diverse the symptoms of waking overmuch may be, "the ordinary causes are heat and drinesse" (2.97). While this assumption provides a natural explanation for why "moistning sleepe" is essential for the humoral body, and for the melancholy body in particular, it in no way simplifies the diagnostic process or prescribed courses of treatment for insomnia. In his section on "Waking and Terrible Dreams Rectified," Burton argues that while nightmares, *incubus*, and troublesome dreams may be caused by the consumption of, for example, venison and other meats that are difficult to digest, they may just as easily be caused by an overactive imagination or a troubled conscience. "All violent perturbations of mind," he suggests, "must in some sort be qualified, before we can hope for any good repose" (2.97). By shifting his focus from the body to the mind, Burton limits the scope of medicinal remedies while at the same time broadening the scope of his discourse on sleep. It is important that his sections on fantasy and perturbations of mind share more in common with ancient and early modern works of philosophy than medicine.[5] When Burton writes that sleep "expells cares" and "pacifies the minde," he participates in a long-standing tradition devoted to the management of the emotions or passions (2.96). Seneca, for example, positions a tranquil sleep as the hard-won product of moral philosophy. In *On Anger*, he exclaims, "And how delightful the sleep that follows this self-examination— how tranquil, how deep and untroubled."[6] In the *Anatomy*, too, a peaceful sleep becomes indicative of a quiet or tranquil soul. In these ways, Burton effectively shifts the focus of his investigation into sleep away from objective truths about the Galenic body and toward subjective experiences governed by the mind.

2

In her recent study of sleep in early modern England, Sasha Handley describes the "persistent vitality of supernatural encounters in sleep and dream reports" to argue that a genuine fear of "diabolical attack" gave rise to a whole series of discreet practices that she refers to as "sleep-piety."[7] Although Handley focuses on the period after 1660, when attitudes toward the physiology of sleep changed in response to new scientific research on the nervous system, her focus on the religious dimensions of sleep makes Burton's earlier and more secular approach to sleep all the more striking. Burton affirms that divine grace is necessary for regulating the humoral body and even compares melancholy to original sin by making it a defining part of the postlapsarian condition of mankind. Still, Burton does not lend credence to the many reports of witches or demons that disrupt sleep (1.122). When he addresses nightmares, which are a common complaint of melancholy individuals, Burton consistently interprets reports about supernatural encounters as the product of human fantasy.

Since Burton often buries his own opinion beneath the diverse authorities whom he cites, sometimes without attribution, readers of the *Anatomy* take notice when his counsel does emerge. For example, when Burton writes of melancholics that "a better meanes in my judgement cannot be taken, then to shew them the causes whence they proceed, not from Divels, as they suppose, or that they are bewitched or forsaken of God, heare or see,

&c. as many of them thinke, but from naturall and inward causes," he specifically aims to supplant fear of what Handley calls "diabolical attack" with knowledge of the body and its natural processes (1.418). Since early modern thinkers believed that the faculties of reason are more easily impaired during sleep, Burton argues that it is necessary to understand how the imagination may contribute to phenomena such as nightmares and night walking. Limiting the devil's power to interfere with sleep reflects Burton's larger argument that those who suffer from melancholy are more susceptible to bouts of religious enthusiasm characterized by extreme fear of death and eternal damnation, not because they are further from God or less deserving of his grace but because they have given full rein to fantasy. Considering Burton's self-identification and professional appointment as a Divine, his shift toward a more secular approach to sleep is unexpected, but it prefigures his larger critique of the increasingly sectarian English Calvinist tradition in the final partition of the *Anatomy* which is devoted to religious melancholy.

When Burton does invoke the devil or other supernatural forces in his discourse on sleep, he often adopts a metaphorical interpretation of the body's primary functions. He writes of melancholy men, for example, that for the "most part it is in the braine that deceives them, although I may not deny, but oftentimes the divell deludes them, takes his opportunity to suggest, and represent vaine objects to melancholy men, and such as are ill affected" (1.426). While Burton's careful caveat may seem to deflect charges of atheism by affirming the existence of the devil, who does not cause melancholy symptoms but may use such natural infirmities to his advantage, Burton's statement only compounds his forceful dismissal of "knavish Impostures of Juglers, Exorcists, Masse Priests, and Mountebankes" (1.426). Rather than attributing the miracles and wondrous feats performed by such men to divine inspiration, Burton foregrounds their susceptibility to delusion as a leading symptom of melancholy madness. Although Burton does not discount the supernatural altogether, he insists that the effects of melancholy can be understood and fully explained in terms of natural physiological processes. "I should rather hold with *Avicenna* and his associats," Burton writes, "that such symptomes proceede from evil spirits, which take all opportunities of humors decayed, or otherwise to pervert the soule of man; and besides the humour it selfe, is *Balneum Diaboli*, the Divells bath, and as *Agrippa* proves, doth intice him to seize upon them" (1.428). Here, the blackness of melancholy may very well suggest the influence of the devil or other evil spirits, but these forces only prey on humors that have already decayed. They should not and cannot be regarded as a true cause of melancholy or attendant nighttime disturbances.

At night, when melancholics report an increase in "diabolical attacks," Burton does not offer them prayers or bedtime rituals that might ward off evil spirits; instead, he offers them an extended digression titled "On the Force of the Imagination." Here, Burton explores how the melancholy imagination, despite its origin in the mind, can directly impact the body. Arguing that distemperature and contaminated organs may especially harm the imagination, Burton suggests that

> this we see verified in sleepers, which by reason of humours and course of vapours troubling the *Phantasy*, imagine many times absurd and prodigious things, and in such as are troubled with *Incubus*, or Witch ridden (as we call it); they lie on their backs, they suppose an old woman rides & sits so hard upon them, that they are almost stifled for want of breath; when there is nothing offends but a concourse of bad humours, which trouble the *Phantasy*. This is likewise evident in such as walke in the night in their sleepe and doe strange feats. (1.250)

Apart from Burton's counsel that sleepers lie on their right side first, then on their left side, sometimes on their belly but never on their back, readers get very little medical advice for dealing with nightmares and night walking. Of all the Galenic nonnaturals, sleeping and waking overlap most with the nonnatural that both classical and early modern thinkers refer to as perturbations of mind. In his digression on the imagination, Burton suggests that inordinate fear causes the nightmares that regularly disrupt the sleep of melancholy men and women, and we later learn that perturbations of mind result similarly from excessive or unruly emotions. Since Burton's discourse on sleep and his discourse on perturbations of mind similarly posit emotion as a primary source of both physical and mental distress, it makes sense that his treatment of the former would flow seamlessly into his treatment of the latter.

For Burton, it is not supernatural phenomena that disrupt sleep but the melancholy imagination of such phenomena. Nevertheless, he argues in "Of the Force of the Imagination" that apparitions of the mind may still produce very real effects on the body. When Burton wonders, for example,

"What will not a fearfull man conceave in the darke; what strange forms of Bugbeares, Divels, Witches, Goblins," he concludes that "most especially in passions and affections, it shewes strange and evident effects" (1.251). As proof that fantasy directly impacts the body, Burton cites examples of expectant mothers who imprint images upon their unborn children, men who have been turned into wolves or women because of the force of their imagination, and diseases such as sciatica or the plague contracted through conceit alone. Without wholly discounting contemporary reports, literary accounts, or historical records of such marvelous phenomena, Burton foregrounds fantasy and imagination as a way to circumvent questions of "diabolical attack." In so doing, he must tread carefully, because the lines drawn between medicine, religion, and philosophy may challenge dominant cultural and institutional norms.

Although shorter in length, Burton's "Of the Force of the Imagination" shares much in common with an essay by the same name, *De la force de l'imagination*, which the French writer Michel de Montaigne composed in the 1570s. While scholars have been somewhat reluctant to posit Montaigne as a direct source of influence for Burton, preferring instead to look at medical texts by earlier English and Continental writers such as Timothy Bright and André du Laurens, this comparison enables us to think differently about the generic designation of Burton's work.[8] Since the quality and duration of sleep may be affected by so many different factors, and since sleep gives fuller range to the imagination, Burton uses the subject of sleep to develop a skeptical stance toward superstition, one that becomes clearer with Montaigne as a precursor. Burton's familiarity with the *Essais* and willingness to identify with Montaigne's authorial voice is clear when he claims, "If I make nothing, as Montaigne said in like case, I will marre nothing; 'tis not my doctrine but my study, I hope I shall doe no body wrong to speake what I thinke, and deserve not blame in imparting my minde" (2.126). In their respective works, both Montaigne and Burton ascribe so much power to the imagination or fantasy that any attempts to treat the body without equal attention to the mind are rendered ineffectual. For Burton, the skeptical form of the essay complements both the indeterminate nature of sleep as an object of study and the desire to undermine dogmatic forms of religious and medical knowledge.

In the case of nightmares, which require that one expel the fear of whatever devil or hobgoblin threatens to disrupt sleep, Burton posits fantasy as both a cause and a potent cure for waking overmuch. Much like his previous suggestion that excessive bouts of sleep may benefit the melancholy individual more than temperance or moderation, Burton's willingness to entertain hypochondriacal concerns and even prescribe placebo treatments to soothe them flies in the face of conventional practices and suggests the precarious nature of human reason, especially in liminal stages of consciousness. While Montaigne does not foreground the problem of sleep to the same degree as Burton, *De la force de l'imagination* similarly limits the scope of human reason and blunts the explanatory force of rational discourses that do not account for the power of fantasy. In this essay, Montaigne offers an extended account of a friend who hears a story of "extraordinary impotence" and "finding himself in a similar situation, was all at once so struck in his imagination by the horror of this story that he incurred the same fate" (1.84).[9] While sexual dysfunction may have a larger psychological component than other forms of physical distress, Burton recounts a variety of cases where other diseases were supposedly contracted through conceit alone. He writes, for example, that "if by some South-sayer, wise-man, fortune-teller, or Physitian, they be told they shall have such a Disease, they will so seriously apprehend it, that they will instantly labour of it" (Burton 1.252–53). Accounts of this kind discount the authority of the medical tradition, in part, by equating doctors with charlatans, but they also help to clarify the role of the imagination in prescribed courses of treatment.

By incorporating essayistic accounts of medical scenarios where imagined causes have given rise to real effects, Burton and Montaigne both use the prose anecdote to test provisional claims about how false cures might be used in an ethical and efficacious manner. From a medical perspective, fantasy completely transforms conventional ideas about contagion and the communicability of disease, since it lends great weight to an individual's perception and experience of a given phenomenon. Burton recounts the story of man who "coming by chance in company of him that was thought to be sick of the Plague (which was not so) fell downe suddainly dead" (1.253). Montaigne, surveying some of the same medical literature, confesses, "I catch the disease that I study and lodge it in me. I do not find it strange that imagination brings fevers and death to those who give it a free hand and encourage it" (Montaigne 1.82). If fantasy, which is especially active during sleep, can have such dangerous and material effects on the body, one logical objective might be to exert greater control over the mind and to cultivate awareness of how easily we are deceived. Neither Burton nor Montaigne, however, adopts this approach. Instead, they recommend the use of imaginary cures to treat imaginary causes. This insight provides a useful lens through which to understand the intersection of superstition and sleep hygiene practices as they develop later in the period.

Burton and Montaigne both demonstrate that while fantasy can cause perfectly healthy individuals to become sick, it can also cause sick individuals to become healthy. This latter capacity opens new possibilities for treatment, which doctors should use to the fullest advantage. On the subject of impotence, Montaigne describes another friend whom he "cured" with the use of a charm described as "a little piece of gold on which were engraved some celestial figures" (1.85). Since the friend had become worried that he would prove unable to consummate his marriage, Montaigne assures him of the efficacy of a very elaborate ritual involving the medal. On his wedding night, Montaigne's friend was to "say certain prayers three times and go through certain motions; each of these three times he should tie the ribbon I was putting in his hand around him and very carefully lay the medal that was attached to it on his kidneys" (1.85). Although Montaigne claims to hate the dissimulation involved in "these monkey tricks," they nevertheless constitute a proven cure (1.86). The base and sexual nature of Montaigne's subject here serves to mask some of the more controversial implications of the attitude that he adopts toward ritual prayer. It follows that if a particular religious rite engages the imagination enough to produce real effects in the practitioner, then the truth claims of the ritual itself are irrelevant.

Since Burton situates his digression on the imagination within the larger context of his treatment of sleep and perturbations of mind, the implicit comparison between pseudoscience and what Handley calls "sleep piety" is much more pointed. Much like Montaigne, who claims that his friend "found some remedy from this fancy by another fancy," Burton argues that "as some are molested by Phantasie; so some againe by Fancy alone, and a good conceit, are as easily recovered" (Montaigne 1.84, Burton 1.253). Considering the efficacy of imaginary cures, especially for those symptoms that might otherwise be interpreted as evidence of diabolical attack, leads Burton also to question the conventional role of certain types of medical practitioners. He comments that "an Empirick oftentimes, and a silly Chirurgian, doth more strange cures then a rationall Physitian" (1.254). As a competing school of ancient medicine, Empiric physicians and philosophers such as

178 | SLEEP AND PERSONHOOD

Sextus Empiricus were often derided by Galen and his followers since they based their practice on experience rather than theoretical knowledge. In some cases, this extreme distrust of dogmatic medical principles gave rise to practices that seem absurd, but it also allowed for greater recognition that the mind and body do not always respond best to reason. As evidence of how one might use fantasy to treat a patient in distress, Montaigne recounts the story of a woman who believed that she had swallowed a pin. He says that "a smart man, judging that it was only fancy and notion derived from some bit of bread that had scratched her as it went down, made her vomit, and, on the sly, tossed a crooked pin into what she threw up" (Montaigne 1.89). Burton claims similarly that "wee see commonly the Tooth-ache, Gout, Falling-sicknesse, biting of a mad Dog, and many such maladies cured by Spells, Word, Characters, and Charmes" (Burton 1.253–54). Burton is no Empiric, but he does acknowledge much more than most that fantasy alters the humoral body and offers natural explanations for (theoretically) super-natural phenomena.

From an epistemological perspective, Burton's apparent lack of concern for scientific legitimacy is alarming, but his argument about fantasy reveals the limitations of reason within a larger medical context and underscores the *Anatomy* as a skeptical form of prose. Referencing the 1621 edition of Sextus Empiricus's *Outlines of Pyrrhonisim*, Angus Gowland argues that in order to understand "the value of skepticism for physicians," we must also under-stand that in the *Anatomy* "the message delivered by the tension between the content of the knowledge concerning disease and the skeptical method of its presentation was that it would only be through an apprehension of its limits, and recognition of its errors, that medicine could be properly adminis-tered."[10] When Burton writes, "'Tis opinion alone (saith Cardan) that makes, or marres Physitians, and hee doth the best cures, according to *Hippocrates*, in whom most trust. So diversely doth this phantasie of ours affect, turne and winde, so imperiously command our bodies," he suggests that opinion is more important in successfully administering a medical treatment than the efficacy of the treatment itself (1.254). This skeptical critique of medi-cine finds a more pointed expression in Montaigne's question, "Why do the doctors work on the credulity of their patient beforehand with so many false promises of a cure, if not so that the effect of the imagination may make up for the imposture of their decoctions?" (Montaigne 1.88–89). Here, Mon-taigne suggests that medicine, as both a practical and theoretical discourse, is no more sound than the knowledge of sorcerers and mountebanks. As playful as it is provocative, this skeptical position is even more surprising in the *Anatomy*, which is styled as a formal medical treatise and comprises separate partitions devoted to dissecting the many causes and cures of melancholy with scientific and analytical precision.[11]

During the night, when sleep impairs both the movement of the body and the rational faculties of the mind, some early moderns believed that they were more susceptible to diabolical attack. While there are many possible responses to such attacks, Burton's understanding of fantasy allows for a wide array of viable treatments. Examining how sleep practices and bedtime rituals changed in response to fears of diabolical attack, Sasha Handley argues that the bed chamber itself began to take on a new spiritual significance during the latter half of the seventeenth century. She describes, as an example, the documented use of coral to protect sleeping children from evil spirits. Commenting on a scene from Ben Jonson's 1609 *Masque of Queens*, in which a witch attempts to steal the breath from sleeping children, Handley writes that "placing protective charms and objects in and around cradles at night appears to have been common practice within many households and this may well have helped to ease fears of destruction during the night."[12] As in the case of most witch-related customs, the evidence that such charms were effective is difficult to produce, but the fear that they reflect is easily documented. Handley specifies that "the power of these objects was thought to be especially strong when they were made of coral," and she then cites examples of coral amulets with which children were adorned, coral teething sticks, and coral rattles.[13] Given Burton's position on the power of fantasy, he need not affirm the healing or protective properties of coral in order to affirm its capacity to allay fears of witches in the night.

In a section called "Pretious Stones, Metals, Minerals, Alterative," Burton considers coral alongside many other natural materials and voices his own skepticism with a quotation from the Swiss physician Thomas Erastus, who claims, "That stones can worke any wonders, let them beleeve that list, no man shall perswade me, for my part I have found by experience there is no vertue in them" (2.219). Regardless of Burton's actual beliefs about coral, we can envision him, much like Montaigne, offering a coral amulet or a coral toy to the anxious parents of a young child so that their own sleep might be sounder. When Burton exclaims in his digression on the imagination that "all the world knows there is no vertue in such Charmes, or Cures, but a strong conceit and opinion alone," he dethrones reason as the primary faculty of the mind (1.254). In many ways, the state of sleep demonstrates just how much of our mental life is governed by opinion rather than knowledge. The humoral body, to the extent that it may be swayed by fantasy, responds only in part to the rational will.

For melancholics, the same propensity to imagine dark and terrifying things at night extends also into the waking hours. Burton claims, for example, that "in time of sleepe this faculty is free, & many times conceaves strange, stupend, absurd shapes, as in sicke men we commonly observe" (1.152). By establishing the pervasive influence of fantasy on the melancholy individual's nighttime encounters with the devil and other supernatural phenomena, Burton lays the groundwork for a more broad-ranging critique of the multiplying Protestant sects who were injecting new forms of religious enthusiasm into the devotional culture of seventeenth-century England. In her work on early modern dreams, Janine Rivière argues, "While the idea of religious madness was not necessarily new, Burton's appropriation of humoral medicine to explain the physiological and psychological causes of 'religious enthusiasm' was a powerful explanatory tool that appealed to writers seeking to undermine the spread of sectarianism and prophetic visions."[14] By shifting the focus of treatment for the various sleep disorders that melancholics regularly encounter from spiritual warfare to emotional management, not fear of the devil but fear itself, Burton creates a new space for therapeutic techniques derived from classical philosophy. While these ancient techniques are mostly secular, Burton explores their application within an early modern devotional context and aims to make them complementary to existing discourse on the humoral body.

3

Although medicinal remedies treat the outward, physiological symptoms of various sleep disorders, Burton argues that the true requisite for a good night's sleep is a tranquil mind. In a section devoted to the rectification of waking and terrible dreams, Burton claims, "He that wil intend to take his rest must goe to bed *animo securo, quieto, & libero*, with a secure and composed minde, in a quiet place" (2.97). Noise, light, or heat might detract from a sleeper's physical comfort during the night, but these disturbances are nothing compared to those disturbances that might weigh upon his soul. "Many cannot sleep for witches & fascinations, which are too familiar in some places," Burton suggests, but "griefe, feares, cares, expectations, anxieties, [and] great businesses" serve as the true underlying causes of such waking (2.97). During the early modern period, the regulation of the passions emerged as an increasingly urgent part of devotional life, with temperance operating as a central moral imperative. In her description of the six Galenic nonnaturals and the emerging genre of seventeenth-century health regimens, Handley notes that "maintaining a strong and well-managed body required self-discipline and it was thus an essential component of personal and Christian identity, being understood as a sign of decency, wisdom and moral virtue."[15] Given this cultural shift toward discipline, what is most remarkable about Burton's extended discourse on perturbations of mind is his focus on pleasure and reluctance to recast classical tranquility in a Christian light.

Having made the argument that sleep requires tranquility, Burton opens the subsequent section on the rectification of perturbations of mind with an explanation of tranquility's philosophical genealogy. He writes, "A quiet mind is that *voluptas*, or *Summum bonum* of *Epicurus*, *non dolere*, *curis vacare*, *animo tranquillo esse*, not to grieve but to want cares, and have a quiet soule is the only pleasure of the World, as *Seneca* truly recites his opinion, not that of eating and drinking which injurious *Aristotle* malitiously puts upon him" (2.99). Burton's desire to deflect criticism of this turn to pagan philosophy, and to Epicurus in particular, suggests an awareness of how controversial some of these teachings proved to be during the early modern period, mainly because of their connection to sensual indulgence and atheism.[16] In the case of melancholy, the suggestion that "whosoever, he is that shall hope to cure this malady in himself or any other, must first rectifie these passions and perturbations of the minde, the chiefest cure consists in them" seems to substitute human effort for God's grace (2.99).

Calling sense perception into doubt, Burton urges melancholy individuals to learn how to exercise control over their fantasy with the aim of regulating the ebb and flow of violent emotions. While he acknowledges that some may insist that melancholy madness resides "within [a person's] blood, his braines, his whole temperature, it cannot be removed," Burton maintains that "he may choose whether he will give way too farre unto it, [or whether] he may in some sort correct himselfe" (2.103). This agency that Burton ascribes to melancholy individuals draws from a philosophical rather than a medical tradition that posits self-cultivation as the primary vehicle for attaining virtue and wisdom. Even allowing for the influence of fantasy, Burton counsels that if "thou thinkest thou hearest and seest divells, black men, &c. 'tis not so, 'tis thy corrupt phantasy, settle thy imagination . . . rule thy selfe then with reason, satisfie thy selfe, accustome thy selfe, weane thy selfe from such fonde conceipts, vaine feares, strong Imaginations, restless thought" (2.103). Sleepers who are roused by a nightmare or who lay awake in the dark of night afraid of an incubus may be unable to help themselves, but they may seek the counsel of a good friend. If fair means do not succeed, Burton gives such a friend license, much like Montaigne, to employ fouler means: "Sometimes againe by some fained lye, strange newes, witty device, artificiall invention, it is not amisse to deceive them" (2.111). In either case, the cure for such perturbations of mind cannot be found in a medicinal remedy or divine power—only in the ability to curb one's fantasy, either alone or with the help of a friend.

From Burton's discourse on the perturbations of mind, we learn that an entire host of unruly emotions can disturb both a sleeping body and a tranquil mind. Concerning covetousness, for example, Burton argues that a miser "cannot sleep for cares and worldly business . . . or if he doe sleepe, 'tis a very unquiet, interrupt, unpleasing sleepe . . . though he be at a banquet, or at some merry feast, *he sighes for griefe of heart* (as *Cyprian* hath it) *and cannot sleepe though it be upon a downe bed; his wearish body takes no rest, troubled*" (1.285). If too much care for money causes anguish and sleepless nights, so, too, can poverty and want. Describing "those base villains, hunger-starved beggars, wandering rogues, those ordinary slaves, and day laboring drudges," Burton comments, "The very care they take to live, to be drudges, to maintaine their poore families, their trouble and anxiety *takes away their sleep*" (1.350). Since both the rich and poor lose sleep over financial matters, Burton suggests that managing anxiety about money is more important than money itself. While perturbations of mind may result from external events, such as the death of a loved one or a loss of liberty, they ultimately reflect the melancholy individual's own capacity to maintain tranquility in the face of uncertain and changing circumstances.

If a good night's sleep truly depended on the tranquility that Burton describes, one would expect reports of sleeplessness during the early modern period to be even more widespread. Although shared by many ancient schools of philosophy, including Stoicism, Skepticism, and Epicureanism, *tranquillitas* or *ataraxia* was not an easy goal to attain. Angus Gowland affirms that in the *Anatomy of Melancholy* "the goal to be attained was tranquility, which appeared throughout the book as the opposite of the anxiety that characterized the experience of the disease," but he also suggests that Burton's work "was simultaneously an attempt to address the absence of tranquility in that world."[17] In her essay on "perfect happiness" in the *Anatomy*, Mary Ann Lund similarly argues, "While Burton's approach to earthly happiness bears a strong debt to classical ethics . . . the *Anatomy* is caught in a tension between skepticism and hopefulness about how far real peace of mind is sustainable."[18] While Gowland and Lund are right to point to this paradox, they both locate tranquility within a primarily neo-Stoic context that emphasizes control of the body through reason. By examining how Burton's discourse on sleep advocates not only for a more thorough understanding of fantasy but also for the strategic use of excess to treat excess, we are better able to see the skeptical and Epicurean underpinnings of his approach to classical tranquility. As in the case of sleep, Burton does not attempt to discipline the body or violently to dispel perturbations of mind. Rather, he uses gentle and practical means to persuade the sleeper that his fears are of his own making and offers natural causes for even the most marvelous supernatural phenomena.

Since Burton recommends this form of tranquility as part of a larger critique of religious enthusiasm, a present and worldly orientation helps much more than hinders its therapeutic ends. To those melancholy individuals who suffer from sleep deprivation and who imagine hobgoblins where there are none, Burton argues, "The best remedy is to eat a light supper, and of such meats as are easie of digestion . . . not to lie on his backe, not to meditate or thinke in the day time of any terrible objects, or especially talke of them before hee goes to bed" (2.98). This dual exhortation to care for the body and the mind reflects the wisdom of a true philosopher-physician and showcases Burton's penchant for extending his inquiry well beyond the confines of Galenic humoral theory and the early modern medical treatise. In the *Anatomy*, readers regularly encounter practical strategies for procuring sleep alongside meditations on sleep's metaphysical significance. "We are never better or freer from cares than when we sleepe," Burton writes, "and yet, which we so much avoid and lament, death is but a perpetuall sleepe, and why should it as *Epicurus* argues, so much affright us? *When we are, death is not, but when death is, then we are not*" (2.178). For Burton, the very

184 | SLEEP AND PERSONHOOD

same strategies that can allay a sleeper's fear of nighttime terrors and diabolical attack may also help to allay fear of death and divine punishment. The practice of tranquility thus serves as preparation both for sleep and for eternal rest.

NOTES

1. Robert Burton, *The Anatomy of Melancholy*, ed. Thomas Faulkner, Nicolas K. Kiessling, and Rhonda L. Blair, commentary by J. B. Bambourgh with Martin Dodsworth, 6 vols. (Oxford: Oxford University Press, 1989–2000). All subsequent references in this chapter are to this edition and will be cited parenthetically by volume and page number. In all Burton quotes, italics were retained from the Oxford edition.

2. In returning to the question of genre, I agree with Mary Ann Lund's recent claim that "Burton's solidly Galenic framework is not an all-encompassing one" and that there is good reason to "move beyond a humoralist explanation of emotion." See "Robert Burton: Perfect Happiness and the *Visio dei*," in *The Renaissance of Emotion: Understanding Affect in Shakespeare and His Contemporaries*, ed. Richard Meek and Erin Sullivan (Manchester: Manchester University Press, 2015), 88. On formalist genre criticism and the *Anatomy* as Menippean satire, paradox, and self-consuming artifact, see especially Northrop Frye, *The Anatomy of Criticism* (Princeton: Princeton University Press, 1957); Rosalie Colie, *Paradoxia epidemica: The Renaissance Tradition of Paradox* (Princeton: Princeton University Press, 1966); and Stanley Fish, *Self-Consuming Artifacts: The Experience of Seventeenth-Century Literature* (Berkeley: University of California Press, 1972).

3. Sasha Handley, *Sleep in Early Modern England* (New Haven: Yale University Press, 2016).

4. Building upon Richard Strier's critique of what he terms the "new humoralism," Stephanie Shirilan suggests that the move in Burton studies away from formalist readings has produced "literalist misreadings" that do not sufficiently consider the stylistic features of the *Anatomy*. The argument that I am making regarding excess and contradiction depends on a close reading of the text and challenges the view of Burton as an unambiguous purveyor of neo-Galenic theory. See Strier, *The Unrepentant Renaissance: From Petrarch to Shakespeare to Milton* (Chicago: University of Chicago Press, 2011), 6–23, and Shirilan, *Robert Burton and the Transformative Powers of Melancholy* (London: Routledge, 2016), 9.

5. On Burton's use of therapeutic strategies, see especially Jeremy Schmidt, *Melancholy and the Care of the Soul: Religion, Moral Philosophy and Madness in Early Modern England* (Aldershot, U.K.: Ashgate, 2007), and Mary Ann Lund, *Melancholy, Medicine and Religion in Early Modern England: Reading "The Anatomy of Melancholy"* (Cambridge: Cambridge University Press, 2010).

6. Seneca, *Moral Essays*, trans. John W. Basore, Loeb Classical Library 214 (Cambridge, Mass.: Harvard University Press, 1928), 1:341.

7. Handley, *Sleep in Early Modern England*, 71.

8. Although much shorter in length, Timothy Bright's *A Treatise of Melancholie* (London: Thomas Vautrollier, 1586) serves as an important precursor for Burton's *Anatomy*, and he regularly cites, under Laurentius, André du Laurens's *Discours de la conservation de la veuë: des maladies melancholique: des catarrhes, et de la viellesse* (Paris, 1597). On Burton as a reader of Montaigne, see especially William H. Hamlin, *Montaigne's English Journey: Reading the Essays in Shakespeare's Day* (Oxford: Oxford University Press, 2013), 82. On

reading in Burton and Montaigne, see Lund, *Melancholy, Medicine and Religion*, 47–50.

9. All subsequent references in this chapter from the *Essays* will be to Michel de Montaigne, *The Complete Works: Essays, Travel Journal, Letters*, trans. Donald Frame (New York: Everyman's Library, 2003) and cited parenthetically by volume and page number.

10. Angus Gowland, *The Worlds of Renaissance Melancholy: Robert Burton in Context* (Cambridge: Cambridge University Press, 2006), 122.

11. Gowland, *Worlds of Renaissance Melancholy*, 100–103, provides some broader context for this form of skepticism in a subsection called "The Humanist Critique of Medicine."

12. Handley, *Sleep in Early Modern England*, 98.

13. Ibid., 98.

14. Janine Rivière, *Dreams in Early Modern England: Visions of the Night*

(London: Routledge, 2017), 108. On Burton's conception of religious melancholy, see the section "Burton: From a Medical Tradition to Religious Controversy" in Michael Heyd, "Melancholy and Enthusiasm: The Sources of the Medical Critique of Enthusiasm," in *"Be Sober and Reasonable": The Critique of Enthusiasm in the Seventeenth and Early Eighteenth Centuries* (Leiden, Netherlands: E. J. Brill, 1995), 44–71.

15. Handley, *Sleep in Early Modern England*, 22.

16. On the influence of Epicurean philosophy during the Renaissance, see especially Ada Palmer, *Reading Lucretius in the Renaissance* (Cambridge, Mass.: Harvard University Press, 2014), and Stephen Greenblatt, *The Swerve: How the World Became Modern* (New York: W. W. Norton, 2012).

17. Gowland, *Worlds of Renaissance Melancholy*, 4.

18. Lund, "Robert Burton," 87.

CHAPTER 9

The Physiology of Free Will

Faculty Psychology and the Structure of the Miltonic Mind

N. AMOS ROTHSCHILD

In Book 5 of *Paradise Lost*, Adam responds to Eve's account of the dream that Satan has inspired by describing in detail the form and workings of the human mind. In particular, the first man offers a nuanced account of the interactions between "the five watchful senses" and two of the mind's faculties: the Fancy and the Reason (5.100–113).[1] Alastair Fowler glosses the speech with a note that Adam voices little more than "common knowledge," and that assessment has helped to shape an editorial consensus that Milton's depictions of faculty science merely rehearse straightforward and widely accepted tenets of mid-seventeenth-century natural philosophy.[2] Scott Elledge deems Milton's treatment of the faculties characteristic of a "neat and simple" early modern physiology and psychology; Roy Flanagan finds that "Milton follows the standard 'faculty psychology' of his day," and both Barbara Lewalski and David Scott Kastan maintain that the poem "summarizes" scientific orthodoxy.[3] However, while it is true that the faculty science of *Paradise Lost* is not radically innovative, it need not follow that Milton simply versifies concepts from a homogenous system. As Harinder Marjara reminds us, Milton neither reinvents nor adheres to available scientific models. Instead, "like every other contemporary writer, [he] introduces

188 | SLEEP AND PERSONHOOD

his own variations and gives his own emphasis to traditional ideas to suit his specific needs."[4] In keeping with the project of early modern historical phenomenology, this chapter seeks to recover some of the complexities of seventeenth-century discourses on faculty psychology, to clarify the subtle variations and emphases that characterize *Paradise Lost*'s engagements therewith, and to uncover the specific poetic needs that such engagements supply.[5]

To resituate *Paradise Lost*'s representations of the faculties within the larger early modern cultural conversation about faculty science is to reveal the special emphasis the poem places on the human mind's balance of enclosure and exposure. Collectively, the poem's references to faculty psychology stress that the layered physiological form of Adam's and Eve's minds renders them impenetrable to forced possession from the outside, yet free to admit knowledge of evil without sin so long as such knowledge remains unapproved. Moreover, the poem also invokes faculty science to juxtapose the structure of the first humans' minds with both the physiological form of the serpent's "heart or head" (9.189) and the macrocosmic form of Eden itself. Through Satan's parallel assaults on the sleeping Eve and the sleeping serpent, Milton's epic works to construct the sufficiency of human minds in opposition to the vulnerability of bestial minds, which lack the layered faculties of their human counterparts. Meanwhile, the poem links the form of the garden and the form of its human inhabitants' minds in quasi-allegorical fashion, emphasizing once more the carefully crafted structures (whether geographical or physiological) that ensure both virtue and sin are accessible, though neither is necessary. *Paradise Lost* thus dramatizes at the minute level of faculty science distinctions between exposure and enclosure, sleeping and wakefulness, beasts and humans to render as robust and precise as possible one of its central foci: the freedom of the will. Milton does not invent an original system of faculty psychology, but his use of existent faculty science is calculated to demonstrate that God did, in fact, form the first humans with minds *structurally* "sufficient to have stood, though free to fall" (3.99). These minds are physiologically equipped to obtain and contain information that might prompt sinful action, yet they are also able to maintain a dynamic state of innocence until the very moment the hand touches the fruit.

Milton's faculty science has received some glancing attention in the copious scholarship that analyzes Eve's dream, but most scholars neglect to connect their insights about the abstract import of the episode explicitly with Adam's concrete account of faculty science.[6] For instance, many scholars take Eve's dream as evidence of what Barbara Lewalski terms Adam and Eve's "perilous exposure." These scholars contest those who read the dream as Milton's attempt to depict an inclination toward sin in the prelapsarian lives of Adam and Eve, arguing that Miltonic innocence is founded upon "radical growth," not "stable serene completeness."[7] Such arguments recast the dream episode as part of a progressive education rather than as evidence of a fall by stages. However, they do little to link the first couple's "exposure" to Adam's description of the mind's physiological structure. For example, Thomas Blackburn offers the important insight that the dream scene demonstrates that "the knowledge of evil [that Adam and Eve] do possess in their innocence is essential to their status as free and responsible moral beings," yet he never investigates how Adam's account of the faculties might bear on the poem's understanding of how the first humans can acquire such dangerous knowledge in the first place.[8]

By contrast, Diane McColley does begin to analyze how the dream's abstract implications connect to the concrete complexities of faculty science that Adam describes.[9] In *Milton's Eve*, McColley offers the following assessment of the dream:

> [Eve] is responsible, with Adam's help, for coping with evil even in her innermost thoughts. Faculty psychology allows the possibility of such a process occurring without sin, which enters, not when the lower faculties desire an action, but when the will prefers it to obeying God. . . . If Adam and Eve were immune to temptation through the senses and the imagination, those faculties would not be free, and the exercise of reason and will would be reduced. For Milton, the keenness, the creativity, the liberty, and therefore the vulnerability of the subordinate faculties and the calling to keep them free by exercise of right reason and upright will are among the risky opportunities for independent virtue that fill life in Paradise with challenge and delight.[10]

McColley presents several important points to support her cogent claim that "faculty psychology allows" Eve to experience the dream that Satan induces "without sin." First, she distinguishes between the preferences of "the will" and the desires of the "lower faculties." More importantly, she points out

190 | SLEEP AND PERSONHOOD

that the "vulnerability of the subordinate faculties" is critical both in order that those faculties remain "free" from the restrictions of divine cloistering and in order that Miltonic innocence involve "challenge and delight" rather than static perfection.

While these telling insights suggest that the discourses of faculty psychology are a crucial component in Milton's attempts to render both free will and innocence, an in-depth treatment of *Paradise Lost*'s faculty science is never McColley's focus.[11] Indeed, though it is true that "if Adam and Eve were immune to temptation through the senses and the imagination, those faculties would not be free," the ramifications of such immunity would be greater still. The exposure of the "lower faculties" is essential not only for the liberty of "those faculties" in particular but also for the freedom of Adam's and Eve's minds in their entireties. Likewise, McColley's contention that Eve "is responsible . . . for coping with evil even in her innermost thoughts" could be more precise. *Paradise Lost* certainly represents the mind as free from divine cloistering, but the poem also insists the mind is not over-exposed (and therefore subject to external compulsion or even demonic possession). In other words, Satan must not be denied access to Eve's "subordinate faculties," but neither can he be allowed direct contact with her "innermost thoughts." McColley's suggestive comments therefore open the way for a further-reaching exploration of precisely how engagement with the discourses of physiology and faculty psychology serve *Paradise Lost* in its efforts to represent the first encounter between free-willed innocence and evil. Before beginning such an exploration, however, it is first helpful to survey briefly the discourses in question.

"MANY WORDS MAKING NOTHING UNDERSTOOD": EARLY MODERN DISCOURSE ON THE FACULTIES

The subversive physician and astrologer Nicholas Culpeper made it his business to disseminate widely medical knowledge ordinarily reserved for the College of Physicians. Exploiting lapses in censorship, he published an unauthorized English translation of the college's central tome of medical lore, the *Pharmacopoeia Londoniensis*, in 1649; until his death in 1654, he supplemented that effort with numerous other translations and original works concerning medicine and herbalism. Culpeper offers his most detailed account of the mental faculties in his *Ephemeris* of 1651, where he describes the form of the mind as divided into three parts—Imagination, Judgment, and Memory—each occupying a different region of the brain:

> Imagination is seated in the fore-part of the Brain, it is hot and dry in quality, quick, active, alwayes working, it receives vapors from the Heart, and coyns them into Thoughts; it never sleeps, but always is working, both when the man is sleeping and waking; only when Judgment is awake it regulates the Imagination which runs at random when Judgment is asleep, and forms any Thought according to the nature of the vapor sent up to it. . . .
>
> Judgment alwayes sleeps when men doth, Imagination never sleeps, Memory somtimes sleeps when men sleeps, and sometimes it doth not. . . .
>
> Judgment is seated in the midst of the Brain, to shew that it ought to bear rule over all the other Faculties; it is the Judge of the little world, to approve of what is good, and reject what is bad; it is the seat of Reason, and the guide of Actions. . . .
>
> Memory is seated in the hinder cell of the Brain, it is the great Register to the little World; and its Office is to Record things either done and past, or to be done.[12]

To say that the account of faculty psychology that Culpeper delivers here is entirely characteristic of Galenic theory as inherited by early modern England would be partially accurate.[13] Yet it is also true that the idea of the mind and its faculties that Culpeper presents was neither universally accepted nor even particularly consistent during the period.[14] As we shall see, there were many variations of and elaborations on the basic tripartite model of mind that Culpeper describes, and many more were being produced all the time. Authors joining the cultural conversation about faculty psychology inevitably tweaked the existent system to suit their needs.[15] In fact, Culpeper's detractors complained that his works were colored by a desire both to foment "Rebellion or Atheism" and "to bring into obloquy the famous Societies of Apothecaries and Chirurgeons."[16] However, while in general Culpeper may have sought to advance such subversive agendas, in the case of his discussion of faculty science, he did so by broadcasting rather than altering the College's arcana. Ironically, then, the radical Culpeper might be understood to offer a reasonably faithful version of the hegemonic account of faculty psychology—an illicit peek at an orthodox strain of discourse.[17]

Of course, the broadly sketched orthodoxies concerning the makeup of the mind that Culpeper brought to the masses were certainly not the limit of the period's cultural conversation concerning faculty psychology. The physician and closet occultist Robert Fludd—an admittee and eventually a ranking officer of the same College of Physicians that Culpeper later sought to undermine[18]—takes up the topic of faculty science in his voluminous *Metaphysical, Physical and Technical History of the Microcosm and Macrocosm* (1617–21). His discussion is accompanied by one of the most minutely detailed visual representations of the faculties that survives the period (see figure).

Even a cursory survey of Fludd's diagram reveals its debts to the same rough model of mind later subversively promulgated by Culpeper. Like Culpeper, Fludd presents the mind as fundamentally tripartite in structure, with imaginative, reasoning, and recollecting faculties arranged from the front to the back of the head. Then again, given that Fludd depicts an expansive halo of world-spheres surrounding a head full of subdivided faculties, it is also obvious that he elaborates substantially on such orthodoxies. Variations in terminology between different representations of the faculties—terming a faculty "Fancy" instead of "Imagination," "Estimation" or "Reason" instead of "Judgment"—are common, but Fludd also divides each conventional faculty into two subfaculties: "Imagination" becomes "Sensitiva" and "Imaginativa," "Judgment" becomes "Cogitativa" and "Æstimativa," and "Memory" becomes "Memorativa" and "Motiva." More importantly, he imagines a system of correspondences in which each facet of the mind pairs with a distinct physical or metaphysical world. In sum, although his version of faculty psychology relies on a largely conventional model, Fludd elaborates on that model so that it serves his titular purpose of exploring the links between microcosmic man and the macrocosm.

Fludd's system is by no means extraordinary for its variations. Indeed, disagreement about issues as basic as the location and number of the faculties was commonplace in the period's discourse on faculty science. In *Mikrokosmographia* (1615), Helkiah Crooke weighs whether Imagination, Reason, and Memory "have distinct & particular mansions provided for every one of them" and concludes in the negative, avouching that "the whole substance of the braine is the seat of them all promiscuously disposed therein."[19]

THE STRUCTURE OF THE MILTONIC MIND | 193

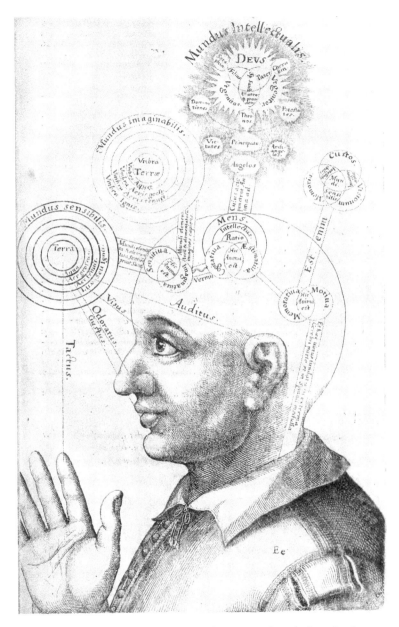

Robert Fludd, "De tripl. anim. in corp. vision." From *Metaphysical, Physical and Technical History of the Microcosm and Macrocosm* (1617–21). Image courtesy Getty Research Institute, Los Angeles (1378-183).

Robert Burton's *The Anatomy of Melancholy* (1621) does locate the faculties in various ventricles, but not all of those faculties match Culpeper's; nor does their placement. Burton reserves "the forepart of the brain [as the] Organ or seat" for the "Common Sense," not the "Phantasie, or Imagination," which he places in the privileged "middle sell of the braine," while the Memory assumes its customary "Seat and Organ" in the "backe part of the braine."[20] Meanwhile, Henry Jackson's 1664 translation of Jacopo Berengario da Carpi's *Mikrokosmographia* crams the "Apprehensive, Cogitative, and Memorative Vertue[s]" into the first ventricle and insists that "the middle Ventricle, is not for the Cogitative Vertue, but is a way for the purging out of many superfluities of the Brain, and for the carrying of spirits to the aforesaid third Ventricle, which spirits serve not to the Memorative Vertue, but to the Motive and Sensitive Vertue."[21]

Such endless rearranging and renaming of faculties earned faculty science its detractors. In the second chapter of his *Leviathan* (1651), Thomas Hobbes sums up writing on the faculties as "many words making nothing understood."[22] He engages with the broader cultural conversation about faculty psychology only to distinguish between the terminology employed therein and the sensory and cognitive phenomena to which such terminology was applied.[23] More drastically still, in *On the Fabric of the Human Body* (1543), the Flemish anatomist Andreas Vesalius—whose work was plagiarized and published in England as early as 1545—reprimands "the crowd of philosophers (and [. . .] theologians) . . . who so ludicrously demean that divine and most wonderful device, the human brain" by inventing for it "a structure of their own that abounds in artless monstrosities!"[24] In short, Vesalius addresses faculty psychology to dismiss it altogether, even as he undertakes the rigorous anatomical study of the brain that would eventually render faculty science obsolete.

As should be made plain by both the exasperation of Hobbes and Vesalius in particular and the preceding survey in general, the various visions of faculty psychology circulating in early modern England comprised a cultural conversation that was anything but "neat and simple."[25] Though Culpeper, Fludd, and their fellow faculty psychologists may rely on an essentially similar schema derived from an inherited Galenic model, they all bring their own small (and not so small) adjustments and shifts in emphasis to that schema. Moreover, it is particularly crucial to note these modifications to a superficially similar system, since—as our brief survey suggests—it is through such adjustments that authors often sought to use the discourses of faculty science to serve the (frequently very different) needs of their projects.

"BUT OPEN LEFT THE CELL / OF FANCY": MILTON AND THE LANGUAGE OF FACULTY PSYCHOLOGY

The faculty science of *Paradise Lost* is no exception. When Adam details in Book 5 the form of the mind—its division into faculties, their names, characteristics, and functions—Milton draws on the same basic system as Culpeper, Fludd, and Burton but emphasizes certain aspects of that system to suit his own ends. Adam prefaces his account of the faculties with a conundrum. He suspects that the "uncouth dream" that Eve describes is "of evil sprung," but his suspicion leaves him confounded as to the origin of said evil: "Yet evil whence?" he asks, since "in [Eve] can harbor none, / Created pure" (5.98–100).[26] By presenting Adam's ensuing explanation of faculty psychology as the first man's effort to grapple with this etiological puzzle, Milton focuses attention on the path by which (and the processes through which) new information—and potentially evil—progresses from the exterior of the body to the interior of the mind:

> But know that in the soul
> Are many lesser faculties that serve
> Reason as chief; among these fancy next
> Her office holds; of all external things,
> Which the five watchful senses represent,
> She forms imaginations, airy shapes,
> Which reason joining or disjoining, frames
> All what we affirm or what deny, and call
> Our knowledge or opinion. (5.100–108)

Adam's description of the faculties proceeds by following sensory data about "external things" inward from the "five watchful senses," to the "fancy," to the "reason." Moreover, Milton stresses the processes such data undergoes at each of the numerous steps of its journey. The senses "represent" any "external things" perceived; the Fancy "forms imaginations" based on those representations; and the Reason "join[s] or disjoin[s]" those imaginations, thereby "fram[ing]" what to "affirm or what deny, and call / Our knowledge or opinion." On the one hand, this description details a mind able to access new information because its component parts form an interconnected whole that links it to the external world. On the other hand, it presents a mind safeguarded against unapproved exterior evil influences because those parts maintain enough modularity to form protective layers.[27] This precarious balance between exposure and enclosure hinges on Fancy's ability to produce "imaginations" of "external things."[28] These "airy shapes" serve as a means by which Reason can access potentially dangerous information about the world, but they also provide crucial distance from it. The mimetic similitude between exterior "thing" and interior "imagination" provides a simultaneous connection to and separation from the world without, thereby allowing Milton to envision a mind free from both cloistering and external necessity.[29]

This is not to say that *Paradise Lost*'s depictions of the Fancy are purely positive. Adam problematizes its role when he turns from the faculties' customary arrangement during waking hours to their more vulnerable configuration during sleep. Reason "retires / Into her private cell when nature rests," he tells Eve in proceeding, and

> Oft in [Reason's] absence mimic fancy wakes
> To imitate her; but misjoining shapes,
> Wild work produces oft, and most in dreams,
> Ill matching words and deeds long past or late. (5.110–14)

Adam's warning is hardly unique in the period in stressing Fancy's unruly aspects, particularly in connection with sleep and dreams.[30] The concern raised by the ascendancy of Fancy during sleep is clear: Fancy is exposed to "external things" via the "represent[ations]" passed on by the senses, and during the night Fancy has free reign to "misjoin" that input without the oversight of Reason.[31] As such, Adam's words engage the anxiety that the reconfiguration of the faculties during sleep might compromise the freedom of the will.

However, Eve's dream and Adam's subsequent explanation together work to contain precisely this concern. *Paradise Lost* frames Adam's description of Fancy's "wild work" such that it is paradoxically reassuring. Fancy might usurp Reason's role during sleep, but, upon waking, the chief faculty can always "disjoin" (5.106) those "shapes" the usurper has "misjoin[ed]." Indeed, the very conversation in which Eve recounts her dream and Adam

THE STRUCTURE OF THE MILTONIC MIND | 197

holds forth about the faculties would seem to accomplish just such a corrective. Perhaps more importantly, Adam concludes that "what in sleep [Eve] didst abhor to dream, / Waking [she] never wilt consent to do" (5.119–21). "Consent" is key. Through this pronouncement, the poem suggests that Eve's dream cannot compromise her free will, regardless of whether Satan has managed to affect her Fancy during sleep. After all, Fancy regularly presents flawed or false information that Reason rejects, particularly after a night of dreams. Only waking "consent" of the Reason can dictate willed action. In juxtaposing the configuration of the faculties during sleep and wakefulness, the poem thus works to demonstrate that Eve possesses a mind whose compartmentalization guarantees the freedom of the will. By allowing Satan an extrabiblical assault on the sleeping Eve, Milton creates not the "dramatic foreshadowing" of the fall to come proposed by William B. Hunter,[32] but a dramatization of humankind's sufficiency to stand.

Descriptions of Fancy elsewhere in *Paradise Lost* also stress the imaginative faculty's simultaneous shortcomings and utility. The narrative voice's account of Satan "close at the ear of Eve; / Assaying by his devilish art to reach / The organs of her fancy" focuses attention on Fancy's dangerous vulnerability as the first faculty to encounter sensory input (4.800–804). However, it also insists that the relative positioning of the faculties interposes the Fancy between the Reason and any threat of exterior intrusion. Likewise, in Book 8, Adam admits to Raphael that "the mind or fancy" is

apt . . . to rove
Unchecked, and of her roving is no end;
Till warned, or by experience taught, she learn,
That not to know at large of things remote
From use, obscure and subtle, but to know
That which before us lies in daily life,
Is the prime wisdom. (8.188–94)

When Adam designates the Fancy as the "roving" part of the mind, Milton reaffirms his emphasis on the faculty's potentially problematic proximity to—and curiosity about—"things remote." Still, the first man's contention that Fancy can be "by experience taught" suggests that though the faculty's contact with the outside world needs to be checked, the faculty is also essential if the first humans are to learn, to change, and to attain "wisdom." In short,

198 | SLEEP AND PERSONHOOD

while Culpeper, Fludd, and many others may situate Fancy as Milton does, *Paradise Lost* stresses how the faculty's peripheral position within the mind renders it exposed, interposed, and essential to learning.

Similarly, Milton adapts faculty psychology to represent the mind as both enclosed and open when Adam describes the dreams in which he first glimpsed Eden (8.287–311) and Eve (8.452–78). The first man experiences both of those glimpses in visions perceived through the Fancy. In the first instance, Adam remembers "a dream, / Whose inward apparition gently moved / [His] fancy" (8.292–94) to envision the Garden to which he relocates. In the second, he recalls that God "open left the cell / Of fancy" so that he might witness "as in a trance" Eve's creation from his rib (8.460–62). It could be argued that, particularly in the former instance, Milton's God encroaches on Adam's free will by actually prompting him to move in his sleep. However, the movement Adam envisions—"in air / Smooth sliding without step" (8.301–2)—would seem to suggest that the Father flies the sleeping Adam to Eden, rather than inspiring Adam to sleepwalk.[33] Alternatively, then, Adam's dream visions might be understood to reaffirm the idea that Milton's God observes the same limited access to the first humans' minds that Satan confronts. In both cases, God works on Adam's Fancy as an "inward apparition" analogous to the "represent[ations]" Adam describes reaching Eve's Fancy through the senses (5.104). The poem thus implies that the Creator leaves Adam's Reason untouched, and the first man remains free to interact with these other creations as he chooses when he awakens (8.309; 8.478–84) to find "before [his] eyes all real, as the dream[s] / Had lively shadowed" (8.310–11).

CONTRASTING FORMS—HUMAN, BESTIAL, AND MACROCOSMIC

However, *Paradise Lost*'s engagement with faculty psychology does not end with its portrayal of human minds. The poem also evokes the language of faculty science and physiology when Satan possesses the serpent. Given Milton's frequent depictions of Satan's protean nature, it is curious Satan claims to require a "Fit vessel . . . in whom / To enter, and his dark suggestions hide / From sharpest sight" (9.89–91). Raphael has already explained that angels can "limb themselves, and colour, shape or size / Assume, as likes them best" (6.152–53). Further, Milton is clear that Satan has suffered no impairment to his shape-shifting abilities due to his fall. During his journey, the archfiend transforms into a cherub of innocent appearance (3.636); mimics a number of "four-footed" creatures in a "sportful herd," depending on which "shape serve[s] best his end" (4.396–98); shifts into a toad (4.800); and even dissipates into a "rising mist" (9.75). Indeed, since his cherubic disguise fools even the most visually oriented of God's faithful servants—the archangel Uriel—his concern with being found out by "sharpest sight" is difficult to take seriously. Milton's decision to have Satan possess a serpent rather than simply transforming into one thus demands a more exacting explanation than that which the devil himself provides.

One such explanation might be found through an examination of the several physiological terms and concepts that appear in the narrative voice's account of the possession. Upon locating the serpent, "in at his mouth" Satan enters, "and his brutal sense, / In heart or head, possessing soon inspire[s] / With act intelligential" (9.187–90). The serpent is said to possess "brutal sense," and only after Satan enters is the beast "inspired / With act intelligential." This last phrase recalls the "intellectual" spirits that facilitate interactions between the faculties high on the archangel Raphael's "gradual scale" (5.479–90).[34] Of course, Raphael also tells Adam that man is the only "creature who not prone / And brute as other creatures, but endued / With sanctity of reason, might erect / His stature" (7.506–9). The serpent's merely "brutal sense" evokes the idea that beasts lack a human's structurally layered faculty psychology. As Burton puts it, "In men [*Phantasie*] is subject and governed by *Reason*, or at least should be; but in Beasts it hath no superior, & is *Ratio Brutorum*, all the reason they have."[35] Without a higher faculty to approve or disapprove of "imaginations" "inspired" by outside forces, it is a small wonder that the serpent is vulnerable to compulsion from without and that Satan is able to infuse himself into the beast's "heart or head." The sleeping serpent in Book 9 thus stands in sharp contrast to the sleeping Eve in Book 4. To borrow Garrett Sullivan's insight, sleep does indeed serve as a "vehicle" through which Milton elaborates a "model of humanness"; however, in this instance, sleep in *Paradise Lost* clarifies rather than "blurs distinctions among man, plant, and animal."[36] Satan's possession of the serpent serves to demonstrate that unwilled compulsion is possible only in the absence of Reason. The insufficiency of the serpent's mind functions to contrast with the structural sufficiency of the human mind—equipped with both exposed Fancy and insulated Reason—that Satan accosts in sleep during the dream episode and attempts awake in the final temptation scene.[37]

If Satan's possession of the serpent complements the poem's representation of human physiology and faculty psychology, so, too, does the archfiend's penetration of Eden's substructure. Indeed, *Paradise Lost*'s descriptions of Eden suggest a macrocosmic anatomical allegory; editors have long noted that the garden's "hairy sides" (4.135) and circular shape (8.304) make it reminiscent of an enormous human head.[38] Kathleen Swaim observes that some scholars have even taken this allegorical reading so far as to read "the first couple in terms of a physiologically based faculty psychology, aligning Eve with the Fancy and Adam with Reason, especially in order to find fault with Eve."[39] However, Milton collapses the allegory aligning the geography of Eden and the physiology of the mind even as he raises it.[40] After all, the only things inside Eden corresponding to Reason and Fancy are not Adam and Eve but the actual faculties of Reason and Fancy that they each individually possess.

Still, Milton redoubles the anatomical resonance of Eden when Satan invades the garden for the second time. As the fiend slips back into the Garden by rising through the waters of the Tigris "involved in rising mist" (9.75), his means of infiltration recall and literalize the simile that the narrative voice uses to describe his prior effort to penetrate Eve's sleeping mind by striving to "taint / The animal spirits that from pure blood arise / Like gentle breaths from rivers pure" (4.804–6). Indeed, Milton reemphasizes the parallel between anatomical and earthly structures when he describes the Tigris rising "through veins / Of porous earth with kindly thirst up drawn" (4.227–28). The "veins / Of porous earth" beneath Eden carry water (and satanic mist) up to the Garden above much as early modern physiology held that bodily veins carried blood and vaporous "spirits" upward to the head (5.480–90).

In rendering Satan as a sort of "animal spirit" within the bloodstream of Eden, Milton achieves more than attractive imagistic layering. Recalling the archangel Raphael's discussion of gustation, the bodily spirits, and the faculties clarifies the significance of the scene:

> flowers and their fruit
> Man's nourishment, by gradual scale sublimed
> To vital spirits aspire, to animal,
> To intellectual, give both life and sense,
> Fancy and understanding, whence the soul
> Reason receives. (5.482–87)

Raphael explains to Adam that, through digestion, food is "sublimed" into the "various forms, various degrees / Of substance" at work within the body (5.473). The archangel assigns each such substance an appropriate place along God's "gradual scale," from the earthy and dense to the "more refined, more spirituous, and pure" (5.475). Through parallel structure, Raphael links the various kinds of bodily spirit with their purposes: "vital spirits" function to "give life," "animal" spirits enable "sense," and "intellectual" spirits animate mental faculties like "Fancy" and, ultimately, "Reason."[41] Within the world of *Paradise Lost*, it is the "animal" spirits, then, that carry information between the body (with its "five watchful senses") and the outermost faculty of the mind: the Fancy. Likewise, the intellectual spirits facilitate communications such as the "imaginations" that Fancy passes on to the Reason. Raphael's "gradual scale" thus bears on Satan's earlier effort to influence the sleeping Eve and his later entry into Eden alike. In the former case, the archangel's system reaffirms that, even if Satan succeeds *both* in his effort "to reach / The organs of [Eve's] fancy" (4.801–2) *and* in his attempt to "taint / [her] animal spirits" (4.804–5), Eve is *still* sinless until her waking Reason either approves or denies the resultant dream. In the latter case, the parallels Satan's infiltration reveals between the structure of the mind and the structure of the garden serve to reemphasize that Milton's God creates all of the boundaries in his universe permeable; his creations are permitted to exercise free will without circumscribed restraint on either the physiological or the geographical level. Just as tainted animal spirits reaching the Fancy do not necessitate sin, so the fallen angel's presence within Eden does not necessitate the fall.

CONCLUSIONS

Paradise Lost engages the discourse on faculty science once more before the temptation scene, when Adam makes his final plea to Eve that they remain together rather than work apart. God's "creating hand / Nothing imperfect or deficient left / Of all that he created, much less man" (9.344–46), Adam assures Eve, but he adds a warning that mankind should not take overmuch comfort in the design of "his" own mind:

> Secure from outward force; within himself
> The danger lies, yet lies within his power:
> Against his will he can receive no harm.

202 | SLEEP AND PERSONHOOD

> But God left free the will, for what obeys
> Reason, is free, and reason he made right,
> But bid her well beware, and still erect,
> Lest by some fair appearing good surprised
> She dictate false, and misinform the will
> To do what God expressly hath forbid. (9.348–56)

Here the poem elaborates on its understanding of free will in light of faculty physiology. Adam again represents the mind in spatial terms—"secure from *outward* force," but imperiled by a danger "*within*" (emphasis added)—positioning the faculty of Reason as the crucial gatekeeper between its outer and inner reaches. Reason cannot be overpowered in the manner of the serpent's "brutal sense" (9.188), so "against his will [mankind] can receive no harm." However, God's "creating hand" could not make the mind perfectly impervious to incursion without cloistering human beings within their own skulls. Adam's earlier account of the faculties explains how the Fancy prevents such hermetic enclosure. The "five watchful senses represent" "external things" to the Fancy, which brings "imaginations" of that sense data to the Reason, which in turn "join[s] or disjoin[s]" that information and "frames / All what we affirm or what deny" (5.103–7). Adam's final warning clarifies the last portion of this chain. After reconfiguring the information that it has received from Fancy, Reason "dictate[s]" to and informs "the will." It is this innermost faculty of the Miltonic mind that has the power to command the body to action—"*To do* [or not to do] what God expressly hath forbid" (emphasis added). If the will is to remain free, Reason must "[keep] strictest watch" for "some specious object" among the "airy shapes" that Fancy has passed along (9.359–63; 5.105). Otherwise, that "fair appearing good" might fool the Reason and make it "dictate false, and misinform the will" to act sinfully.

Taken collectively then, the accounts of Reason and Fancy in *Paradise Lost* suggest that Milton engages with faculty science to represent a robust and precise physiology of free will. He emphasizes both the insulated condition of Reason—that the faculty can contact potential evil only indirectly via the "imaginations" of "external things" that Fancy "forms" and passes on (5.103–5)—and the exposed and interposing situation of Fancy to render a model of the mind free from total sequestration and total vulnerability alike. This model divides and orders the faculties in typical fashion. However, it stresses that those faculties remain simultaneously discrete enough that the Fancy can act as a protective layer to safeguard the Reason against unapproved impingement by exterior evil influences, yet interconnected enough that new information may still reach the Reason via the Fancy so that the mind as a whole is not cloistered but capable of learning and changing. The wills of the first humans are free because their minds contain both Fancy and Reason, the latter sheltered—though not sequestered—by the mediating presence of the former. When Adam concludes his description of the faculties in Book 5 by declaring that "evil into the mind of . . . man / May come and go, so unapproved, and leave / No spot or blame behind" (5.117–19), his pronouncement is therefore far more rigorous than it may first appear. Evil may enter "into the mind" in that it may enter the Fancy, the faculty exposed to contact with external influences. Likewise, it "may come and go . . . and leave / No spot of blame behind" because it remains safely contained within that outermost faculty and never touches Reason directly so long as it remains "unapproved" by the chief faculty. *Paradise Lost* thus bends faculty science in an effort to create a model nuanced enough to explain how the possibility of sin can exist within the mind, yet leave that mind sinless until the precise moment of transgression.

NOTES

1. Quotations from *Paradise Lost* are cited parenthetically throughout. Unless otherwise noted, they follow Alastair Fowler's second edition (London: Longman, 1998). Though Adam refers to the "soul" (5.100) while discussing the faculties, he concludes his discourse on faculty psychology with a statement about the "mind" (5.117). For clarity's sake, I use "mind" in my discussions of faculty science throughout. For a transhistorical study of the complex entanglement of conceptions of "soul," "mind," and "brain," see Carl Zimmer, *Soul Made Flesh: The Discovery of the Brain—and How It Changed the World* (London: William Heinemann, 2004).

2. Milton, *Paradise Lost*, ed. Fowler, 287n. The view of Milton's faculty science solidified by such editorial assessments appears to have been popularized by Kester Svendsen, who describes Milton echoing a largely homogenous vision of "physiology and psychology . . . set forth in dozens of medical treatises, schoolbooks and popular literature." See *Milton and Science* (New York: Greenwood, 1956), 37.

3. Milton, *Paradise Lost*, ed. Scott Elledge (New York: W. W. Norton, 1993), 463; ed. Roy Flannagan (Boston: Houghton Mifflin, 1998), 478n; ed. Barbara Lewalski (Oxford: Blackwell, 2007), 142n; ed. David Scott Kastan (Indianapolis: Hackett, 2005), 148n. Elledge cites Fowler in glossing 5.100–113 and includes an appendix on Milton's "Physiology and Psychology" (463–64).

4. Harinder Singh Marjara, *Contemplation of Created Things: Science in "Paradise Lost"* (Toronto: University of Toronto Press, 1992), 235.

5. Sean McDowell voices precisely my concerns about editorial consensus on Milton's faculty science in his effort to define

the emerging field of historical phenomenology in early modern studies: "Historical phenomenologists quarrel with the older scholarship generally for over-simplifying complex Renaissance ideas about the body and thereby misleading modern readers about the nuances of early modern psychological thought." See McDowell, "The View from the Interior: The New Body Scholarship in Renaissance / Early Modern Studies," *Literature Compass* 3/4 (2006): 784–85. McDowell praises the work historical phenomenologists such as Michael Schoenfeldt have done to generate "new insights into the nuances of early modern psychophysiological theory . . . [through] focus on organs, body parts, humors, and/or passions"; however, McDowell also admits that when Schoenfeldt examines texts such as *Paradise Lost*, he too often "omits detailed consideration of the senses, imagination, common sense, memory, will and understanding—the faculties that participate . . . in the transactions between the rational powers, the body, and the material world" (786–87). This chapter would begin to answer McDowell's concluding call for work that addresses this omission.

6. For an excellent review of criticism on Eve's dream, see Diana Treviño Benet, "Milton's Toad, or Satan's Dream," *Milton Studies* 45 (2006): 38, 50–51n.

7. Barbara Kiefer Lewalski, "Innocence and Experience in Milton's Eden," in *New Essays on "Paradise Lost,"* ed. Thomas Kranidas (Berkeley: University of California Press, 1971), 88. Scholarship on the dream has primarily focused either on what the episode reveals about Milton's efforts to grapple with the etiological difficulties of sin's advent, or what it reveals about the nature of Miltonic innocence. See E. M. W. Tillyard and Millicent Bell for arguments that Eve's exposure to satanic influence during the dream suggests that Milton is more interested in dramatic credibility than in justifying the ways of God to man: Tillyard, *Studies in Milton* (London: Chatto & Windus, 1960), and Bell, "The Fallacy of the Fall in *Paradise Lost*," *Publications of the Modern Language Association* 68 (1953): 863–83. John Diekhoff, Stanley Fish, and

Diane McColley—to name a few—join Lewalski in arguing that Eve remains innocent after the dream and in suggesting that Miltonic innocence is changeable. They point out that earlier analysis of the dream by A. J. A. Waldock, Tillyard, and Bell relies on a static and absolute understanding of innocence. See Diekhoff, "Eve's Dream and the Paradox of Fallible Perfection," *Milton Quarterly* 4 (1970): 5–7; Fish, *Surprised by Sin: The Reader in "Paradise Lost"* (New York: St. Martin's, 1967); McColley, "Eve's Dream," *Milton Studies* 12 (1978): 25–45.

8. Thomas H. Blackburn, "'Uncloister'd Virtue': Adam and Eve in Milton's Paradise," *Milton Studies* 3 (1971): 132.

9. Besides McColley's work, articles by Diana Treviño Benet, Robert Wiznura, and Maura Smyth also offer some discussion of *Paradise Lost*'s physiology and faculty psychology. Benet touches on faculty psychology but focuses on Milton's disagreements with "the animal spirits theory of [his] era" (Benet, "Milton's Toad," 38). Though I agree with Benet's claim that Milton "fashioned the dream episode in Books Four and Five to deny Satan's power to curtail the freedom of the will" (49), I argue that Milton's use of animal spirits theory is secondary to his engagement with faculty science in crafting that denial. Maura Smyth explores the political implications of Milton's faculty psychology, arguing for a Milton who uses Fancy both to identify "the weaknesses of God's political order" and "to legitimize a mode of female authority that [becomes] an intrinsic part of the English political system": Smyth, *Women Writing Fancy: Authorship and Autonomy from 1611 to 1812* (London: Palgrave Macmillan, 2017), 97. In an older article, William Hunter discusses Milton's faculty science in connection with early modern dream and demon lore, concluding that Eve's dream is causally connected to her fall. See Hunter, "Eve's Demonic Dream," *English Literary History* 13 (1946): 255–65.

10. Diane McColley, *Milton's Eve* (Urbana: University of Illinois Press, 1983), 90.

11. In quibbling with this observation about the import of Milton's faculty

psychology, I do not intend to suggest that McColley is unaware that Eve's physiological design allows her to remain free from both necessary virtue *and* necessary sin. Rather, I attempt to clarify and extend McColley's argument by exploring further the effects of the physiological terms that Milton employs.

12. Nicholas Culpeper, *An ephemeris for the yeer 1651, Amplified with Rational Predictions from the Book of the Creatures* (London: Peter Cole, 1651), 4–5.

13. On the inherited version of Galen and the tripartite theory of mind, see Zimmer, *Soul Made Flesh*, 16–23, and E. Ruth Harvey, *Inward Wits: Psychological Theory in the Middle Ages and the Renaissance* (London: Warburg Institute, 1975), 10, 17, 35, 69. For a more extensive account of faculty psychology as a "synthesis of ideas from many different sources" including Aristotle, Galen, St. Augustine, the Arabic writers Avicenna and Averroes, and many others, see Katharine Park, "The Organic Soul," in *The Cambridge History of Renaissance Philosophy*, ed. Charles B. Schmitt, Quentin Skinner, Eckhard Kessler, and Jill Kraye (Cambridge: Cambridge University Press, 1988), 465.

14. Indeed, Culpeper's writings are not even internally consistent on the subject. As Park notes, "The tradition of philosophical psychology was highly pluralistic" ("Organic Soul," 480).

15. For an account of the ways in which early modern physiology could serve political ends, see John Rogers, *The Matter of Revolution: Science, Poetry, and Politics in the Age of Milton* (Ithaca: Cornell University Press, 1998). For an analysis of the relationship between politics and faculty psychology in the period, see Todd Wayne Butler, *Imagination and Politics in Seventeenth-Century England* (Burlington, Vt.: Ashgate, 2008).

16. According to *The Oxford Dictionary of National Biography*'s entry on Culpeper, these accusations appeared in the royalist newssheet *Mercurius Pragmaticus* on September 4–9, 1649. See Patrick Curry, "Culpeper, Nicholas (1616–1654)," in *The Oxford Dictionary of National Biography*,

ed. Lawrence Goldman (Oxford: Oxford University Press, 2004).

17. The *Oxford Dictionary of National Biography* claims that it "would be hard to overstate Culpeper's importance for the medical practice and health education (in the widest sense) of his time and place" and credits him with putting "the orthodox medicine of his day . . . into the realm of public discourse."

18. If anything, Fludd's relationship with the College of Physicians suggests that even membership in that organization did not necessarily indicate a shared homogenous vision regarding matters physiological. Indeed, the *ODNB* notes that Fludd's unorthodox views on Galenic medicine in particular made his membership a tumultuous one; he was initially denied admittance because he "was not well enough versed in Galenic medicine," he was later "secretly denounced as an anti-Galenist," and he even temporarily "had his license withdrawn for his allegedly arrogant support of anti-Galenic opinions." Still, his name appears among the authorizing fellows of the *Pharmacopoeia Londoniensis*—the very compendium Culpeper illegally translated and published. See Ian Maclean, "Fludd, Robert (*bap.* 1574, *d.* 1637)," in *The Oxford Dictionary of National Biography*, ed. H. C. G. Matthew and Brian Harrison (Oxford: Oxford University Press, 2004).

19. Helkiah Crooke, *Mikrokosmographia, A description of the Body of Man. Together with the controversies and Figures thereto belonging. Collected and Translated out of all the Best Authors of Anatomy, Especially out of Gasper Bauhinus and Andreas Laurentius,* 2nd ed. (London: William Jaggard, 1616), 504–5.

20. Robert Burton, *The Anatomy of Melancholy*, ed. Thomas Faulkner, Nicolas Kiessling, and Rhonda Blair (Oxford: Clarendon, 1989), 1:152. The middle cell of the brain—highest and closest to God— is often deemed preeminent in the period, as in Culpeper's assertion that "Judgment is seated in the midst of the Brain, to shew that it ought to bear rule over all the other Faculties" (Culpeper, *Ephemeris*, 4.) That Burton situates "*Phantasie*" at the mind's

center is thus telling. Although he argues that, in humans, *"Phantasie"* is "subject and governed by *Reason*, or at least should be," his emphasis on the imaginative faculty's potential power is clear; much as Fludd adjusts faculty science to suit his needs, Burton privileges *"Phantasie"* over the other faculties in order to further his anatomization of melancholy.

21. Jacopo Berengario da Carpi, *Mikrokosmographia: or, A description of the Body of Man being a Practical Anatomy, shewing the Manner of Anatomizing from Part to Part; The like hath not been set forth in the English Tongue. Adorned with many demonstrative Figures,* trans. Henry Jackson (London: Livewell Chapman, 1664), 301.

22. Thomas Hobbes, *Leviathan,* ed. G. A. J. Rogers and Karl Schuhmann (New York: Continuum, 2005–6), 1:20.

23. For example, in his discussion of "imagination" and "memory," Hobbes explains, "After [an] object is removed, or the eye shut, wee still retain an image of the thing seen, though more obscure than when we see it. . . . This *decaying sense,* when wee would express the thing it self, (I mean *fancy* it selfe,) wee call *Imagination,* . . . But when we would express the *decay,* and signifie that the Sense is fading, old, and past, it is called *Memory"* (*Leviathan,* 1:15–16, italics in original).

24. Andreas Vesalius, *On the Fabric of the Human Body,* trans. William F. Richardson and John B. Carman (Novato, Calif.: Norman, 2009), 163. The gorgeous plates that accompanied Vesalius's work were reproduced to accompany a plagiarized Latin text in 1545 and borrowed again to adorn an English physiology treatise detailing the very sort of elaborate system of faculty psychology that Vesalius mocked.

25. Scott Elledge describes faculty science with these words in an appendix to his edition of *Paradise Lost* (463).

26. As Fowler notes in his edition of *Paradise Lost,* the conundrum with which Adam struggles concerns the distinction between external (procatarctic) and internal (proegumenal) causes (288n). See Fowler's introduction (37) for a discussion

of Milton's interest (or lack thereof) in the causes of the fall and for references to criticism on the topic.

27. Hobbes's physiological system offers an excellent contrast with Milton's emphasis on the mind's balance of exposure and enclosure. In describing the process of sensation, Hobbes asserts that "the cause of Sense, is the Externall Body, or Object, which presseth the organ proper to each Sense, either immediately, as in the Tast and Touch; or mediately, as in Seeing, Hearing, and Smelling: which pressure, by the mediation of the Nerves, and other strings, and membranes of the body, continued inwards to the Brain" (*Leviathan,* 1:13). Moreover, according to his system, seemingly voluntary actions—such "as to *go,* to *speak,* to *move* any of our limbes"—are caused by "motion in the organs and interiour parts of mans body, [which are themselves] caused by the action of the things wee See, Heare, &c" (1:42, italics in original). Hobbes thus presents a vision of the mind as utterly exposed to external influence and necessity.

28. While I will not pursue the idea here, connections between Milton's simultaneously positive and wary renderings of the image-maker Fancy in *Paradise Lost* and the "conflict between iconophilia and iconophobia" that Kristie Fleckenstein detects elsewhere in Milton's work warrant further consideration: see Fleckenstein, "Between Iconophilia and Iconophobia: Milton's *Areopagitica* and Seventeenth-Century Visual Culture," in *Rhetorical Agendas: Political, Ethical, Spiritual,* ed. Patricia Bizzell (Mahwah, N.J.: Lawrence Erlbaum Associates, 2006), 72.

29. I am not invested in proclaiming the originality of Milton's attempt to grapple with the freedom of the will by way of engagement with the discourses of faculty science. Indeed, the Cambridge philosopher and theologian John Smith offers the following distinction concerning the relative accessibility of the faculties in his *Select Discourses* (1660): "[The] pseudo-prophetical spirit only flutters below upon the more terrene parts of a man's soul—his passions and fancy. The prince of darkness comes not within the

sphere of light and reason to order affairs there." See John Smith, *Select Discourses*, ed. Henry Griffon Williams, 4th ed. (Cambridge: Cambridge University Press, 1859), 207.

30. For the suggestion that Milton's treatment of Fancy in the poem is quasi-positive, see Lee Jacobus, who notes that such a perspective is remarkable considering "the fact that imagination and fancy were considerably distrusted in Milton's time": Jacobus, *Sudden Apprehension: Aspects of Knowledge in "Paradise Lost"* (Paris: Mouton, 1976), 76. For two older but still essential accounts of the sixteenth- and seventeenth-century anti-imagination discourses to which Jacobus alludes, see Murray Bundy, "The Theory of Imagination in Classical and Medieval Thought," *University of Illinois Studies in Language and Literature* 12 (1927): 1–289, and William Rossky, "Imagination in the English Renaissance: Psychology and Poetic," *Studies in the Renaissance* 5 (1958): 49–73.

31. As Garrett Sullivan puts it, "The significance of sleep's status as largely outside of reason's influence cannot be overestimated": Sullivan, *Sleep, Romance and Human Embodiment: Vitality from Spenser to Milton* (Cambridge: Cambridge University Press, 2012), 18. I would deepen our sense of that significance by considering the implications of sleep's challenge to reason for Milton's representations of free will.

32. Hunter, "Eve's Demonic Dream," 265.

33. While it may seem inconsequential how Adam physically reaches Eden while he dreams, I would submit that the prospect of a sleepwalking Adam is profoundly problematic for *Paradise Lost*. After all, if Fancy—the dominant faculty during sleep—were able to prompt action during sleep, it would open the possibility of a somnambulant Adam consuming the forbidden fruit as a sleep snack, with no consent from his Reason and thus no freedom of will. As foolish as such speculations may seem, early moderns took quite seriously the questions raised about the relationship between sleep, reason, and free will by phenomena like sleepwalking. Indeed, no less a personage

than King James compelled the physician Richard Haydocke to atone for his charlatanic sleep-preaching by recording and supplementing the king's views on the controversy. The resultant manuscript treatise, *Oneirologia* (1605), examines sleepwalking, sleep-talking, and much more in an effort at "discoveringe howe farre the reasonable Soule exerciseth her operations in the time of Sleepe: And prooveinge that in Sleepe there can bee noe reasonable and Methodicall speech." See Alexander Marr, "Richard Haydocke's *Oneirologia*: A Manuscript Treatise on Sleep and Dreams, Including the 'Arguments' of King James I," *Erudition and the Republic of Letters* 2 (2017): 152.

34. I analyze the implications of Raphael's scale in detail later in this section.

35. Burton, *Anatomy of Melancholy*, 1.152 (italics in original).

36. Sullivan, *Sleep, Romance, and Human Embodiment*, 1.

37. Satan's choice to possess a serpent rather than transform into one may allow Milton to juxtapose bestial insufficiency with sufficiency, but the poet seems uneasy that God punishes the serpent despite the fact that it has *no choice* but to participate in Eve's temptation (see Fowler, *Paradise Lost*, 548n). I believe that the subsequent metamorphosis of the devils into serpents (10.504–45) allows Milton to keep the physiological juxtaposition of bestial and human minds while salvaging some semblance of divine justice. See Karen Edwards for a detailed analysis of "Milton's complicated serpents" in the metamorphosis scene (*Milton and the Natural World* [Cambridge: Cambridge University Press, 1999], 85–99).

38. See *Paradise Lost*, ed. Fowler, 222n, and ed. Flannagan, 445n; both cite C. S. Lewis's contention that "the happy garden is an image of the human body" (Lewis, *A Preface to "Paradise Lost,"* ed. Mohit K. Ray [New Delhi: Atlantic, 2005], 46).

39. Kathleen M. Swaim, *Before and After the Fall: Contrasting Modes in "Paradise Lost"* (Amherst: University of Massachusetts Press, 1986), 227. Swaim cites Fredson Bowers as one such reader, but then seems to join the ranks herself, albeit with the mild corrective that "Adam's stolid reason

would stagnate" without the enlivening input provided by "Eve's fanciful nature" (228).

40. For a detailed account of Milton's collapsing allegories, see Catherine Martin, *The Ruins of Allegory: "Paradise Lost" and the Metamorphosis of Epic Convention* (Durham: Duke University Press, 1998).

41. For more on Milton's use of spirit theory, see Benet, "Milton's Toad"; Hunter, "Eve's Demonic Dream," 49; and W. Reavley Gair, "Milton and Science," in *John Milton: Introductions*, ed. John Broadbent (Cambridge: Cambridge University Press, 1973), 29–30.

Afterword

Beyond the Lost World: Early Modern Sleep Scenarios

GARRETT A. SULLIVAN JR.

In a 2002 article, Carol M. Worthman and Melissa K. Melby discuss how their fellow anthropologists had until that point all but ignored the topic of sleep: "Sleep, in its ubiquity, seeming nonsociality, apparent universality, and presumed biologically driven uniformity, has been overlooked as a background variable. Amazingly, it has not engaged a discipline dedicated to the study of human behavior, human diversity, and their cultural biological bases."[1] Since Worthman and Melby's article was first published, sleep has become a subject of inquiry in a range of humanistic and social scientific disciplines. The authors identify a major reason for this: scholars have come to realize that, rather than being defined by "biologically driven uniformity," sleep has a "cultural biological" basis. Every living human sleeps, but how she does so, and what others make of her doing so, is profoundly informed by culture. In this regard, and as the essays in *Forming Sleep: Representing Consciousness in the English Renaissance* so admirably demonstrate, sleep is a worthy object of scrutiny for literary and historical as well as anthropological investigation.

And yet, in early modern studies, sleep's "cultural biological" nature has sometimes been simplistically rendered in the service of a problematic distinction between how we slept then versus how we sleep now. We see this in the wake of the historian A. Roger Ekirch's trailblazing work on sleeping patterns prior to the Industrial Revolution. Ekirch's major claim is that people slept differently in the preindustrial period than they do today, dividing their slumbers into "first" and "second" sleeps, with an intervening period of wakefulness. Ekirch's argument is genuinely illuminating, but it lends itself to a narrative in which a "natural" way of sleeping has been rudely disrupted by industrial modernity. (In this regard, it is worth noting that Ekirch's findings were first published with a title redolent of a historical fall from grace: "Sleep We Have Lost.")[2] Ekirch's work has had a wide impact, having been picked up in outlets such as the *New Yorker*, *NPR*, and the *New York Times*. In a *BBC News Magazine* article from February 2012 that considers the research of Ekirch and others, Stephanie Hegarty suggests that "a growing body of evidence from both science and history suggests that the eight-hour sleep may be unnatural."[3] We learn in this article that, in the 1990s, a psychiatrist named Thomas Wehr "plunged [a group of subjects] into darkness for 14 hours every day for a month"; starting in the fourth week, those subjects "slept first for four hours, then woke for one or two hours before falling into a second four-hour sleep." Here we encounter "natural" sleep—the "sleep we have lost"—(re-)created in the lab. In generating this result, Wehr's experiment sacrifices only one thing: the actual, variable sleeping habits of human beings.

To put it another way, Thomas Wehr produces in his experiment a particular *sleep scenario* that chimes in some ways with Ekirch's findings.[4] In this scenario, culture is putatively checked at the door. This includes the various aspects of the sleep subjects' lives that inform how they usually slumber: whether they work two jobs or late at night, or have young children, or are commuting long distances, or live in apartments with paper-thin walls and loud, night-owl neighbors. My point is not to deny the value of Wehr's findings; it is instead to suggest, first, that the particular sleep scenario in which those findings are produced helps to shape them and, second, that the scenario's bracketing of culture is also, paradoxically, revelatory of what our culture values: a scientific "truth" generated in indifference to our quotidian experience as slumberers.

As we have seen, Wehr's study reinforces Ekirch's findings about preindustrial sleep. This would seem to suggest that, for all my quibbling about his method, Wehr has indeed re-created the "sleep we have lost." The only problem is that segmented sleep is best understood not as "natural" but as a template for sleeping that was unevenly adhered to in practice. The historian Sasha Handley puts it this way: "Early modern bedtimes, as far as they are recoverable, form a complex jigsaw that combines individual opportunities for determining sleep's timings with personal preferences and religious sensibilities. . . . I do not offer an alternative 'system' of sleeping habits [to that of segmented sleep] . . . but insist instead on a more flexible and multilayered understanding of sleep's timings that could vary on a daily basis, according to key transitions in the individual life cycle, and that took account of a diverse range of personal and religious sensibilities."[5] Handley's brilliant study draws heavily on household records, especially probate inventories. As she herself notes, "A broader range of sleeping environments would certainly offer important points of comparison to the households examined here. Parallel research into sleep's management within prisons, hospitals and workhouses may also tell a different story to developments within household life."[6] One major conclusion to be drawn from Handley's work, though, is that there is no such thing as a "natural" conception of sleep whose historical passing we might be tempted to mourn. Instead, there were in the early modern period a range of sleep practices, and we do a conceptual violence to sleep's variety when we seek to abstract from it a single idea, no matter how widely championed, about "how they slept back then."

I have been arguing *against* an idealist conception of sleep grounded in appeals to nature and *for* a view of it as interwoven with culture. Such a view requires that we approach sleep not as a "biologically driven uniformity" that would operate the same way in all human beings if only culture didn't get in the way but as a variable somatic practice that is functionally inextricable from the social. My emphasis thus far has been on the way in which culture informs different sleeping habits. However, one could make much the same point about the representation and the phenomenological experience of sleep: both are inseparable from, and are rendered legible by, the sleep scenarios in which they are embedded.[7] In an early modern literary context, this helps to explain one of the fascinating elements of sleep, which is the remarkable extent to which it is open to multiple and often conflicting interpretations. As I have argued elsewhere, sleep in the early modern period can betray a clean conscience or a guilty one; it can connote piety or sinfulness; it signifies either the suspension of sensory activity or the overindulgence of the senses; a commonplace metaphor for death, sleep also encodes (animal or, especially, vegetal) life.[8] How and what sleep can mean in a given literary work depends in large part upon the particular scenario in which it is embedded. This is not to posit that sleep's meanings are transparent if one is sensitive to the nature of a given scenario; it is instead to suggest that the scenario provides a horizon of expectations for the way in which sleep might be thought within it.[9]

In the first canto of Book 1 of *The Faerie Queene*, Edmund Spenser presents us with two conflicting sleep scenarios, each of which centers upon Redcrosse's sleep on a particular night.[10] The first scenario emphasizes sleep's unregulability, the way in which it can descend upon and overtake the subject. Spenser associates sleep's unruliness with classical epic through the agency of Morpheus, who looms large in this canto: "The drouping Night thus creepeth on them fast, / And the sad humor loading their eye liddes, / As messenger of *Morpheus* on them cast / Sweet slombring deaw, the which to sleepe them biddes" (1.1.36.1–4). If sleep here overwhelms Redcrosse and Una—we are told that *they* do *its* bidding—three stanzas earlier it makes a rhetorical appearance as a crucial aspect of self-care. Una says to Redcrosse, "Then with the Sunne take Sir, your timely rest, / And with new day new worke at once begin: / Vntroubled night they say giues counsell best" (1.33.1–3). Una is the spokesperson for "timely rest," a sleep associated with self-regulation and shaped in accordance with the demands of the next day's "new worke." Moreover, insofar as it is Una that advocates for "timely rest," we are to believe that this is the sleep of the Protestant true believer.

The brilliance of Spenser's depiction of sleep resides in the conceptual tensions that, at least for a time, he leaves unresolved.[11] On the one hand, Redcrosse and Una go to bed shortly after she speaks in praise of timely rest. In doing so, they perform their status as adherents of the true faith. On the other hand, their timely rest is shadowed by the compulsory sleep whose bidding they both do. In presenting the same phenomenon through the lenses of two different sleep scenarios, Spenser subtly undercuts a confident interpretation of Redcrosse's slumber as connoting self-regulation. Instead, he shows how self-regulation is closely shadowed by its failure. And similar shadows are routinely cast over sleep in Book 1. For example, consider the way in which Arthur's dream vision of Gloriana, which he describes in terms of his hart "steal[ing] away" while he was "slombring soft" (9.13.6), is troublingly anticipated by Redcrosse's "fit false dreame, that can delude the sleepers sent [senses]" (1.43.9)—a dream that led Redcrosse's "manly heart

[to] melt away" (47.5). While we are seemingly supposed to credit the former and discount the latter, their similarity forces us to consider the possibility that Arthur's dream might be as specious as Redcrosse's. The two distinct sleep scenarios threaten to dissolve into each other. At stake here is not only the question of how we interpret sleep but also the extent to which we are capable of maintaining the model of self-regulation that Spenser associates with (timely rest and) the true faith.[12]

In representing the dreams of Arthur and Redcrosse, Spenser attends to both the sleep practice of these characters—for instance, Arthur sleeps on "verdant gras" (9.13.3) with his pillow as his helmet—and their oneiric activity. Intriguingly, the content of their dreams is underrepresented; what the dream *depicts* is less important than what it *does*, which in Redcrosse's case entails "bath[ing him] in wanton blis and wicked ioy" (1.47.6).[13] This is, of course, not the only way in which dreams are presented to us in early modern literature; one can think of numerous examples in which the content of a dream takes precedence over either the circumstances of its generation or the nature of its somatic efficacy. The broader point is that, in early modern literature, both dreams specifically and consciousness more generally have variable roles to play in different sleep scenarios. It is in this regard that the contributors to this volume perform such an invaluable service.

The essays in *Forming Sleep* present us with a range of literary sleep scenarios in which the relationship among sleep, sleeplessness, and consciousness is provocatively explored. The contributors to this volume eloquently attest to the surprisingly variegated nature of sleep's cultural biological basis. Sleep appears within these pages as a register of "the felt experience of consciousness" (Giulio Pertile), as both an emblem and eroder of social division (Brian Chalk), and as a "launchpad for allegory" (Nancy Simpson-Younger). While many of these essays draw upon natural philosophical treatises, their authors are attuned to the way in which the sleep scenarios they investigate are as shaped by genre and form as they are by Galenic humoralism or faculty psychology (Margaret Simon, Jennifer Lewin, Cassie Miura, N. Amos Rothschild). It's also worth noting that two contributors (Benjamin Parris and Timothy A. Turner) situate sleep and sleeplessness within the genealogy of biopower (and also, in Parris's case, of capital). Contextualized in this way, early modern sleep practices gesture not toward a lost world but to an emergent one.

In *24/7: Late Capitalism and the Ends of Sleep*, Jonathan Crary identifies sleep as the final frontier of a relentlessly consumerist society: "In its profound uselessness and intrinsic passivity, with the incalculable losses it causes in production time, circulation, and consumption, sleep will always collide with the demands of a 24/7 universe. The huge portion of our lives that we spend asleep, freed from a morass of simulated needs, subsists as one of the great human affronts to the voraciousness of contemporary capitalism."[14] Crary also observes of sleep that it "is a ubiquitous but unseen reminder of a premodernity that has never been fully exceeded, of the agricultural universe which began vanishing 400 years ago."[15] An exhilaratingly polemical work, *24/7* astutely isolates the challenge sleep poses to late capitalism even if it also sometimes overstates that challenge and homogenizes present-day sleep practice.[16] In associating sleep with a slowly vanishing "agricultural universe," however, Crary flirts with the "sleep we have lost" brand of idealism discussed at the beginning of this essay.[17] *Forming Sleep* serves as a puissant antidote to such idealizing impulses. The essays in this collection also demonstrate that the literary sleep scenario is not primarily a mimetic one. Instead of merely reflecting natural philosophical knowledge, such scenarios produce new ways of thinking about the relationship between, on the one hand, literary form or genre and, on the other, sensation, embodiment, consciousness, humanness, ethics, and agency. *Forming Sleep* invites us both to abandon our efforts to conjure up a lost world of "natural" slumber and to move beyond medical explanations for a somatic phenomenon whose meanings and significance far exceed that which is dreamt of in natural philosophy. This invitation is a welcome one, and, in taking it up, the contributors to this volume help us to see just how rich, complex, and even contradictory early modern sleep scenarios could be.

NOTES

1. Carol M. Worthman and Melissa K. Melby, "Toward a Comparative Developmental Ecology of Human Sleep," in *Adolescent Sleep Patterns: Biological, Social, and Psychological Influences*, ed. Mary A. Carskadon (Cambridge: Cambridge University Press, 2002), 69–117, esp. 69.

2. A. Roger Ekirch, "Sleep We Have Lost: Pre-Industrial Slumber in the British Isles," *American Historical Review* 106, no.

2 (April 2001): 343–86. See also Ekirch, *At Day's Close: Night in Times Past* (New York: W. W. Norton, 2005).

3. Stephanie Hegarty, "The Myth of the Eight-Hour Sleep," *BBC News Magazine*, February 22, 2012, http://www.bbc.com/news/magazine-16964783.

4. By using the term *scenario*, I intend two things: to invite us, first, to think of sleep not as an isolable action unto itself

but as a somatic operation usually (but not always) experienced and construed as part of a bodily habitus; and second, to consider both to attend to the "where, when, how and why" of sleep, not to mention the "with (or without) whom." In the case of a literary sleep scenario, an analysis of it would likely take up matters of genre and form.

5. Sasha Handley, *Sleep in Early Modern England* (New Haven: Yale University Press, 2016), 9.

6. Ibid., 218.

7. In making this claim, I do not mean to discount the significance of either broader cultural or discourse-specific meanings of sleep that inform these scenarios.

8. For more on sleep's range of signification in this period, see my book *Sleep, Romance, and Human Embodiment: Vitality from Spenser to Milton* (Cambridge: Cambridge Univeristy Press, 2012).

9. The term *horizon of expectations* is derived from the reception theory of Hans Robert Jauss.

10. I develop the significance of unregulable sleep in a forthcoming essay entitled "Sleeping in Error in Spenser's *Faerie Queene*, Book One." Quotations from Spenser are drawn from *The Faerie Queene*, ed. A. C. Hamilton et al. (New York: Pearson/Longman, 2007).

11. Starting later in this canto, the scales are tipped in the favor of sleep's uncontrollability. Redcrosse's alienation from Una is linked to his (Archimago-enhanced) fitful slumbers.

12. For a persuasive discussion of Spenser's pathologized version of self-care in Book 3 of *The Faerie Queene*, see Benjamin Parris's essay in this volume.

13. Compare Giulio Pertile's point, made in this collection, about sleep's primacy over dreams in the Renaissance sonnet sequence.

14. Jonathan Crary, *24/7: Late Capitalism and the Ends of Sleep* (London: Verso, 2013), 10.

15. Ibid., 11.

16. Crary does not emphasize the ways in which sleep represents an opportunity for late capitalism, as witnessed by the burgeoning market for white-noise machines or hypoallergenic pillows or mattresses that can be modified to match the comportment of the individual sleeper. Regarding the homogenization of sleep in 24/7, Benjamin Reiss points out that "[Crary] ignores the fact that bourgeois Westerners have numerous sleep-related advantages that previous generations—or most living in the developing world—could only envy: climate-controlled homes, improved bedding, fewer pests, advances in medicine and hygiene, reduced fear of fire, private bedrooms, labor laws" (Reiss, "Sleep's Hidden Histories," *Los Angeles Review of Books*, February 15, 2014, https://lareviewofbooks .org/article/sleeps-hidden-histories/

17. As Reiss puts it, Crary's conception of sleep embattled by capitalism "implies nostalgia . . . for a preindustrial age, when sleep was more 'natural,' running free like the now-despoiled waters that run through our valleys" ("Sleep's Hidden Histories").

BIBLIOGRAPHY

All early modern texts have been accessed through the Early English Books Online database (EEBO), between July 2015 and March 2019, unless otherwise labeled.

Adams, John Henry. "Agentive Objects and Protestant Idolatry in *Arden of Faversham.*" *Studies in English Literature, 1500–1900* 57, no. 2 (2017): 231–51.

Agamben, Giorgio. *Homo Sacer: Sovereign Power and Bare Life.* Translated by Daniel Heller-Roazen. Stanford: Stanford University Press, 1998.

An Alarme to Wake Church Sleepers. London: Matthew Symmons, 1644.

Aristotle. *Aristotle on Sleep and Dreams.* Translated by David Gallop. Warminster, U.K.: Aris & Phillips, 1996.

———. *De anima.* Translated by J. A. Smith. Oxford: Clarendon Press, 1931.

———. *Nicomachean Ethics.* Translated by Sarah Broadie and Christopher Rowe. Oxford: Oxford University Press, 2002.

———. "On Dreams." In *On the Soul; Parva naturalia; On Breath,* translated by W. S. Hett, 348–73. Cambridge, Mass.: Harvard University Press, 1957.

———. *The Politics and the Constitution of Athens.* Translated by Benjamin Jowett. Edited by Stephen Everson. Cambridge: Cambridge University Press, 1996.

———. *Rhetoric.* Translated by John Henry Freese. Loeb Classical Library 193. Cambridge, Mass.: Harvard University Press, 1939.

Arjava, Antti. "Paternal Power in Late Antiquity." *Journal of Roman Studies* 88 (1998): 147–65.

Augustine. *The Works of Saint Augustine: A Translation for the 21st Century.* Translated by Maria Boulding, OSB. Edited by Boniface Ramsey. New York: New City Press, 2004.

Barrough, Phillip. *The Method of Phisick, Conteyning the Causes, Signes, and Cures of Inward Diseases in Mans Body* [. . .]. London: Richard Field, 1601.

———. *The Methode of Phisicke, Conteyning the Causes, Signes, and Cures of Inward Diseases in Mans Body.* London: Thomas Vautroullier, 1583.

Bates, Thomas. *The True Relation of Two Wonderfull Sleepers.* 1646. Reprinted in *Reprints of English Books, 1475–1700,* edited by Joseph Arnold Foster, no. 42. East Lansing, Mich.: 1945. [Source text: British Museum, E.349.]

Bell, Millicent. "The Fallacy of the Fall in *Paradise Lost.*" *Publications of the Modern Language Association* 68 (1953): 863–83.

Bembo, Pietro. *Prose e rime.* Edited by Carlo Dionisotti. Turin, Italy: Unione Tipografico-Editrice Torinese, 1960.

Benet, Diana Treviño. "Milton's Toad, or Satan's Dream." *Milton Studies* 45 (2006): 38–52.

BIBLIOGRAPHY

Bennett, Jane. *Vibrant Matter: An Ecology of Things*. Durham: Duke University Press, 2010.

Berengario da Carpi, Jacopo. *Mikrokosmographia: or, A description of the body of man being a practical anatomy, shewing the manner of anatomizing from part to part, the like hath Not been set forth in the English tongue: Adorned with many demonstrative figures*. Translated by Henry Jackson. London: Livewell Chapman, 1664.

Berger, Harry, Jr. *The Allegorical Temper*. New Haven: Yale University Press, 1957.

Bevington, David. "Asleep Onstage." In *From Page to Performance: Essays in Early English Drama*, edited by John A. Alford, 51–83. East Lansing: Michigan State University Press, 1995.

Bèze, Théodore de. *The Psalmes of David*. Translated by Anthony Gilby. London: John Harison and Henrie Middleton, 1580.

Blackburn, Thomas H. "'Uncloister'd Virtue': Adam and Eve in Milton's *Paradise*." *Milton Studies* 3 (1971): 119–37.

Bodenham, John. *Englands Helicon casta placent superis, pura cum veste venite, et manibus puris sumite fontis aquam*. Edited by A. B. London: J. R[oberts] for John Flasket, 1600.

Boose, Lynda. "Scolding Brides and Bridling Scolds: Taming the Woman's Unruly Member." *Shakespeare Quarterly* 42, no. 2 (1991): 179–213.

Bowers, Fredson. "Adam, Eve, and the Fall in *Paradise Lost*." *Publications of the Modern Language Association* 84 (1969): 264–73.

Brathwait, Richard. "Of Sleepe." In *A New Spring Shadowed in Sundry Pithie Poems*, D2v–D3r. London: G. Eld., 1619.

Bright, Timothy. *A Treatise of Melancholie*. London: Thomas Vautrollier, 1586.

Bristol, Michael, ed. *Shakespeare and Moral Agency*. New York: Continuum, 2010.

Brooks, Harold. Introduction to *A Midsummer Night's Dream*, edited by Harold Brooks, xxi–cxliii. London: Thomson Learning, 2006.

Brown, Peter, ed. *Reading Dreams: The Interpretation of Dreams from Chaucer to Shakespeare*. Oxford: Oxford University Press, 1999.

Brown, Russell M. "Sidney's *Astrophil and Stella*: Fourth Song." *Explicator* 29, no. 6 (1971): item 48.

Browne, Sir Thomas. *Religio Medici*. In *The Major Works*, edited by C. A. Patrides, 57–162. London: Penguin, 1977.

Budra, Paul, and Clifford Werier, eds. *Shakespeare and Consciousness*. New York: Palgrave Macmillan, 2016.

Bundy, Murray. "The Theory of Imagination in Classical and Medieval Thought." *University of Illinois Studies in Language and Literature* 12 (1927): 1–289.

Burton, Robert. *The Anatomy of Melancholy*. Oxford, 1621.

———. *The Anatomy of Melancholy*. Edited by Thomas Faulkner, Nicolas K. Kiessling, and Rhonda L. Blair. Commentary by J. B. Bambough with Martin Dodsworth. 6 vols. Oxford: Oxford University Press, 1989–2000.

Butler, Samuel. *Hudibras written in the time of the late wars*. London, J.G. for Richard Marrist, 1663.

Butler, Todd Wayne. *Imagination and Politics in Seventeenth-Century England*. Burlington, Vt.: Ashgate, 2008.

Cahill, Patricia. *Unto the Breach: Martial Formations, Historical Trauma, and the Early Modern Stage*. Oxford: Oxford University Press, 2008.

Calhoun, Joshua. "Ecosystemic Shakespeare: Vegetable Memorabilia in the Sonnets." *Shakespeare Studies* 39 (2011): 64–73.

Calvin, John. *The Psalmes of David and Others: With M. John Calvins Commentaries*. Translated by Arthur Golding. London: [Thomas East and Henry Middleton for Lucas Harison and George Byshop], 1571.

Campbell, Lily B. *Shakespeare's Tragic Heroes: Slaves of Passion.* Cambridge: Cambridge University Press, 1930.

Campion, Thomas. "The Second Book of Thomas Campion's Epigrams." In *The Latin Poetry of Thomas Campion,* edited by Dana F. Sutton. Birmingham, U.K.: Philological Museum, 2016. http://www.philological.bham.ac.uk/campion/epigrams_2_trans.html.

———. *Thomae Campiani poemata.* London: Richard Field, 1595.

———. *The Works of Thomas Campion.* Edited by Walter R. Davis. London: Doubleday, 1969.

Canetti, Elias. *Crowds and Power.* Translated by Carol Stewart. Harmondsworth, U.K.: Penguin, 1973.

Canguilhem, Georges. *A Vital Rationalist: Selected Writings from Georges Canguilhem.* Edited by Francois Delaporte. New York: Zone Books, 1994.

Carrai, Stefano. *Ad somnum: L'invocazione al sonno nella lirica italiana.* Padua, Italy: Antenore, 1990.

Casey, Edward. *The Fate of Place: A Philosophical History.* Oakland: University of California Press, 1997.

Cavell, Stanley. "Epistemology and Tragedy: A Reading of *Othello.*" *Daedalus* 103, no. 3 (1979): 27–43.

———. *Pursuits of Happiness: The Hollywood Comedy of Remarriage.* Cambridge, Mass.: Harvard University Press, 1981.

Cefalu, Paul. "The Burdens of Mind Reading in Shakespeare's *Othello*: A Cognitive and Psychoanalytic Approach." *Shakespeare Quarterly* 64, no. 3 (2013): 265–94.

Chan, Mary. "The Strife of Love in a Dream and Sidney's Second Song in *Astrophil and Stella.*" *Sidney Newsletter* 3, no. 1 (1982): 3–9.

Cicero. *On Old Age; On Friendship; On Divination.* Translated by W. A. Falconer. Loeb Classical Library 154. Cambridge, Mass.: Harvard University Press, 1923.

Clarke, Danielle. "Mary Sidney Herbert and Women's Religious Verse." In *Early Modern English Poetry: A Critical Companion,* edited by Patrick Cheney, Andrew Hadfield, and Garrett A. Sullivan, 184–94. Oxford: Oxford University Press, 2007.

Cogan, Thomas. *The Haven of Health, Chiefly gathered for the comfort of students, and consequently of all those that have a care of Their health, amplified upon five words of Hippocrates, written Epid. 6. Labour, cibus, potio, somnus, Venus.* London: Henrie Midleton for William Norton, 1584.

———. *The Haven of Health [. . .].* London, 1596.

———. *The Haven of Health [. . .] Hereunto Is added a preservation from the pestilence, with a short censure of the late sicknes at Oxford.* London: Anne Griffin for Roger Ball, 1636.

Colie, Rosalie. *Paradoxia epidemica: The Renaissance Tradition of Paradox.* Princeton: Princeton University Press, 1966.

Cook, Eleanor. "'Methought' as Dream Formula in Shakespeare, Milton, Wordsworth, Keats, and Others." *English Language Notes* 32, no. 4 (1995): 34–46.

Coren, Pamela. "In the Person of Womankind: Female Persona Poems by Campion, Donne, Jonson." *Studies in Philology* 98, no. 2 (Spring 2001): 225–50.

Craighero, Laila. "The Role of the Motor System in Cognitive Functions." In *The Routledge Handbook of Embodied Cognition,* edited by Lawrence Shapiro, 51–58. New York: Taylor and Francis, 2014.

Craik, Katharine A., and Tanya Pollard, eds. *Shakespearean Sensations: Experiencing Literature in Early Modern England.* Cambridge: Cambridge University Press, 2013.

Crary, Jonathan. *24/7: Late Capitalism and the Ends of Sleep.* London: Verso, 2013.

Crooke, Helkiah. *Mikrokosmographia, a description of the body of man, together with the controversies and figures thereto belonging / collected and translated out of all the best authors of anatomy, especially out of Gasper Bauhinus and Andreas Laurentius.* 2nd ed. London: William Jaggard, 1616.

Culpeper, Nicholas. *An ephemeris for the yeer 1651, amplified with rational predictions from the book of the creatures.* London: Peter Cole, 1651.

Curran, John E., Jr. "'Duke Byron Flows with Adust and Melancholy Choler': General and Special Character in Chapman's 'Byron' Plays." *Studies in Philology* 108, no. 3 (2011): 345–78.

Curry, Patrick. "Culpeper, Nicholas (1616–1654)." In *The Oxford Dictionary of National Biography*, edited by Lawrence Goldman. Oxford: Oxford University Press, 2004. https://doi-org.prox.lib.ncsu.edu/10.1093/ref:odnb/6882.

Daniel, Drew. *The Melancholy Assemblage: Affect and Epistemology in the English Renaissance.* New York: Fordham University Press, 2013.

Daniel, Samuel. *Poems and "A Defence of Ryme."* Edited by Arthur Colby Sprague. Cambridge, Mass.: Harvard University Press, 1930.

———. *Selected Poetry and "A Defense of Rhyme."* Edited by Geoffrey G. Hiller and Peter L. Groves. Asheville, N.C.: Pegasus Press, 1998.

Dawson, Antony, and Paul Yachnin. *The Culture of Playgoing in Shakespeare's England: A Collaborative Debate.* Cambridge: Cambridge University Press, 2001.

Della Casa, Giovanni. *Rime.* Edited by Stefano Carrai. Milan: Mimesis, 2014.

Della Porta, Giambattista. *Natural Magick.* London: John Wright, 1669.

Descartes, René. *Meditations on First Philosophy.* Translated and edited by John Cottingham. Cambridge: Cambridge University Press, 2017.

Desportes, Philippe. *Les Amours d'Hippolyte.* Edited by Victor E. Graham. Geneva: Droz, 1960.

Detmer, Emily. "Civilizing Subordination: Domestic Violence and *The Taming of the Shrew.*" *Shakespeare Quarterly* 48, no. 3 (1997): 273–94.

Diekhoff, John S. "Eve's Dream and the Paradox of Fallible Perfection." *Milton Quarterly* 4 (1970): 5–7.

Dimsdale, Joel E. "Sleep in *Othello.*" *Journal of Clinical Sleep Medicine* 5, no. 3 (2009): 280–81.

Doelman, James. "Circulation of the Late Elizabethan and Early Stuart Epigram." *Renaissance and Reformation* 29, no. 1 (Winter 2005): 59–73.

Dolven, Jeff. "Besides Good and Evil." *Studies in English Literature, 1500–1900* 57, no. 1 (Winter 2017): 1–22.

Dowd, Michelle. "Shakespeare's Sleeping Workers." *Shakespeare Studies* 41 (2013): 148–76.

The drowsie disease, or, an alarum to wake church sleepers. London: J. D., 1638.

Dubrow, Heather. *The Challenges of Orpheus.* Baltimore: Johns Hopkins University Press, 2008.

Edwards, Karen. *Milton and the Natural World.* Cambridge: Cambridge University Press, 1999.

Ekirch, A. Roger. *At Day's Close: Night in Times Past.* New York: W. W. Norton, 2005.

———. "Sleep We Have Lost: Pre-Industrial Slumber in the British Isles." *American Historical Review* 106, no. 2 (April 2001): 343–86.

Elwood, Christopher. *The Body Broken: The Calvinist Doctrine of the Eucharist and the Symbolization of Power in Sixteenth-Century France.* Oxford: Oxford University Press, 1999.

Elyot, Sir Thomas. *The Castel of Helthe gathered and made by Syr Thomas Elyot knyghte, out of the chiefe authors of physyke, wherby euery manne may knowe the state of his owne body, the preseruatio[n] of helthe, and how to instructe welle his physytion in syckenes that he be Not deceyued.* London: Thomas Berthelet, 1539.

———. *The Castell of Health corrected, and in some places augmented by the first author thereof, Sir Thomas Elyot Knight.* London: Widdow Orwin, 1595.

Empson, Jacob. *Sleep and Dreaming.* New York: Palgrave Macmillan, 2002.

Falk, Florence. "Dream and Ritual Process in *A Midsummer Night's Dream.*" *Comparative Drama* 14, no. 3 (1980): 263–79.

Ferry, Anne. *The "Inward" Language: Sonnets of Wyatt, Sidney, Shakespeare, Donne.* Chicago: University of Chicago Press, 1983.

Fiedrowicz, Michael. Introduction to *Augustine's Expositions of the Psalms, 1–32*, edited by John E. Rotelle, 13–66. New York: New City Press, 2000.

Fineman, Joel. *Shakespeare's Perjured Eye: The Invention of Poetic Subjectivity in the Sonnets.* Berkeley: University of California Press, 1986.

Fish, Stanley E. *Self-Consuming Artifacts: The Experience of Seventeenth-Century Literature.* Berkeley: University of California Press, 1972.

———. *Surprised by Sin: The Reader in "Paradise Lost."* New York: St. Martin's, 1967.

Fleckenstein, Kristie S. "Between Iconophilia and Iconophobia: Milton's *Aeropagitica* and Seventeenth-Century Visual Culture." In *Rhetorical Agendas: Political, Ethical, Spiritual*, edited by Patricia Bizzell, 69–76. Mahwah, N.J.: Lawrence Erlbaum Associates, 2006.

Florio, John. *A worlde of wordes, or Most copious, and exact dictionarie in Italian and English, collected by John Florio.* London: Arnold Hatfield for Edward Blount, 1598.

Floyd-Wilson, Mary. *English Ethnicity and Race in Early Modern Drama.* Cambridge: Cambridge University Press, 2003.

Fludd, Robert. *Utriusque cosmi, maioris scilicet et minoris, metaphysica, physica, atque technica historia.* Frankfurt: Theodor De Bry, 1617–21.

Foucault, Michel. *The History of Sexuality.* Vol. 1, *An Introduction.* Translated by Robert Hurley. New York: Vintage Books, 1990.

———. *The Order of Things: An Archaeology of the Human Sciences.* New York: Random House, 1970.

Foxe, John. *The Whole Workes of W. Tyndall, John Frith, and Doct Barnes three worthy martyrs, and principall teachers of this Churche of England collected and compiled in one tome togither, beyng Before scattered, [and] now in print here exhibited to the Church. To the prayse of God, and profite of all good Christian readers.* London: John Daye, 1573.

Fretz, Claude. "'Either his notion weakens, or his discernings / Are lethargied': Sleeplessness and Waking Dreams as Tragedy in *Julius Caesar* and *King Lear.*" *Études Épistémè* 30 (2016): 1–33.

Frost, Robert. *The Poetry of Robert Frost: The Collected Poems.* Edited by Edward Latham. New York: Holt Paperbacks, 2002.

Frye, Northrop. *The Anatomy of Criticism.* Princeton: Princeton University Press, 1957.

———. *Northrop Frye on Shakespeare.* Edited by Robert Sandler. New Haven: Yale University Press, 1986.

Gair, W. Reavley. "Milton and Science." In *John Milton: Introductions*, edited by John Broadbent, 120–43. Cambridge: Cambridge University Press, 1973.

Garber, Marjorie. *Dream in Shakespeare: From Metaphor to Metamorphosis.* 1974. Reprint, New Haven: Yale University Press, 2013.

Gibson, Kristen. "The Order of the Book: Materiality, Narrative and Authorial Voice in John Dowland's *First Booke of Songs or Ayres.*" *Renaissance Studies* 26 (2012): 13–33.

Gil, Daniel Juan. *Shakespeare's Anti-Politics: Sovereign Power and the Life of the Flesh.* Basingstoke, U.K.: Palgrave Macmillan, 2013.

Gilby, Anthony. "Epistle dedicatorie." In *The Psalmes of David*, translated by Théodore de Bèze, iir–vr. London: John Harison and Henrie Middleton, 1580.

Gish, Dustin. "Taming the Shrew: Shakespeare, Machiavelli, and Political Philosophy." In *Shakespeare and the Body Politic*, edited by Bernard

J. Dobski and Dustin Gish, 197–220. Lanham, Md.: Lexington Books, 2013.

Golding, Arthur. "Epistle dedicatorie." In *The Psalmes of David and Others: With M. John Calvins Commentaries*, translated by Arthur Golding. London: [Thomas East and Henry Middleton for Lucas Harison and George Byshop], 1571.

Gowland, Angus. *The Worlds of Renaissance Melancholy: Robert Burton in Context*. Cambridge: Cambridge University Press, 2006.

Greenblatt, Stephen. *Renaissance Self-Fashioning: From More to Shakespeare*. Chicago: University of Chicago Press, 1980.

———. *The Swerve: How the World Became Modern*. New York: W. W. Norton, 2012.

Greene, Roland. "Sir Philip Sidney's Psalms, the Sixteenth-Century Psalter, and the Nature of Lyric." *Studies in English Literature, 1500–1900* 30, no. 1 (1990): 19–40.

Guilhamet, Leon. "*A Midsummer-Night's Dream* as the Imitation of an Action." *Studies in English Literature, 1500–1900* 15, no. 2 (1975): 266–71.

Hamilton, Christopher. *Living Philosophy: Reflections on Life, Meaning and Morality*. Edinburgh: Edinburgh University Press, 2001.

Hamlin, Hannibal. "'The highest matter in the noblest forme': The Influence of the Sidney Psalms." *Sidney Journal* 23, no. 1–2 (2005): 133–57.

———. *Psalm Culture and Early Modern English Literature*. Cambridge: Cambridge University Press, 2004.

Hamlin, William H. *Montaigne's English Journey: Reading the Essays in Shakespeare's Day*. Oxford: Oxford University Press, 2013.

Handley, Sasha. *Sleep in Early Modern England*. New Haven: Yale University Press, 2016.

Hannay, Margaret. "'House-Confined Maids': The Presentation of Woman's Role in the Psalmes of the Countess of Pembroke." *English Literary Renaissance* 24, no. 1 (1994): 44–71.

———. *Philip's Phoenix: Mary Sidney, Countess of Pembroke*. Oxford: Oxford University Press, 1990.

———. "Re-revealing the Psalms: Mary Sidney, Countess of Pembroke, and Her Early Modern Readers." In *Psalms in the Early Modern World*, edited by Linda Phyllis Austern, David Orvis, and Kari Boyd McBride, 219–34. Farnham, U.K.: Ashgate, 2011.

Hanson, Elizabeth. *Discovering the Subject in Renaissance England*. Cambridge: Cambridge University Press, 1998.

Hardt, Michael, and Antonio Negri. *Multitude: War and Democracy in the Age of Empire*. New York: Penguin Press, 2004.

Harvey, E. Ruth. *Inward Wits: Psychological Theory in the Middle Ages and the Renaissance*. London: Warburg Institute, 1975.

Harvey, Gabriel. *Four letters, and certaine sonnets especially touching Robert Greene, and other parties by him abused*. London: John Wolfe, 1592.

Heath, James. *Torture and English Law: An Administrative and Legal History from the Plantagenets to the Stuarts*. Westport, Conn.: Greenwood Press, 1982.

Heath, Robert. *Clarastella; Together with Poems Occasional, Elegies, Epigrams, Satyrs*. London: Humphrey and Mosely, 1650.

Hegarty, Stephanie. "The Myth of the Eight-Hour Sleep." *BBC News Magazine*, February 22, 2012. http://www .bbc.com/news/magazine16964783.

Heyd, Michael. "Melancholy and Enthusiasm: The Sources of the Medical Critique of Enthusiasm." In *"Be Sober and Reasonable": The Critique of Enthusiasm in the Seventeenth and Early Eighteenth Centuries*, 44–71. Leiden, Netherlands: E. J. Brill, 1995.

The Historie and Life of King James the Sext. Edinburgh: James Ballantyne, 1825.

Hobbes, Thomas. *Leviathan*. Edited by G. A. J. Rogers and Karl Schuhmann. 2 vols. New York: Continuum, 2005–6.

Hobson, Allan. *Sleep and Dreams*. Burlington, N.C.: Carolina Biology Supply, 1992.

Hoeniger, F. David. *Medicine and Shakespeare in the English Renaissance*. Newark: University of Delaware Press, 1992.

Holland, Peter. Introduction to *A Midsummer Night's Dream*, edited by Peter Holland, 1–118. Oxford: Oxford University Press, 1995.

Hooker, Richard. *Of the Laws of Ecclesiastical Polity: A Critical Edition*. Edited by Arthur Stephen McGrade. Oxford: Oxford University Press, 2013.

Howard, Henry, Earl of Surrey. *Poems*. Edited by Emrys Jones. Oxford: Clarendon Press, 1964.

Hunter, William B. "Eve's Demonic Dream." *English Literary History* 13 (1946): 255–65.

Ing, Catharine. *Elizabethan Lyrics: A Study in the Development of English Metres and Their Relation to Poetic Affect*. London: Chatto and Windus, 1951.

Iovan, Sarah. "Singers and Lutes, Lutes and Singers: Musical Performance and Poetic Discourse in Early Modern Songs." *Sixteenth Century Journal* 47, no. 3 (2016): 535–55.

Jacobus, Lee A. *Sudden Apprehension: Aspects of Knowledge in "Paradise Lost."* Paris: Mouton, 1976.

King, Ros. "Minds at Work: Writing, Acting, Watching, Reading *Hamlet*." In *Shakespeare and Consciousness*, edited by Paul Budra and Clifford Werier, 139–62. New York: Palgrave Macmillan, 2016.

Kingdon, Robert N., ed. *The Execution of Justice in England*, by William Cecil, and *A True, Sincere, and Modest Defense of English Catholics*, by William Allen. Ithaca: Cornell University Press, 1965.

Knoll, Gillian. "How to Make Love to the Moon: Intimacy and Erotic Distance in John Lyly's *Endymion*." *Shakespeare Quarterly* 65, no. 2 (2014): 164–79.

Kuzner, James. *Open Subjects: English Renaissance Republicans, Modern Selfhoods and the Virtue of Vulnerability*. Edinburgh: Edinburgh University Press, 2012.

Langbein, John H. *Torture and the Law of Proof: Europe and England in the Ancién Regime*. Chicago: University of Chicago Press, 1977.

Lanyer, Aemylia. *The Poems of Aemylia Lanyer: Salve Deus Rex Judaeorum*. Edited by Susanne Woods. Oxford: Oxford University Press, 1993.

Larson, Katherine R. "From Inward Conversation to Public Praise: Mary Sidney Herbert's Psalmes." *Sidney Journal* 24, no. 1 (2006): 21–43.

Laurens, André du. *Discours de la conservation de la veuë: des maladies melancholique; des catarrhes, et de la viellesse*. Paris, 1597.

Lavater, Ludwig. *Of Ghostes and Spirites Walking by Nyght and of Strange Noyses, Crackes, and Sundry Forewarnynges, Whiche Commonly Happen Before the Death of Menne, Great Slaughters, [and] Alterations of Kyngdomes*. London: Henry Benneyman for Richard Watkins, 1572.

Leitch, Megan. "'Grete luste to slepe': Somatic Ethics and the Sleep of Romance from *Sir Gawain and the Green Knight* to Shakespeare." *Parergon* 32, no. 1 (2015): 103–28.

Lemnius, Levinus. *The Touchstone of Complexions, Generallye appliable, Expedient and Profitable for all Such, as be Desirous & Carefull of Their Bodylye health: Contayning Most Easie Rules & Ready Tokens, Whereby Every One May Perfectly Try, And Throughly Know, as Well the Exacte State, Habite, Disposition, and Constitution, of his owne Body Outwardly: As also the Inclinations, Affections, Motions, & Desires of his Mynd Inwardly*. Translated by Thomas Newton. London: Thomas Marsh, 1576.

Leo, Russ. "Medievalism Without Nostalgia: Guyon's Swoon and the English Reformation *Descensus ad Inferos*." *Spenser Studies* 39 (2014): 105–47.

Levack, Brian P. *The Witch-Hunt in Early Modern Europe.* 3rd ed. Abingdon, U.K.: Routledge, 2006.

Levin, Carole. *Dreaming the English Renaissance: Politics and Desire in Court and Culture.* New York: Palgrave Macmillan, 2008.

Levinas, Emmanuel. *Existence and Existents.* Translated by Alphonso Lingis. Dordrecht, Netherlands: Kluwer, 1988.

——. *Of God Who Comes to Mind.* Translated by Bettina Bergo. Stanford: Stanford University Press, 1998.

——. *Time and the Other.* Translated by Richard Cohen. Pittsburgh: Duquesne University Press, 1985.

Levine, Caroline. *Forms: Whole, Rhythm, Hierarchy, Network.* Princeton: Princeton University Press, 2015.

Lewalski, Barbara Kiefer. "Innocence and Experience in Milton's Eden." In *New Essays on "Paradise Lost,"* edited by Thomas Kranidas, 86–117. Berkeley: University of California Press, 1971.

——. *Writing Women in Jacobean England.* Cambridge, Mass.: Harvard University Press, 1993.

Lewin, Jennifer. "Murdering Sleep in *Macbeth.*" *Shakespearean International Yearbook* 5 (2006): 181–88.

——. "'Your Actions Are My Dreams': Sleepy Minds in Shakespeare's Last Plays." *Shakespeare Studies* 31 (2003): 184–204.

Lewis, C. S. *A Preface to "Paradise Lost."* Edited by Mohit K. Ray. New Delhi: Atlantic, 2005.

Lindley, David. *Thomas Campion.* Leiden, Netherlands: E. J. Brill, 1986.

Lund, Mary Ann. *Melancholy, Medicine and Religion in Early Modern England: Reading "The Anatomy of Melancholy."* Cambridge: Cambridge University Press, 2010.

——. "Robert Burton, Perfect Happiness and the *Visio dei.*" In *The Renaissance of Emotion: Understanding Affect in Shakespeare and His Contemporaries,* edited by Richard Meek and Erin Sullivan, 86–109.

Manchester: Manchester University Press, 2015.

Lupton, Julia Reinhard. "Animal Husbands in *The Taming of the Shrew.*" In *Thinking with Shakespeare: Essays on Politics and Life,* 25–67. Chicago: University of Chicago Press, 2011.

Lydgate, John. *The Governall of Helthe with ye medecyne of ye stomacke.* London: Wynkyn de Worde, 1506.

Macey, David. "Rethinking Biopolitics, Race, and Power in the Wake of Foucault." *Theory, Culture, and Society* 26, no. 6 (2009): 186–205.

Macias, Teresa. "'Tortured Bodies': The Biopolitics of Torture and Truth in Chile." *International Journal of Human Rights* 17, no. 1 (2013): 113–32.

Maclean, Ian. "Fludd, Robert (*bap.* 1574, *d.* 1637)." In *The Oxford Dictionary of National Biography,* edited by H. C. G. Matthew and Brian Harrison. Oxford: Oxford University Press, 2004. https://doi-org.prox.lib.ncsu.edu/10.1093/ref:odnb/9776.

Macrobius. *Commentary on the Dream of Scipio.* Translated by William Harris Stahl. New York: Columbia University Press, 1952.

Marjara, Harinder Singh. *Contemplation of Created Things: Science in "Paradise Lost."* Toronto: University of Toronto Press, 1992.

Marotti, Arthur. "'Love is not Love': Elizabethan Sonnet Sequences and the Social Order." *English Literary History* 49 (1982): 396–428.

——. *Print, Manuscript, and the English Renaissance Lyric.* Ithaca: Cornell University Press, 1995.

Marr, Alexander. "Richard Haydocke's *Oneirologia*: A Manuscript Treatise on Sleep and Dreams, Including the 'Arguments' of King James I." *Erudition and the Republic of Letters* 2 (2017): 113–81.

Martin, Catherine G. *The Ruins of Allegory: "Paradise Lost" and the Metamorphosis of Epic Convention.* Durham: Duke University Press, 1998.

Marx, Karl. *Capital: A Critique of Political Economy*. Vol. 1. Translated by Ben Fowkes. London: Penguin, 1976.
———. *Capital*. New York: Penguin Classics, 1990.

Masten, Jeffrey. "'Shall I turne blabb?': Circulation, Gender, and Subjectivity in Mary Wroth's Sonnets." In *Reading Mary Wroth: Representing Alternatives in Early Modern England*, edited by Naomi J. Miller and Gary Waller, 67–87. Knoxville: University of Tennessee Press, 1991.

Maus, Katherine Eisaman. *Inwardness and Theatre in the English Renaissance*. Chicago: University of Chicago Press, 1995.

McCleave, Sarah. "The Moment of Morpheus: The Role of Sleep Scenes in Restoration and Georgian Musical Drama." In *Tanz und Bewegung in der barocken Oper*, edited by Sibylle Dahms and Stephanie Schroedter, 107–24. Vienna: Studien Verlag, 1996.

McColley, Diane K. "Eve's Dream." *Milton Studies* 12 (1978): 25–45.
———. *Milton's Eve*. Urbana: University of Illinois Press, 1983.

McDowell, Sean. "The View from the Interior: The New Body Scholarship in Renaissance / Early Modern Studies." *Literature Compass* 3/4 (2006): 778–91.

McWhorter, Ladelle. "Sex, Race, and Biopower: A Foucauldian Genealogy." *Hypatia* 19, no. 3 (2004): 38–62.

Meek, Richard, and Erin Sullivan. Introduction to *The Renaissance of Emotion: Understanding Affect in Shakespeare and His Contemporaries*, edited by Richard Meek and Erin Sullivan, 1–24. Manchester: Manchester University Press, 2015.

Mikics, David. "Poetry and Politics in *A Midsummer Night's Dream*." *Raritan* 18, no. 2 (1998): 99–119.

Miller, Naomi J. *Changing the Subject: Mary Wroth and Figurations of Gender in Early Modern England*. Lexington: University Press of Kentucky, 1996.

Miller, Nichole E. "The Sexual Politics of Pain: Hannah Arendt Meets Shakespeare's Shrew." *Journal for Cultural and Religious Theory* 7, no. 2 (2006): 18–32.

Milton, John. *Paradise Lost*. Edited by Scott Elledge. New York: W. W. Norton, 1993.
———. *Paradise Lost*. Edited by Roy Flannagan. Boston: Houghton Mifflin, 1998.
———. *Paradise Lost*. Edited by Alastair Fowler. 2nd ed. London: Longman, 1998.
———. *Paradise Lost*. Edited by David Scott Kastan. Indianapolis: Hackett, 2005.
———. *Paradise Lost*. Edited by Barbara K. Lewalski. Oxford: Blackwell, 2007.

Montaigne, Michel de. *The Complete Essays of Montaigne*. Translated by Donald M. Frame. Stanford: Stanford University Press, 1998.
———. *The Complete Works: Essays, Travel Journal, Letters*. Translated by Donald Frame. New York: Everyman's Library, 2003.
———. *The Essayes of Montaigne: John Florio's Translation*. Edited by Bennett A. Cerf and Donald S. Klopfer. New York: Modern Library, 1933.
———. *Essays*. Translated by John Florio. London: Val. Sims for Edward Blount, 1603.

Montrose, Louis Adrian. "'Shaping Fantasies': Figurations of Gender and Power in Elizabethan Culture." *Representations* 2 (Spring 1983): 61–94.

Morrison, Sara, and Deborah Uman, eds. *Staging the Blazon in Early Modern English Theater*. London: Routledge, 2016.

Nashe, Thomas. *The Terrors of the Night*. London: John Danter for William Jones, 1594.

Nelson, T. G. A., and Charles Haines. "Othello's Unconsummated Marriage." *Essays in Criticism: A Quarterly Journal of Literary Criticism* 33, no. 1 (1983): 1–18.

Norton, Thomas. *A Declaration of the Favourable Dealing of Her Majesties Commissioners Appointed for the*

Examination of Certaine Traitours, and of Tortures Unjustly Reported to be Done on them for Matters of Religion. London: C. Barker, 1583.

Nyquist, Mary. "Reading the Fall: Discourse and Drama in *Paradise Lost*." *English Literary Renaissance* 14 (1984): 199–229.

Oram, William A. "Spenserian Paralysis." *Studies in English Literature, 1500–1900* 41, no. 1 (2001): 49–70.

Orgel, Stephen. *Imagining Shakespeare: A History of Texts and Visions*. New York: Palgrave Macmillan, 2003.

Osherow, Michele. "Mary Sidney's Embroidered Psalms." *Renaissance Studies* 29, no. 4 (2015): 650–71.

Ovid. *Times and Reasons: A New Translation of Fasti*. Translated by Anne Wiseman and Peter Wiseman. Oxford: Oxford University Press, 2011.

Palmer, Ada. *Reading Lucretius in the Renaissance*. Cambridge, Mass.: Harvard University Press, 2014.

Paolucci, Anne. "The Lost Days in *A Midsummer Night's Dream*." *Shakespeare Quarterly* 28, no. 3 (1977): 317–26.

Park, Katharine. "The Organic Soul." In *The Cambridge History of Renaissance Philosophy*, edited by Charles B. Schmitt, Quentin Skinner, Eckhard Kessler, and Jill Kraye, 464–84. Cambridge: Cambridge University Press, 1988.

Parker, Patricia. "Black *Hamlet*: Battening on the Moor." *Shakespeare Studies* 31 (2003): 127–64.

Parris, Benjamin. "'The body is with the King, but the King is not with the body': Sovereign Sleep in *Hamlet* and *Macbeth*." *Shakespeare Studies* 40 (2012): 101–42.

———. "'Watching to banish Care': Sleep and Insomnia in Book 1 of *The Faerie Queene*." *Modern Philology* 113, no. 2 (2015): 151–77.

Paster, Gail Kern. *The Body Embarrassed: Drama and the Disciplines of Shame in Early Modern England*. Ithaca: Cornell University Press, 1993.

———. *Humoring the Body: Emotions and the Shakespearean Stage*. Chicago: University of Chicago Press, 2004.

Pertile, Giulio. "'And all his senses stound': The Physiology of Stupefaction in Spenser's *Faerie Queene*." *English Literary Renaissance* 44, no. 3 (2014): 420–51.

———. *Feeling Faint: Affect and Consciousness in the Renaissance*. Evanston: Northwestern University Press, 2019.

———. "*King Lear* and the Uses of Mortification." *Shakespeare Quarterly* 67, no. 3 (Fall 2016): 319–43.

Petrarca, Francesco. *Canzoniere*. Edited by Marco Santagata. Milan: Mondadori, 2004.

———. *Petrarch's Lyric Poems: The "Rime sparse" and Other Lyrics*. Translated and edited by Robert M. Durling. Cambridge, Mass.: Harvard University Press, 1976.

Politiano, Angelo. *Magni Athanasii opusculum in Psalmos*. London: for Sebastian Gryph of Germany, 1528.

Pollard, Tanya. *Drugs and Theater in Early Modern England*. Oxford: Oxford University Press, 2005.

Poynter, F. N. L. *A Seventeenth Century Doctor and His Patients*. Bedfordshire, U.K.: The Society, 1951.

Prescott, Anne Lake. *French Poets and the English Renaissance: Studies in Fame and Transformation*. New Haven: Yale University Press, 1978.

———. "'King David as a Right Poet': Sidney and the Psalmist." *English Literary Renaissance* 19, no. 2 (1989): 134–46.

Presti, Roberto Lo. "'For sleep, in some way, is an epileptic seizure' (*somn. vig.* 3, 457a9–10)." In *The Frontiers of Ancient Science: Essays in Honor of Heinrich von Staden*, edited by Brooke Holmes and Klaus-Dietrich Fischer, 339–96. Berlin: Walter de Gruyter, 2015.

Puttenham, George. *The Art of English Poesy*. Edited by Frank Whigham and Wayne A. Rebhorn. Ithaca: Cornell University Press, 2007.

Quere, Ralph W. "Changes and Constants: Structure in Luther's Understanding of the Real Presence in the 1520's."

Sixteenth Century Journal 16, no. 1 (1985): 45–78.

Quitslund, Beth. "'Teaching Us How to Sing?': The Peculiarity of the Sidney Psalter." *Sidney Journal* 23, no. 1–2 (2005): 83–110.

Rainholde, Richard. *A Booke Called the Foundacion of Rhetorike: because all other partes of rhetorike Are grounded thereupon, every parte sette forthe in an oracion upon questions, verie profitable to bee knowen and redde*. London: John Kingston, 1563.

Rather, L. J. "The 'Six Things Non-Natural': A Note on the Origins and Fate of a Doctrine and a Phrase." *Clio Medica* 3 (1968): 337–47.

Rees, Joan. *Samuel Daniel: A Critical and Biographical Study*. Liverpool: Liverpool University Press, 1964.

Reiss, Benjamin. "Sleep's Hidden Histories." *Los Angeles Review of Books*, February 15, 2014. https://lareviewofbooks.org/article/sleepshiddenhistories/#!.

Reitenbach, Gail. "'Maydes Are Simple, Some Men Say': Thomas Campion's Female Persona Poems." In *The Renaissance Englishwoman in Print: Counterbalancing the Canon*, edited by Anne M. Haselkorn and Betty Travitsky, 80–96. Amherst: University of Massachusetts Press, 1990.

Rejali, Darius. *Torture and Democracy*. Princeton: Princeton University Press, 2009.

Reyes, Hernán. "The Worst Scars Are in the Mind: Psychological Torture." *International Review of the Red Cross* 89, no. 867 (2007): 591–617.

Rivière, Janine. *Dreams in Early Modern England: Visions of the Night*. London: Routledge, 2017.

Roberts, Dorothy. "Torture and the Biopolitics of Race." *University of Miami Law Review* 62, no. 2 (2008): 229–47.

Roberts, William Clare. *Marx's Inferno: The Political Theory of "Capital."* Princeton: Princeton University Press, 2016.

Robertson, Jean. "Macbeth on Sleep: 'Sore Labour's Bath' and Sidney's *Astrophil and Stella*." *Notes and Queries* 14 (1967): 139–41.

Rogers, John. *The Matter of Revolution: Science, Poetry, and Politics in the Age of Milton*. Ithaca: Cornell University Press, 1998.

Rossky, William. "Imagination in the English Renaissance: Psychology and Poetic." *Studies in the Renaissance* 5 (1958): 49–73.

Ruvoldt, Marie. *The Italian Renaissance Imagery of Inspiration: Metaphors of Sex, Sleep, and Dreams*. Cambridge: Cambridge University Press, 2004.

Sanchez, Melissa. *Erotic Subjects: The Sexuality of Politics in Early Modern English Literature*. Oxford: Oxford University Press, 2011.

Sannazaro, Jacopo. *Opere volgari*. Edited by Alfredo Mauro. Bari, Italy: Laterza, 1961.

Scarry, Elaine. *The Body in Pain: The Making and Unmaking of the World*. New York: Oxford University Press, 1985.

Schalkwyk, David. "Othello's Consummation." In *Othello: The State of Play*, edited by Lena Cowen Orlin, 203–33. London: Bloomsbury, 2014.

Schmidt, Jeremy. *Melancholy and the Care of the Soul: Religion, Moral Philosophy and Madness in Early Modern England*. Aldershot, U.K.: Ashgate, 2007.

Schoenfeldt, Michael. *Bodies and Selves in Early Modern England: Physiology and Inwardness in Spenser, Shakespeare, Herbert, and Milton*. Cambridge: Cambridge University Press, 1999.

Schuler, Robert M. "Bewitching *The Shrew*." *Texas Studies in Language and Literature* 46, no. 4 (2004): 387–431.

Scianna, Ferdinando. *To Sleep, Perchance to Dream*. New York: Phaidon, 1997.

Scott, George Ryley. *The History of Torture Throughout the Ages*. London: Luxor Press, 1959.

Scott-Bauman, Elizabeth, and Ben Burton, eds. *The Work of Form: Poetics and Materiality in Early Modern Culture*. Oxford: Oxford University Press, 2014.

228 | BIBLIOGRAPHY

Searle, John. "The Mystery of Consciousness." *New York Review of Books*, November 2, 1995.

Seneca. *Epistles*. Vol. 3, *Epistles 93–124*. Translated by Richard M. Gummere. Loeb Classical Library 77. Cambridge, Mass.: Harvard University Press, 1925.

———. *Letters on Ethics*. Translated by Margaret Long and A. A. Graver. Chicago: University of Chicago Press, 2015.

———. *Moral Essays*. Vol. 1. Translated by John W. Basore. Loeb Classical Library 214. Cambridge, Mass.: Harvard University Press, 1928.

Shakespeare, William. *King Lear*. Edited by R. A. Foakes. London: Bloomsbury Arden Shakespeare, 2013.

———. *A Midsummer Night's Dream*. Edited by Peter Holland. Oxford: Oxford University Press, 1995.

———. *The Norton Shakespeare*. 2nd ed. Edited by Stephen Greenblatt et al. New York: W. W. Norton, 2008.

———. *The Norton Shakespeare*. 3rd ed. Edited by Stephen Greenblatt et al. New York: W. W. Norton, 2016.

———. *The Riverside Shakespeare*. Edited by G. Blakemore Evans. Boston: Houghton Mifflin, 1997.

Shaw, Brent. "Raising and Killing Children: Two Roman Myths." *Mnemosyne* 54, no. 1 (2001): 31–77.

Shirilan, Stephanie. *Robert Burton and the Transformative Powers of Melancholy*. London: Routledge, 2016.

Shuger, Deborah. "'Gums of Glutinous Heat' and the Stream of Consciousness: The Theology of Milton's Maske." *Representations* 60 (1997): 1–21.

Sidney, Sir Philip. *Astrophil and Stella*. In *English Sixteenth-Century Verse: An Anthology*, edited by Richard S. Sylvester, 417–95. New York: W. W. Norton, 1984.

———. *The Correspondence of Sir Philip Sidney*. Edited by Roger Kuin. Oxford: Oxford University Press, 2012.

———. *The Countess of Pembroke's Arcadia (the Old Arcadia)*. Edited by Jean Robertson. Oxford: Clarendon Press, 1973.

———. *The Major Works*. Edited by Katherine Duncan-Jones. Oxford: Oxford University Press, 2008.

———. *Poems of Sir Philip Sidney*. Edited by William A. Ringler. Oxford: Clarendon Press, 1962.

———. *Sir P. S. His Astrophel and Stella: Wherein the excellence of sweete Poesie Is concluded*. London: Thomas Newman, 1591.

Sidney, Sir Philip, and Mary Sidney Herbert. *The Sidney Psalter*. Edited by Hannibal Hamlin, Michael G. Brennan, Margaret P. Hannay, and Noel J. Kinnamon. Oxford: Oxford University Press, 2009.

Simon, Margaret. "Collaborative Writing and Lyric Interchange in Philip Sidney's *Old Arcadia*." *Early Modern Literary Studies* 19, no. 2 (2017): 1–16.

———. "Refraining Songs: The Dynamics of Form in Philip Sidney's *Astrophil and Stella*." *Studies in Philology* 109, no. 1 (Winter 2012): 86–102.

Simpson-Younger, Nancy. "'The Garments of Posthumus': Identifying the Non-responsive Body in *Cymbeline*." In *Staging the Blazon in Early Modern Theater*, edited by Sara Morrison and Deborah Uman, 177–88. Farnham, U.K.: Ashgate, 2013.

———. "'I become a vision': Seeing and the Reader in Sidney's *Old Arcadia*." *Sidney Journal* 30, no. 2 (2012): 57–85.

———. "Watching the Sleeper in *Macbeth*." *Shakespeare* 12, no. 3 (2016): 260–73.

Sloan, LaRue Love. "'I'll watch him tame, and talk him out of patience': The Curtain Lecture and Shakespeare's *Othello*." In *Oral Traditions and Gender in Early Modern Literary Texts*, edited by Mary Ellen Lamb and Karen Bemford, 85–99. Aldershot, U.K.: Ashgate, 2008.

Smith, Bruce R. *Phenomenal Shakespeare*. Chichester, U.K.: Wiley-Blackwell, 2010.

Smith, John. *Select Discourses*. Edited by Henry Griffon Williams. 4th ed.

Cambridge: Cambridge University Press, 1859.

Smyth, Maura. *Women Writing Fancy: Authorship and Autonomy from 1611 to 1812*. London: Palgrave Macmillan, 2017.

Spenser, Edmund. *The Faerie Queene*. Edited by A. C. Hamilton et al. New York: Pearson/Longman, 2007.

———. *The Faerie Queene*. Edited by Thomas P. Roche. New York: Penguin, 1987.

Steadman, John M. "The 'Inharmonious Blacksmith': Spenser and the Pythagoras Legend." *Publications of the Modern Language Association* 79, no. 5 (1964): 664–65.

Strier, Richard. *The Unrepentant Renaissance: From Petrarch to Shakespeare to Milton*. Chicago: University of Chicago Press, 2011.

Sugg, Richard. *The Smoke of the Soul: Medicine, Physiology and Religion in Early Modern England*. New York: Palgrave Macmillan, 2013.

Sullivan, Garrett A., Jr. *Sleep, Romance, and Human Embodiment: Vitality from Spenser to Milton*. Cambridge: Cambridge University Press, 2012.

Svendsen, Kester. *Milton and Science*. New York: Greenwood, 1956.

Swaim, Kathleen M. *Before and After the Fall: Contrasting Modes in "Paradise Lost."* Amherst: University of Massachusetts Press, 1986.

Swann, Joel S. "Copying Epigrams in Manuscript Miscellanies." In *Manuscript Miscellanies in Early Modern England*, edited by Joshua Eckhardt and Daniel Starza Smith, 151–68. London: Ashgate, 2016.

Sylvester, Richard, ed. *Anchor Anthology of Sixteenth-Century Verse*. London: Peter Smith, 1974.

Teske, John A. "From Embodied to Extended Cognition." *Zygon* 48, no. 3 (2013): 759–87.

Tillyard, E. M. W. *Studies in Milton*. London: Chatto & Windus, 1960.

Tilmouth, Christopher. "Passions and Intersubjectivity in Early Modern Literature." In *Passions and Subjectivity in Early Modern Culture*, edited by Brian Cummings and Freya Sierhuis, 13–32. Farnham, U.K.: Ashgate, 2013.

Toft, Robert. "Musicke a Sister to Poetrie: Rhetorical Artifice in the Passionate Airs of John Dowland." *Early Music* 12, no. 2 (May 1984): 190–97, 99.

Totaro, Rebecca. "Securing Sleep in *Hamlet*." *Studies in English Literature, 1500–1900* 50, no. 2 (2010): 407–26.

Trillini, Regula Hohl. "The Gaze of the Listener: Shakespeare's Sonnet 128 and Early Modern Discourses of Music and Gender." *Music and Letters* 89, no. 1 (March 20, 2008): 1–17.

A True Relation, of the Proceedings Against John Ogilvie, a Jesuit. Edinburgh: Andro Hart, 1615.

Trull, Mary. "'Theise Dearest Offrings of My Heart': The Sacrifice of Praise in Mary Sidney Herbert, Countess of Pembroke's Psalms." In *English Women, Religion, and Textual Production, 1500–1625*, edited by Micheline White, 37–58. Abingdon, U.K.: Routledge, 2011.

Tuberville, George. *The Book of Falconrie or Hauking, for the Onely Delight and Pleasure of all Noblemen & Gentlemen: Collected out of the Best Aucthors as well Italians as Frenchmen, and some English practices Withall Concerning Faulconrie*. London: Christopher Barker, 1575.

Turner, Timothy. "Othello on the Rack." *Journal for Early Modern Cultural Studies* 15, no. 3 (2015): 102–36.

van der Eijk, Philip. *Medicine and Philosophy in Classical Antiquity*. Cambridge: Cambridge University Press, 2005.

Vasiliauskas, Emily. "The Outmodedness of Shakespeare's Sonnets." *English Literary History* 82, no. 3 (2015): 759–87.

Vesalius, Andreas. *On the Fabric of the Human Body*. Translated by William F. Richardson and John B. Carman. Novato, Calif.: Norman, 2009.

Vickers, Nancy J. "Diana Described: Scattered Woman and Scattered Rhyme."

Critical Inquiry 8, no. 2 (Winter 1981): 265–89.

Vitkus, Daniel. "Turning Turk in *Othello*: The Conversion and Damnation of the Moor." *Shakespeare Quarterly* 48, no. 2 (1997): 145–76.

Vives, Juan Luis. *Somnium et vigilia in "Somnium Scipionis" (Commentary on "The Dream of Scipio").* Translated by Edward V. George. Greenwood, S.C.: Attic Press, 1989.

Waldock, A. J. A. *"Paradise Lost" and Its Critics.* Cambridge: Cambridge University Press, 1966.

Waller, Gary. *The Sidney Family Romance: Mary Wroth, William Herbert, and the Early Modern Construction of Gender.* Detroit: Wayne State University Press, 1993.

———. "The Text and Manuscript Variants of the Countess of Pembroke's Psalms." *Review of English Studies* 26, no. 101 (1975): 8–18.

Warley, Christopher. *Sonnet Sequences and Social Distinction in Renaissance England.* Cambridge: Cambridge University Press, 2005.

Watson, Amanda. "Off the Subject: Early Modern Poets on Rhyme, Distraction, and Forgetfulness." In *Forgetting in Early Modern English Literature and Culture: Lethe's Legacies,* edited by Christopher Ivic and Grant Williams, 83–96. London: Routledge, 2004.

Westbrook, Raymond. "*Vitae necisque potestas.*" *Historia: Zeitschrift für Alte Geschichte* 48, no. 2 (1999): 203–23.

Williams, George. "Sleep in Hamlet." *Renaissance Papers* (1964): 17–20.

Wilson, Christopher. *Words and Notes Coupled Lovingly Together.* New York: Garland, 1989.

Wilson, Christopher, and Michela Calore, eds. *Music in Shakespeare: A Dictionary.* London: A & C Black, 2014.

Windeatt, Barry. "The Art of Swooning in Middle English." In *Medieval Latin and Middle English Literature,* edited by Christopher Canon and Maura Nolan, 211–30. Cambridge: Brewer, 2011.

Wiseman, Susan. *Writing Metamorphosis in the English Renaissance, 1500–1700.* Cambridge: Cambridge University Press, 2013.

Wiznura, Robert. "Eve's Dream, Interpretation, and Shifting Paradigms: Books Four and Five of *Paradise Lost.*" *Milton Studies* 49 (2008): 108–23.

Worthman, Carol M., and Melissa K. Melby. "Toward a Comparative Developmental Ecology of Human Sleep." In *Adolescent Sleep Patterns: Biological, Social, and Psychological Influences,* edited by Mary A. Carskadon, 69–117. Cambridge: Cambridge University Press, 2002.

Wright, Leonard. *A Summons for Sleepers, Wherein most Grievous and Notorious Offenders Are Cited to Bring Forth True Frutes of Repentance, Before the Day of the Lord Now at Hand. Hereunto Is Annexed a Pattern for Pastors, Deciphering Briefly the Dueties Pertaining to that Function.* London: J. Wolfe, 1589.

Wroth, Lady Mary. *The Poems of Lady Mary Wroth.* Edited by Josephine A. Roberts. Baton Rouge: Louisiana State University Press, 1983.

Wyatt, Sir Thomas. *The Complete Poems.* Edited by R. A. Rebholz. New York: Penguin, 1985.

Young, David. *Something of Great Constancy.* New Haven: Yale University Press, 1966.

Young, Michael B. *King James and the History of Homosexuality.* New York: New York University Press, 2000.

Zim, Rivkah. *English Metrical Psalms: Poetry as Praise and Prayer, 1535–1601.* Cambridge: Cambridge University Press, 1987.

Zimmer, Carl. *Soul Made Flesh: The Discovery of the Brain—and How It Changed the World.* London: William Heinemann, 2004.

CONTRIBUTORS

Brian Chalk is Associate Professor at Manhattan College. He is the author of *Monuments and Literary Posterity in Early Modern Drama* (2015) and has published essays on Shakespeare and his contemporaries in journals including *Studies in Philology* and *Studies in English Literature, 1500–1900*. He is currently at work on a book-length study examining the relationship between dream experience and theatrical experience in Shakespeare's plays and poems.

Jennifer Lewin is Lecturer at the University of Haifa, Israel. Her essays and reviews on Spenser, Milton, Shakespeare, eighteenth-century poetry, and twentieth-century New Criticism have appeared in *Shakespeare Studies, Renaissance Quarterly, International Shakespeare Yearbook, Spenser Review*, Blackwell's *Companion to Twentieth-Century Poetry in English*, and *Never Again Would Birds' Song Be the Same*, a collection of essays in honor of John Hollander, which she also edited. She has articles forthcoming in the *Shakespeare Encyclopedia*, and her poetry has appeared in *Raritan*.

Cassie Miura is Lecturer in Culture, Arts, and Communication at the University of Washington, Tacoma. She received her PhD in comparative literature from the University of Michigan in 2016. Her research interests include early modern British literature, theories of the emotions, and classical reception. She is working on a monograph titled *The Humor of Skepticism: Therapeutic Laughter from Montaigne to Milton*, which argues that laughter becomes integral to the reception of skepticism and broader conceptions of medical and philosophical therapy beginning in mid-sixteenth-century France and concluding in the early English Restoration.

Benjamin Parris is Visiting Assistant Professor of English at the University of Pittsburgh. His research focuses on conceptions of bodily life and ethical care in early modern thought, and his work has appeared in *Shakespeare Quarterly, Modern Philology*, and *Studies in English Literature, 1500–1900*. He is currently at work on his first book project, *Vital Strife: Sleep, Insomnia, and Early Modern Sensation*.

Giulio Pertile is Lecturer at the University of St. Andrews, Scotland, where he teaches early modern literature. He is the author of *Feeling Faint: Affect and Consciousness in the Renaissance* (2019). His articles have appeared in journals including *English Literary Renaissance, The Seventeenth Century*, and *Shakespeare Quarterly*.

N. Amos Rothschild is Associate Professor of English at St. Thomas Aquinas College. He is presently at work on a book project examining representations of erudition in early modern England.

Margaret Simon is Associate Professor of English at North Carolina State University. Her research focuses on sixteenth- and seventeenth-century English literature, material cultures, history of the emotions, and the history and literary representation of early modern writing practices. Her current scholarship concerns materiality and comparative media studies, looking to how early modern printed texts rendered objects in language and graphic technologies. Her work has appeared in *Studies in Philology, Studies in English Literature, 1500–1900, Early Modern Literary Studies, The Sidney Journal*, and *Renaissance Papers*, among other venues.

Nancy Simpson-Younger is Assistant Professor at Pacific Lutheran University. She joined the faculty there in 2015 as a specialist in medieval and early modern literature, with a particular focus on Shakespeare and Sir Philip Sidney. She is currently working on a book project about requital, consciousness, and embodiment in the early modern era. Her work has been published in *Studies in Philology, Shakespeare, The Sidney Journal*, and the edited collection *Staging the Blazon*.

Garrett A. Sullivan Jr. is Liberal Arts Professor of English at the Pennsylvania State University. He is the author of *Sleep, Romance, and Human Embodiment: Vitality from Spenser to Milton* (2012) and has written extensively on early modern drama, memory, and environment. In addition to several monographs, his work has appeared in venues including *English Literary History, Shakespeare Quarterly, Renaissance Drama*, and *Spenser Studies*.

Timothy A. Turner is Associate Professor of English at the University of South Florida Sarasota-Manatee. He has published essays on the representation of torture on the early modern stage in the *Journal for Early Modern Cultural Studies, Studies in English Literature, 1500–1900*, and *Explorations in Renaissance Culture*. Most recently, his chapter on the "Painter Addition" to *The Spanish Tragedy* was included in the edited collection *Shakespeare and the Visual Arts: The Italian Influence* (2017).

INDEX

Page numbers in italics refer to figures.

affect, 24–26, 31–32, 42, 57, 71–73
affection, 118, 120, 124
Agamben, Giorgio, 90, 93, 107n35
agency, 12, 16n18, 43, 51, 54, 60, 75–76, 168,
    181, 212
    female, 52
    loss of, 23, 59, 144
    male, 45
    moral, 112
Alarme to Wake Church-Sleepers, An, 7
allegory, 70, 72, 80,
    and Spenser, 149–52, 156–58, 161–63
    and Milton, 188, 200
Anatomy of Melancholy (Burton), 13, 100,
    167–83, 194
Aristotle, 48n8, 66n8, 89–90, 93
    On Dreams, 36
    and sleep, 23–24, 36–37, 151, 155
    and torture, 94–95
Aristotelian form, 7
Aristotelian soul, 4
Astrophil and Stella (Sidney), 21, 24, 37, 40,
    44, 56, 111
Augustine of Hippo, Saint, 77–79
awareness, 3, 22–23, 27, 36–37, 40, 43, 47,
    66n8
    See also consciousness

Barrough, Philip, 5–6, 141
    The Method of Phisicke (1583), 5
Bates, Thomas, 8, 83n1
    *The True Relation of Two Wonderfull
        Sleepers*, 7–9
biocultural, 2, 6, 10, 14, 89
biology, 90–94, 104–5, 131, 151–52, 154–56, 170
biopolitics, 13, 92, 96, 105, 106n33, 164
    and Marxist theory, 150

and *The Faerie Queene*, 150–55
    See also Foucault, Michel
biopower, 11–12, 223
    in *The Faerie Queene*, 150–52
    in *Othello*, 90–96, 100, 103–4
blazon, 29, 28, 51–52, 56
    and Christ, 43
body, 1–8, 55, 61, 84n20, 96, 104, 108n64,
    128–29, 143, 150–51, 156–59, 164, 183,
    204n5, 206n27
    animal body, 71
    of Christ, 72
    and divine encounters, 70, 82
    embryonic body, 76
    female body, 52
    humoral body, 22, 169, 171–72, 178, 180
    knowledge of, 173
    metaphorical body, 70
    and mind, 15n11, 100, 104, 195, 201
    processes of, 16n23, 77–83
    representations of, 53
    resting body, 3, 57
    sleeping body, 4, 146n23, 168, 182
    and suffering, 90
    unconscious body, 80–81
body natural, 128–29, 131, 135, 139
    See also biopolitics
body politic, 128–29, 131, 135, 143, 146n31
Booke of Ayres, A (Campion), 52, 54
Bright, Timothy, 101, 104, 138, 175
    A Treatise of Melancholie, 101, 138
Browne, Thomas, 143
Burton, Robert, 13, 100, 167–83, 194–95, 199,
    Anatomy of Melancholy, 13, 100, 167–83, 194

Calvin, Jean, 70, 72–3, 76, 78–9
Calvinism, 73, 173
Campion, Thomas, 51–65
    A Booke of Ayres, 52, 54

234 | INDEX

Christ, 43, 71–73, 77
Christian, 5, 69, 71, 75, 81, 164, 181
choleric temperament, 97, 101
   See also humors.
Cogan, Thomas, 4–5, 89–90, 97, 100, 129
   Haven of Health, The, 4, 89, 129
coma, 5, 11
   coma-like, 132
   comatose, 69, 75
   coma sleep, 141
conscience, 9, 171, 211
consciousness, 22–24, 26, 29, 31–36, 38–42,
   45–47, 69–70, 131, 143, 176
   and agency, 60, 112
   feigned, 64
   and God, 73–76, 81–83
   and the stage, 90
   states of, 52, 89, 94
control
   of the body, 183
   desire for, 110, 113
   of environment, 111, 122
   loss of, 36, 40
   narrative, 96
   of others, 59, 97, 103, 105n7, 114–16, 119,
   123, 150
   of self, 124, 165n18, 168
   over sleep, 110
Crooke, Helkiah, 192, 205n19
   Mikrokosmographia, 192
Culpeper, Nicholas, 190–92
   Ephemeris, 190–91
   Pharmacopeoia Londoniensis, 190
cultural biological approach, 209, 213

Daniel, Samuel, 34–37, 44–45, 111
   Delia (1592), 34–35, 111
death, 1–2, 79, 99, 121, 183
   fear of, 173, 184
   feigning death, 54
   little death, 54, 58
   and resurrection of Christ, 77
   and sleep, 81, 109–10, 128–30, 139, 143–
   44, 211
Delia (Daniel), 34–35, 111
Della Casa, Giovanni, 29, 30–35, 38–41, 44
   Rime (1558), 54, 29, 30, 41
Desportes, Phillipe, 23, 32–35
   Les Amours d'Hippolyte, 32
devil, the, 69, 173, 175, 180
   See also Satan
diagnosis (diagnosing the sleeper), 3–4, 12

   physical (or medical), 8–9, 171
   spiritual, 7–8
dotage, 133–34, 142
dreams, 27, 36, 45, 113, 123
   and awareness/consciousness, 37, 42, 54
   bad dreams, 167, 171, 180 (*see also*
     nightmares)
   dream poetry, 23, 28–30, 32–39
   dreamlike state, 129
   in *The Faerie Queene,* 212–13
   in *King Lear,* 133–34, 142–43
   in *Paradise Lost,* 187–89, 196–99
   sharing dreams, 141
   and vision, 113, 122
   waking dream, 138

Elyot, Thomas Sir, 6–7, 97, 100–101, 142–43
   The Castell of Health (1539), 97, 100,
   142
embodiment, 54, 57, 63, 69–74, 76–79,
   81–83
   and consciousness, 22
   female, 52
   and form, 64
   and music, 61
epigram, 52, 62–64
erotics, 27–29, 43, 52–54, 57, 59–60, 63–65
evil, 136, 173–74, 190, 195–96, 202–3
   knowledge of, 71, 188
evil spirits, 174, 179
exhaustion, 23, 122, 131–34, 139, 143–44, 154

faculties, the, 112, 173, 179, 187–90, 192, 194–
   97, 199–203
   and Culpeper, 190–92, 194, 206n20
   and Fludd, 192, *193,* 195
faculty psychology, 74, 187–82, 194–95, 198–
   200, 204n9, 205n13
Faerie Queene, The (Spenser), 15n13, 149–
   64, 212
Fancy, 14, 187, 192, 195–203
   See also dreams; imagination
female, 38, 43, 51–2, 55, 114, 119
   agency, 52
   and manipulation, 114
fetal life, 80–82
free will, 75, 190, 197–98, 201–02
Fludd, Robert, 192–93
   "De tripl. anim. in corp. vision," *193*
   *Metaphysical, Physical and Technical
   History of the Microcosm and Macrocosm,* 192

form
  embodied, 7, 47, 71, 151, 158
  literary, 6, 24–25, 31–32, 34, 40, 54, 58, 61, 64, 213–14
  of the mind, 188, 191, 195
Foucault, Michel, 90, 95–96, 105, 155
  The History of Sexuality, 90, 96, 155

Galen, 55
  Galenic nonnaturals, 167–69, 174, 181
  Galenic body, 172
  Galenic humoral theory, 189, 191, 213
  Galenic model, 194
genre, 9–14, 109–11, 213–14
gaze, 38–39, 43
  gendered, 24
  objectifying, 29
  Petrarchan, 38 (*see also* Petrarch)
  and vision, 25
God, 8, 69–83, 181, 188
  and embodiment, 73
  and free will, 75–76
  knowledge of, 70–74, 76–83
  in *Paradise Lost*, 198, 201–02

half-sleep, 52, 54–55, 58–59, 63, 65
Haven of Health, The (Cogan), 4, 89, 129
Haydocke, Richard, 54–55
2 Henry IV, 109, 128–31, 135, 142, 146n31
Hobbes, Thomas, 194, 206n23, 206n27
  Leviathan (1651), 194
humors, 22, 97, 101, 103–4, 108n50, 170, 174
humoral theory, 92, 96–97, 100–101, 104–5, 183
  See also Galen

imagination, 33, 167, 171, 174–79, 182, 191–92, 195–96, 199, 201–2, 207n30
  See also Fancy
insomnia, 23, 39, 165n20
  and Della Casa, 29–30, 32–35, 41
  and *The Faerie Queene* (Spenser), 149–52, 155, 157, 162, 164
  and labor, 150
  and lovers, 25, 38
  and Shakespearean kings, 128, 130–31, 134, 140, 145n4
  and sonnets, 34–35, 46
  treatment for, 171
insomniac, 23, 39
  as speaker, 34, 40
  visions of, 38
kings, in Shakespeare's work, 128, 131, 140

labor, 150, 152–53, 160–61 164
liminal states/conditions, 23–24, 36, 57, 64–65, 169, 176
  of bodies, 52
  in *King Lear*, 143
  of sleepers, 110

Marx, Karl, 152–55, 161
  and biopolitics, 155
  Capital, 152
Marxist, 150, 155, 161
manipulation, 102, 118–19, 123
  and biopower, 100, 103
  and gender, 114
  of humors, 97, 100, 103
  vulnerability to, 112–13 (*see also* vulnerability)
  See also torture
melancholy, 100–102, 108n50, 108n59, 168–70, 172–74, 176, 180–83, 185n14, 206n20
  See also humors
metaphor, 1–2, 61, 64, 70–74, 77–79, 82, 83n2, 98, 130, 133, 143, 211
metaphysical, the, 131, 169, 183
  bonds, 128
  ideas, 70
  knowledge, 71
  sight, 73
  world, 192
Method of Phisicke, The (Barrough), 5
Midsummer Night's Dream, A (Shakespeare), 110, 112, 116, 121, 124
Mikrokosmographia (Crooke), 192
Milton, John, 187–90, 195–202
  and innocence, 189–90, 204n7
  and the mind, 202
  Paradise Lost, 187–88, 190, 195–203
mind, the, 38, 41, 73, 172–76, 187–88, 190–92, 195–203
  and body, 100, 104, 171, 178 (*see also* body)
  and the divine, 81
  deterioration of, 134
  faculties of the, 179–80, 201 (*see also* faculties, the)
  perturbations of the, 167–69, 172, 174, 177, 181–83
  tranquil, 168, 180, 182
Montaigne, Michel de, 2–3, 66n10, 141, 175–79, 182
  De la force de l'imagination, 175
  On Sleep, 141
music, 52, 57–61, 64, 168

nightmares, 34, 133, 138, 169, 171–75, 182
  See also dreams: bad dreams

Othello (Shakespeare), 89, 91–93, 96–97,
  103–4, 110
Ovid, 55–56

patriarchy, 90, 91, 95–96, 114, 120, 122
Petrarch, 25–29, 44
  Rerum Vulgarium Fragmenta, 25, 27
Psalms, 69–82
  Psalm 51, 76
  Psalm 139, 70, 76–77, 79, 85n35

race, 92, 96–97, 101–5
reason, 24, 25, 47, 69, 173–78, 180, 183, 187,
  192, 195–203
rhyme, 52, 57–61, 64–65, 80

Sannazzaro, Jacopo, 28–29
  Rime 61, 29
  Sonnettie e canzoi 62, 28
Satan, 187–90, 197–201
  See also devil, the
senses, the, 5, 23–24, 41–42, 45, 197–98
  "the five watchful senses," 187, 195–96,
    201–2
  and God, 73–74
  and insomnia, 39
  loss of, 111, 129, 156, 163
  sensory experience, 135
  sensory objects, 23
  sensory perception, 39, 75, 132, 195, 211
Shakespeare, William, 92, 100, 102, 104–5,
    108n50, 112, 119, 121, 139, 150
  Antony and Cleopatra, 134
  2 Henry IV, 109, 128–31, 135, 142, 146n31
  Hamlet, 128–29, 143
  Henry V, 130
  King Lear, 93, 129–32, 134–35, 143, 146n31
  Merchant of Venice, 95
  A Midsummer Night's Dream, 110, 112,
    116, 121, 124
  Macbeth, 110, 128, 143
  Othello, 89, 91–93, 96–97, 103–4, 110
  Richard III, 109–10
  the *Sonnets*, 22; Sonnet 43, 111, 119
  The Taming of the Shrew, 89–94, 96–97,
    110, 150
Sidney, Sir Philip, 39–43, 56–57, 59, 72–76
  Arcadia, 56

Astrophil and Stella, 21, 24, 37, 40, 44,
    56, 111
  Morpheus sonnets, 24, 37, 40–41, 111
Sidney Herbert, Mary, 69–70, 72, 75–83
sight, 29, 39, 41, 43, 73
sin, 71, 74, 80, 172, 188–89, 201, 203
sonnets, 21, 24, 27, 31, 34, 41
  about or addressed to sleep, 22–23, 35,
    37–38, 43
  form of the, 24, 34, 40, 46–47
  nocturnal, 29, 39, 44
Spenser, Edmund, 7, 149–52, 155–64, 212–13
  The Faerie Queene, 15n13, 149–64, 212
sleep
  and age, 128, 130–31
  and children, 140, 179
  and control, 38, 56, 97, 110, 113, 116, 119,
    151
  daily sleep, 163, 81
  of death, 81, 146n31 (*see also* death)
  desire for, 31, 142, 144 (*see also*
    insomnia)
  and erotic experiences, 27, 45, 52–55, 63,
    65 (*see also* erotics)
  and gender, 25, 46, 55, 92
  hygiene and practices, 4, 167–68, 177
  of monarchs, 127–32, 136, 139, 142
  near sleep, 23, 36, 44 (*see also* half-sleep)
  need for, 100, 129–30, 133, 135–36, 139,
    142
  proximity to, 24–25, 27, 34, 36, 39, 43
  resisting onset of, 44–45
  restorative properties of, 110, 112, 129,
    142, 150–52, 154, 161–63
  states of, 2, 4–6, 23–24, 52, 55, 61–63, 69
sleep deprivation, 92, 96, 98, 137, 139
  and biopower, 90–94, 96, 100, 103
  dangers of, 89
  effects of, 90–91, 94, 97, 99–100, 140,
    145n18
  and humors, 99–103, 108n48, 183
  and manipulation, 97
  as torture, 91–94, 103, 106n13
  See also insomnia; sleeplessness
sleepers, 7–9, 27, 32, 55, 109–10, 113, 121, 129,
    145n23, 174, 180, 182–84
  and divine protection, 74–75
  and manipulation, 120
sleeplessness, 92, 99, 138, 169, 182
  forced, 94
  See also insomnia
sleeping sickness, 69

sleep-waking, 52–54, 60
  See also half-sleep
sloth, 71, 170
sounding. See swooning
soul, 9
speculation, 10
stillborn children, 75–76
subjectivity, 21–22, 24, 38, 92
  forms of, 25, 43–45, 47
swooning, 2, 6
Symcotts, John, 8–9
syncope, 2, 6

Taming of the Shrew, The (Shakespeare),
  89–94, 96–97, 110, 150
torture, 90–97, 99, 103–4
  See also sleep deprivation
Treatise of Melancholie, A (Bright), 101, 138
The True Relation of Two Wonderfull Sleepers (Bates), 7, 9

unconscious, 2–3, 5, 8–9, 14, 74–76, 80–81,
  120, 156, 164, 168
unconsciousness, 34, 54, 69–70, 80

virtue, 121, 130, 151–52, 155, 157, 159–60, 163–
  64, 170, 182, 188
vision (sense), 23–25, 38, 40–41, 46
vision, 28, 32, 40, 49n26, 113, 212
  See also dreams
vulnerability, 76, 109–13, 129, 143, 188, 199
  of body, 81, 95, 143
  to death, 110
  of faculties, 190, 196–97 (see also facul-
    ties, the)
  ignorance of, 113
  of monarchs, 128
  sleep as a means of preventing, 111
  to surroundings, 109

watch, 5–6, 70, 93, 98–100, 103, 151
  See also sleeplessness
watchfulness, 75, 116
work, 155–56, 160–62
Wroth, Mary, 24–25, 34, 42–47, 49n35
  Pamphilia to Amphilanthus, 24, 42–44,
    49n28
Wyatt, Thomas, 29, 37, 60
  "Unstable Dream," 29, 37

CPSIA information can be obtained
at www.ICGtesting.com
Printed in the USA
LVHW091952140420
653438LV00002B/4